D0195163

Protect
Your Estate

SECOND EDITION

Definitive Strategies for Estate and Wealth Planning
from the Leading Experts

Robert A. Esperti

Attorney and Counsellor at Law

Renno L. Peterson

Attorney and Counsellor at Law

McGraw-Hill

New York   San Francisco   Washington, D.C.   Auckland   Bogotá
Caracas   Lisbon   London   Madrid   Mexico City   Milan
Montreal   New Delhi   San Juan   Singapore
Sydney   Tokyo   Toronto

McGraw-Hill

*A Division of The **McGraw·Hill** Companies*

1   2   3   4   5   6   7   8   9   0   AGM / AGM   9   0   3   2   1   0   9   8

ISBN 0-07-135198-1

The sponsoring editor for this book was Susan Barry, the editing supervisor was Fred Dahl, and the production supervisor was Elizabeth Strange. It was set in New Baskerville by Inkwell Publishing Services.

Printed and bound by R. R. Donnelley & Sons.

McGraw-Hill books are available at special quantity discounts to use as premiums and sales promotions, or for use in corporate training programs. For more information, please write to the Director of Special Sales, McGraw-Hill, 11 West 19th Street, New York, NY 10011. Or contact your local bookstore.

 This book is printed on recycled, acid-free paper containing a minimum of 50% recycled, de-inked fiber.

For Liz and Karen

Contents

Introduction

Our objective in writing this book is to familiarize you with the estate planning process; to impart a good understanding of that process; and to give you a level of comfort and security that will motivate you to accomplish your planning objectives by seeking the assistance of estate planning professionals.

We do not believe that you should attempt to plan your estate by yourself; estate planning loners generally do not achieve good planning results. A little bit of knowledge can be very dangerous with regard to the estate planning process—dangerous if it is viewed as complete or ultimate knowledge. On the other hand, a little bit of knowledge can go a long way if it is used to initiate the selection and monitoring of good professionals to assist you in accomplishing your objectives.

How-to-do-it books may be fun to read, but using fill-in-the-blank estate planning or canned software can be worse than doing no planning at all. Good planning necessitates a motivated and knowledgeable client who interacts with professional advisers to bring out the very best in them with respect to their knowledge.

Some people are unfamiliar with what kinds of professionals they should look for to assist them in planning their estates; others know what kinds of professionals they need but do not know how to go about selecting them.

We believe that estate planning should be a collaborative effort consisting of the following professional players:

an estate planning attorney;

an accountant who is well-versed in tax law and knows your affairs;

a professional life insurance agent who knows the estate planning process and the general techniques used within it; and

a financial adviser, if you have one.

Today, attorneys are called upon to deal with an enormous volume of law created by an ever-growing and complicated society. In truth, most attorneys tend to get very good at dealing with selected areas of the law. They tend to specialize because of their ability to acquire extraordinary skills in specific legal areas.

In searching for an attorney to plan your estate, always look for a specialist: an attorney who practices in the area of estate planning to the exclusion of most other legal areas. Attorneys who readily fall into this category are tax attorneys.

Some tax attorneys specialize only in the area of income tax planning; but the majority spend a significant amount of their time in estate planning as well. There are also nontax attorneys who, because of their clients' needs and because of their desire and experience, are excellent estate planners. They know a lot about tax too.

The problem most people have is that they don't know where to find that specialist, because many attorneys do not advertise. People who find themselves in this predicament should ask other advisers for a referral or lead. Accountants, life insurance professionals, and financial advisers have usually had significant dealings with attorneys (both good and bad) and, based on their knowledge and experience, most will be delighted to make a recommendation or two. If you do not have other advisers, discuss the matter with the trust officials of your local bank's trust department. Trust officers are generally knowledgeable about local estate planning attorneys.

We have helped to establish a national organization of attorneys who are dedicated to high-quality estate planning. The National Network of Estate Planning Attorneys is a growing affiliation of attorneys who share common beliefs about how proper estate planning is accomplished. By seeking out a Network member, you can better address your estate planning needs. A select number of Network attorneys pursue a postdoctoral estate planning curriculum sponsored by the Esperti Peterson Institute. These attorneys are trained in all aspects of working with individuals and families who have large estates. We highly recommend using one of these attorneys. Please see the Authors' Note if you would like more information.

Our advice on the selection of an attorney applies equally to the selection of an accountant, a life insurance professional, and other financial advisers. Always select knowledgeable specialists with the assistance of your other advisers. The fact that one of your current advisers is a friend or relative or someone you trust does not make that adviser an estate planning expert. Do not be afraid to expand your planning team.

Professional advisers should be selected for the knowledge they possess within their disciplines. All your advisers should participate in the estate planning process and should work well not only with you but also with each other. In our opinion, there is no room for the professional loner, regardless of expertise.

Encourage all your advisers to work together harmoniously for your benefit. The estate planning team should identify the best ideas of each of the professional players and coordinate them into one overall plan that meets your objectives to your satisfaction.

Over the years we have found that many times a team is not enough. The worlds of legal and financial services are changing dramatically. No longer can one readily differentiate between professions in all situations. Accountants and, to a lesser extent, attorneys can take commissions for the sale of life insurance and other financial products. Accountants are also slowly getting into the practice of law, as are large financial institutions and even banks.

Because of the massive changes in how legal and financial services are now being delivered, we are convinced that the time has come for the professions to band together in new types of collaborative organizations. We see a real danger in going to an accounting firm, law firm, bank, or brokerage firm for legal, accounting, insurance, and financial advice. While this one-stop shopping approach is appealing, there is a tendency for the institution to dictate what is sold and how it is sold. Large companies, despite their best efforts, too often have a built-in conflict of interest.

We advocate that independent professionals join in associations that we call collaboratives. These advisors can retain their independence because they have a primary alliance to the client. Each professional owns his or her own firm, thus reducing or eliminating any allegiance to a greater organization. There is no push or motivation to use techniques, products, or services that are provided by a larger, umbrella company for whom the professionals work.

By creating collaboratives, professionals and clients get the best of all worlds. They get independent professionals who share a common culture and are highly trained in all aspects of estate and financial planning. Attorneys remain attorneys, accountants remain accountants, and financial professionals remain financial professionals. However, each professional understands the functions of the others. By sharing a common culture and knowledge base, the professionals can truly work together. All ideas can be explored without conflicts of interest. New concepts that are the product of the minds of many different professionals can continually be invented and implemented.

An organization known as Quantum Alliance[3] reflects this concept of collaboration and independence. It is an amalgamation of many professionals in diverse disciplines who work together for the betterment of all. We are affiliated with this organization and have been instrumental in its conception. It is the estate and wealth strategies organization of the future.

This book was first written in 1981 for the benefit of our clients. The Economic Recovery Tax Act of 1981 had just been passed. Its impact on planning was massive. In response, we literally shut down our law firm and retooled almost everything we were doing. The first edition of this book, titled *The Handbook of Estate Planning*, was born out of our desire to communicate all the changes to our clients.

Since we wrote *The Handbook of Estate Planning*, we have revised it four times. This is the fifth edition. The title of the book was changed in 1993 to *Protect Your Estate*. That title reflected the changing nature of estate planning. Why the change? The planning landscape is totally new. Massive wealth is trading generational hands. Cornell University estimates that more than $13 trillion will pass to the baby boomers and generations beyond them in the next few decades. As we mentioned, the delivery of financial and legal services is also being revolutionized.

Now, more than ever, knowledge is king. Please treat this book as a survey of what can be. After reading it, you will be prepared to work within your own planning collaborative. You do not have to be an expert, but you should understand some of the tools with which your advisors will work. With your knowledge and the expertise of the professionals you hire, you can enhance the quality of your life, knowing that you have preserved and protected your estate and planned for the new millennium.

Acknowledgments

We wish to acknowledge the technical editing efforts of our colleague and partner, David K. Cahoone.

We dedicate this book to David. His professional expertise, winsome and gentle spirit, and untiring efforts as our partner and colleague in our national law, design, and consulting firms, as well as in the leadership of the National Network of Estate Planning Attorneys, the Esperti Peterson Institute of Estate & Wealth Strategies Planning, and Quantum Alliance[3] (a multidisciplinary collaboration), have been enormously helpful to us for many years, and are greatly appreciated.

Thank you, David.

—Bob and Renno

Authors' Note

Consumers and estate planning professionals have continually told us over the last four decades that they need more and better information, and more practical education in estate planning. To meet these needs, we established the National Network of Estate Planning Attorneys and the Esperti Peterson Institute, and became involved with the Quantum Alliance[3].

The National Network of Estate Planning Attorneys

The Network is an educational and practice resource that enables member attorneys to responsibly provide proper estate planning acumen to their clients. Network attorneys embrace the principles of effective counseling, active listening, and relationship building with clients and other collaborative professionals. They are taught to be counselors of the planning law rather than merely its technical providers.

Attorneys who are Network members are educated in the theory and practice of estate planning and thoroughly trained in estate planning strategies. They use state-of-the-art computer models and software so that they can provide the most current documentation to their clients. The Network provides call-in technical support to its members, and provides them with periodic technical bulletins to ensure the quality of their practice fitness. It also provides an expansive curriculum of practical professional course offerings held throughout the United States.

Network members range from board-certified estate planners to veteran general practitioners seeking to develop specialist skills to serve their clients' estate planning needs. Members view themselves as practitioners who expand their horizons and secure a rewarding and enriching way of practicing estate planning law that focuses on the client.

The Esperti Peterson Institute of Estate and Wealth Strategies Planning

The Esperti Peterson Institute was founded in 1994 to meet the growing need of experienced specialist practitioners to know ever more about cutting-edge issues in the planning world. Today, the Institute is a globally respected think tank that offers fellowships in advanced postdoctoral planning curricula specifically directed to the needs of affluent client families.

The Institute's 100-plus fellows are carefully selected attorneys, accountants, life insurance professionals, and financial advisors whose professional contributions are evidence of their expertise. With hard work and expansive experimental case studies, these professionals matriculate through an intense three-year program that provides them with new insights into collaborative planning possibilities.

Institute course work provides highly specialized multidisciplinary training devoted exclusively to the high net worth family, centered on the Esperti-Peterson Model of Estate & Wealth Strategies Planning. It not only provides professional training in the profession's most advanced technical techniques, but also provides postdoctoral training in how practitioners can meet the needs of affluent client families in the areas of intrafamily counseling and goal setting, and how these special families may effectively use interdisciplinary, collaborative models to build effective family offices.

Quantum Alliance[3]

QA[3] consists of a number of professional member organizations, including the National Network of Estate Planning Attorneys, the American Academy of Estate Planning Attorneys, and the Esperti Peterson Institute of Estate and Wealth Strategies Planning. QA[3] is the world's foremost estate and wealth strategies organization, devoted exclusively to multidisciplinary planning. It allows professionals from the legal, accounting, life insurance, and financial professions to practice together collaboratively at a level unparalleled in the professional world. Its principles and ethical standards ensure that each practitioner not only retains his or her professional independence, but also becomes part of a much larger support organization devoted exclusively to holistic planning excellence.

QA[3]'s overall structure and academic ontology encourage independent, third-party, objective professional counseling. The independence of its thousands of participating professionals enables them to provide objective advice with collaborative access to the best accounting, legal, financial, and insurance practitioners. Together, these professionals can offer tailored family counseling products and services that are unmatched in their quality and integrity.

If you are an estate planning professional or a client in search of one, and would like more information about the National Network of Estate Planning Attorneys, the Esperti Peterson Institute, or Quantum Alliance[3], call (800) 638-8681 for more information.

1

What Is Estate Planning?

"It's More Than Money"

Estate planning is people: spouses, children, grandchildren, favorite family members, and close friends; their security and prosperity without you. It is state and federal taxes: income, death, and gift. It is lawyers, accountants, insurance people, banks, and financial planners. It is society's rules along with the red tape and courts of law that accompany those rules. It is a world of advisers busily accomplishing things that most people do not understand. It is time and money!

Estate planning takes time: a little now or a lot later; time to identify and accomplish goals that are personally important; or time to react to a host of external forces that may have their own interests rather than those of your loved ones at heart.

Estate planning involves money, business, and finance. It involves dollars, lots of dollars, to create and maintain a lifestyle for you and your family while you are alive and for your loved ones after your death. It involves the sacrifice of dollars to purchase life insurance or to invest in a portfolio, in lieu of personal indulgences, with the sincere belief that you are creating security for you and your loved ones.

Estate planning is human ambition and the fulfillment of that ambition by acquiring and holding property. It is a life statement of commitment to others, while maintaining a lifestyle that is comfortable for you.

Estate planning is living planning. It is your attempt to use your resources to create an environment for yourself and others that will be sufficient for you and will extend beyond your life. It is the ability to share your success with others. Estate planning allows you the opportunity to control your success both during life and after death.

1

We always ask our clients, "What do you want done with your property and insurance after you're gone?" The responses have been different, but they all contained thoughts that could be summarized as follows:

"I would like to give my property to whom I want, in precisely the way I want. Further, I wish my beneficiaries to receive my property when I wish them to receive it.

"But, and this is very important to me, I want to save every last tax dollar, both state and federal, in accomplishing my objectives. Oh yes, I also want to avoid, or at the least reduce, attorneys' fees and court costs.

"Finally, I don't want myself or my family involved in a lot of red tape that prevents my objectives from being accomplished quickly."

You probably know what you want to do with your property both during life and on death. You are sensitive to the red tape imposed by society's rules. You need professional help in accomplishing your planning objectives.

You are unique; therefore, planning for your estate must be unique. Planning, to be good, must fit you; it must be comfortable, like a favorite pair of shoes. You must understand the estate planning process, for without understanding there can be no comfort. Planning without understanding results, more often than not, in uncertainty and anxiety.

Our main objective is to assist you in understanding the rules, to take the magic out of planning and replace it with knowledge and comfort. We hope to expand your planning horizons.

Your understanding is our mandate. With the comfort of knowledge, you should be able to confidently seek out the professional advisers and products you need. You should have the ability to communicate your goals and objectives to your advisers. On completing this book, you should have a good grasp of the estate planning process and the techniques it utilizes. You should be able to discern between the knowledgeable professional and the not-so-knowledgeable professional. We hope to give you enough understanding of the estate planning process to enable you to participate in a meaningful dialogue with your advisers in accomplishing your estate planning objectives.

We have heard the question many times, "Why do today what I can put off until tomorrow?" In estate planning, tomorrow may instantly become today. None of us can predict the timing of our own deaths with certainty. Death sneaks up on most of us and respects no time parameters. Statistically, there may be a tomorrow, but don't plan on it! Planning *now* is mandatory.

Estate planning is a process that begins within your life and can continue far after death. It is not unique or indigenous to any economic class. Its audience is America, and its players are Americans. How often we have heard, "Estate planning for me? Heavens, I don't need an estate plan! I have so little." Really? No loved ones, no disposition toward a favorite family member, close friend, or institution (charitable or otherwise)? No property, no insurance or pension plan? No personal possessions, mementos, or family heirlooms that require a loving pass-on? No debts?

Estate planning is virtually for everyone, and it is getting more complex every day. When this book was first written in 1981, the Economic Recovery Tax Act of 1981, which was given the acronym ERTA, had just been passed. It revolutionized federal gift and estate tax laws. Since the passage of ERTA there have been no fewer than 126 tax laws passed. Each time, the new laws were to reform, simplify, or reduce taxation. Each time, the laws became more complicated, and more people were affected. The good news is that the laws have led to the ability to reduce gift, income, and estate taxes.

In many ways, gift and estate taxes are voluntary. Those with the knowledge of and access to expert professionals can escape most of these taxes. Legislation, some old, some new, and creative lawyers, accountants, and other planners have developed very effective strategies for estate planning. In fact, the planning landscape has changed so radically that we and our colleagues in the Esperti Peterson Institute now refer to estate planning as wealth strategies planning. Why? Because estate planning encompasses so many different disciplines and so many different techniques. This book includes discussions of important new planning techniques. It is designed to get you thinking about the incredible opportunities for planning: planning to make your life more enjoyable, planning to escape some of the immense problems of disability, and planning to reduce or eliminate federal estate and gift taxes. It is our hope that this book will motivate you to plan the right way and right away. The time for planning, using these new and exciting opportunities, is now.

2
Title

"How Do You Own It?"

"I don't know how I own it" is an answer we frequently receive from our clients when we ask in whose names their various assets are held. One of the major problems confronting estate planners is that people frequently buy and sell assets without the foggiest idea of how those assets should properly be held.

Not understanding how property should be owned makes estate planning a frustrating and impossible exercise. You cannot plan for property that you do not own; and if for some reason you do attempt to do planning with what you do not own (and this does happen), your attempt will be to no avail.

There are three often-used methods by which an adult takes ownership of property: fee simple, tenancy in common, and joint tenancy with right of survivorship. We will explain each method.

The concept of fee simple ownership is easy. To own something in fee simple is to completely own it by yourself. The fee simple owner is a sole and absolute owner.

To own property in tenancy in common is to own it with one or more other people. As a tenant in common, you cannot be a fee simple owner of the entire asset. An example of this form of ownership is if you and a friend own a 100-page book. You own the book as tenants in common. Each of you owns 50 percent of the book; that is, each of you owns 50 pages. Each of you would be able to leave half, 50 pages, on death to anyone. Each of you while alive could give your 50 pages away to anyone. Each of you owns absolutely 50 percent of that book. Each of you is a tenant in common with the other.

There is no limit to the number of tenants who can own something with others in a tenancy in common; 100 people could be tenants in common in the ownership of a 100-page book. Each would then own one-hundredth, or one page, of the book.

The only real problem occasioned by tenancy in common is the fact that if one of the tenants wants to sell his or her interest and the buyer wants to know what he or she is purchasing, the selling tenant in common does not know which of the 100 pages is owned. All the seller knows is that he or she owns one-hundredth of the book.

Of course, we very seldom see 100 tenants in common. Generally, we see two, three, or four people who have bought something together, with each owning a half, third, or quarter of the property. Should a proposed sale by one of the tenants pose a problem as to what pages that tenant actually owns, the local court will have to become involved. The court's solution is called partition. The court takes the asset and makes an actual, physical division based on each tenant's percentage of ownership.

That technique does not always work well. Does one tenant get every other page of the book? The front half? The rear half? Generally, it is better for the quarreling tenants to sell the book to a third person and divide the cash according to their percentage of ownership.

All in all, tenancy in common is a frequently used method of owning property. The important thing to understand about this method of owning property is that if you are a tenant in common, you absolutely own your percentage share in the property. Your percentage share can be sold or given away during your lifetime and can be left to your chosen beneficiaries at your death.

A potential drawback of this form of ownership is that the other tenants may not particularly like the person to whom the deceased tenant has left the percentage share in the property. We commonly refer to this problem as the "breaks of the game." If an individual chooses this form of ownership, that person's co-owners and beneficiaries may face co-owners they do not like.

The third form of ownership commonly used in the marketplace is joint tenancy with right of survivorship. In our experience, this method of taking title is greatly misunderstood by the public. In fact, it is a form of ownership that is extremely confusing.

Joint tenancy with right of survivorship is a great deal like tenancy in common, yet totally different in its results. For example, we again have two people, each of whom owns 50 percent of that 100-page book; now, however, they own it as joint tenants with right of survivorship. This method of ownership does not mean, like tenancy in common, that each of them owns 50 percent of that book; each of them does not own half of the book, or 50 pages. If they own the book in joint tenancy with right of survivorship, they each own *100 percent* of the book for purposes of title holding. Both of them own the whole thing? Yes, that is correct.

Joint ownership, or joint property as it is commonly called, is a *fictional* form of ownership created by English common law heritage. It is fictional in that two or more people can own the whole thing. What occurs to breathe realism into this fictional method of owning property is the added survivorship feature. Remember the proper name of this method of ownership: joint tenancy with right of survivorship. The survivorship feature means that as each individual joint tenant dies, that person simply falls off the ownership charts. Upon death, title is in the hands of the surviving joint tenants. Each of the survivors now owns a greater percentage of the property. Specifically, if there were three tenants and one died, the remaining two would own the asset. It is almost as if the deceased tenant never really owned the property in the first place.

"My word," you say, "do you mean to tell me that if I own a mountain cabin with my brother in joint tenancy with right of survivorship, upon my death, my spouse and children have absolutely no right to that cabin? That it all belongs to my brother? That once I die, I am removed from ownership, and since my brother survived, it is all his? That my family has absolutely no rights to that cabin? Is that what you mean?" Yes, that is exactly what we mean. Surprised? Many of our clients certainly have been.

Joint tenancy with right of survivorship is an automatic method of planning for property because this method of taking title functions as a mini estate plan. It automatically passes ownership by law to the surviving tenants. Please realize that there is no reason to plan your jointly held interest in your will or trust. As long as there is a joint tenant who survives you, the passage of the asset is already planned. So, if you have the opportunity to buy into a 100-page book as a joint tenant with 99 other people for the price of $1,000, and the total value of that book is $100,000, it might not be a good bargain. On the other hand, if the 99 other people are all 80 years of age or older and you are only 21, that might suggest a good deal. As each joint owner passes away, the remaining joint owners then own the book as 99 joint tenants with right of survivorship; 98 joint owners with right of survivorship; 97, and so on, right down to the last one to survive, which, in this example, might be you. What a deal. What a crazy form of ownership!

Now, on the other hand, from a living point of view, let us assume that you are a joint tenant who wishes to sell your interest to someone else. You certainly could and, in most states, you would not have to receive the permission of the other joint owners; but what if you, as a joint tenant, wanted to carve out your interest for your sole and personal use? You would have to go to the local courthouse and ask the judge to apply that old legal remedy of partition. You would have to ask the judge to divide the property; or you could hire a lawyer to come up with a complicated and technical solution. Amazingly enough, jointly held assets, when viewed from a living point of view (without the survivorship feature), function just like assets held in tenancy in common. It is the survivorship feature that distinguishes the two.

There is another offshoot to joint ownership, a special kind of joint ownership called tenancy by the entirety. It is used in some states by a husband and wife to hold real estate. For most practical reasons, it works the same as joint tenancy. The major difference between the two is that generally, under tenancy by the entirety, there is no right to split the property during marriage unless both spouses consent. For our purposes, think of tenancy by the entirety as joint tenancy, except that tenancy by the entirety is only available for spouses. As we will see in Chapter 32, tenancy by the entirety is a method that can be used for asset protection. If you do own assets in tenancy by the entirety, consult your attorney, because your state's laws are probably unique.

Many times a client will ask, "What if I just put my name and someone else's name on a piece of property and don't specify whether it is owned in tenancy in common or joint tenancy; which method have I elected, if any?" In our jurisdiction, that property would be held in tenancy in common. In others, it would be held in joint tenancy with right of survivorship. The answer, therefore, depends on the law of your state. Each state has its own laws. Do not assume anything; find out the correct answer from your advisers.

Always know how you wish to take title to assets and properly communicate that intent to others. Is it fee simple, tenancy in common, or joint tenancy with right of survivorship? Know what you are doing in this area, because taking proper title to property is very serious business, as you will see throughout this book.

Types of Title: A Summary

Fee simple

You own *all* of it.

You can:

> Give it away.
>
> Sell it.
>
> Leave it on death.

Tenancy in common

You own *part* of it.

You can:

>Give your part away.
>
>Sell your part.
>
>Leave your part on death.

Joint tenancy

You own *all* of it with someone else.

But you can:

>Give your interest away.
>
>Sell your interest.

You *cannot* leave your interest on death.

3

Jointly Held Property

"Common but Complicated"

For years, professionals have been taking pot shots at joint tenancy as an ownership technique. Even the *Reader's Digest* has vigorously attacked it as a trap or pitfall to avoid.

Joint ownership has some apparently good attributes. Joint tenancy is a convenient form of ownership. It is a form of ownership that has been encouraged in the marketplace by financial institutions, by merchants, and, to some extent, by professional advisers.

Joint ownership appears to be psychologically pleasing to people, particularly to married couples. Its very name implies "the two of us," a partnership, a marriage of title as well as of love. On the surface, at least, it has appeared as the right way to take title to property between people who care for each other.

Because of its survivorship feature, joint ownership creates an instant mini estate plan for joint owners. We saw in Chapter 2, Title, that if two people own a book jointly and one of them dies, the other continues to own the entire book. There is no need to pass title. By law, title simply remains with the survivor.

Jointly held property requires no will, trust, or other estate planning device. It does not go through probate court on the death of the first joint tenant. In fact, this has been one of its main selling points: "If there is no probate, owning property jointly has got to be good."

Jointly held property has been most attractive among close family members. What the heck; easy to do; natural and loving in name (jointly); a mini estate plan; and no probate court. What an estate plan!

However, there are significant problems with this form of property ownership.

Jointly held property can pass property to the wrong folks, to the other joint tenant rather than to chosen beneficiaries. On the death of a joint tenant there is absolutely no question as to where that property interest is going. It is going to the surviving owner by operation of law. On death, a joint owner cannot control the way the property passes nor the time of its passage.

Death has its own timing. Who will outlive whom is an unknown. So are the results of owning property jointly. As we see it, it is one big roll of the dice. Assume the following fact situation:

A widow with three adult children meets and marries a widower with one adult child. They combine their assets and title them jointly. One day later the widow dies.

What is the result of joint ownership in this situation? That is easy. The widower receives *everything*, the widow's children *nothing*.

Joint ownership only works if there is a surviving joint tenant. What happens if the joint owners die at the same time? Most states have adopted the Uniform Simultaneous Death Act. Under this law, joint property generally is distributed in proportion to the number of joint tenants. Only four states, Alaska, Louisiana, Montana, and Ohio, have not adopted the Uniform Simultaneous Death Act. In addition, Puerto Rico has not adopted this act.

Simultaneous death and joint ownership do not mix well. Remember the survivorship feature. If one owner outlives the other by one second, the property goes to the heirs of the one who survived by one second. Because of the survivorship problem, critics allege that jointly owned property may go to unintended heirs.

Jointly owned property is generally beneficial to creditors of the owners. Property taken in both names is generally seizable on the default or misdeed of either owner. Either or each joint owner could lose ownership in the property, which is not good estate creditor planning.

There is another hurdle to get over with jointly held property, the federal estate and gift tax.

Historically, federal gift tax laws attempted to tax property that was put into joint tenancy with right of survivorship. For married couples, the gift occurred when the property was titled in the names of both spouses. For nonspousal relationships, the same was true. The joint tenant who put up money to buy property was taxed when he or she added the name of someone else to the property's title if that other person did not put up money to pay for his or her share.

The federal estate tax laws attempted to tax all the jointly held property, even property held by spouses, in the estate of the first owner to die. When the remaining tenant died, it was taxed all over again. Joint property was generally taxed twice—in other words, 200 percent taxable! There were some exceptions; but in our experience, they seldom seemed to apply to the situation at hand. Federal estate tax and joint property simply did not mix very well.

Today, spouses who are citizens of the United States can acquire property jointly without incurring a federal gift tax. The law is absolutely clear on this point, and there are no limits to the amounts involved. Regardless of which spouse's funds are used, no federal gift tax will result from U.S. citizen spouses taking property jointly.

The law states that unlimited tax-free gifts are allowed between U.S. citizen spouses. This unlimited gifts rule between U.S. citizen spouses is referred to as an unlimited lifetime marital deduction.

If the spouse receiving the gift is not a U.S. citizen, there is no unlimited lifetime marital deduction. There is instead an exclusion from the gift tax of the first $100,000 (adjusted yearly for inflation) in the value of gifts to the noncitizen spouse. This limited exception for noncitizen spouses is discussed further in Chapter 11.

Interspousal property transfers, when made to a U.S. citizen spouse, are no longer of federal gift tax consequence. Do not, however, make the mistake of neglecting to check your state's gift tax laws, as they may apply to jointly held assets.

Many states do have gift taxes and tax jointly held property much like the federal government used to. States sometimes follow the example of the federal tax laws. Keep in mind, though, that there have been, and probably will continue to be, states that elect to go their own way in spite of what the federal laws say.

The law has not materially changed with respect to owning property jointly with people other than your spouse. For most types of assets, when the person who owns property adds another person to the title, and that person has not paid his or her fair share, a gift has been made. A common example of this type of gift occurs between a parent and a child. If Mom owns a home in her name and decides to put her daughter's name on the deed as a joint tenant, Mom has made a potentially taxable gift of one-half of the value of the home to her daughter. While there may have been no intention to make a gift, lack of intent is immaterial.

For some types of assets, such as bank accounts, just putting another's name on the account is generally not a gift. However, if the other person takes money out of the account, a gift occurs immediately. This gift may well create a gift tax liability.

Unfortunately, transactions in which inadvertent gifts are made are common. We see them in our practice regularly. Sometimes, the effects of the gifts are difficult to rectify. Some people try to change the title back to its original form. Not a good idea! When the transaction is reversed, it is a gift back to the original owner. In this case, two wrongs make a catastrophe. If you are in this situation, you need to see your professional advisor so that together you can work out a solution. We will tell you ahead of time that it is not easy to cure this tax problem.

For federal estate tax purposes, there is a presumption that the full value of the property is included in the estate of the first joint tenant to die. The estate must then overcome this presumption by proving that the other joint tenant or tenants contributed to the property and therefore owned part of it. To the extent the others owned a portion of the property, the estate of the first joint tenant to die is reduced. Because of the adverse tax and practical effects of joint tenancy with right of survivorship between people who are not spouses, most knowledgeable advisors do not recommend its use.

As to spouses, the estate of the first spouse to die will include only *half* the value of the jointly held property. When the second spouse dies, the estate will be taxed on the value of the entire asset. Why? Because of the survivorship feature, jointly held property automatically belongs to the surviving tenant. If it all belongs to the survivor, it will all be taxed in the survivor's estate.

If, however, the surviving spouse is not a U.S. citizen, the estate of the first spouse to die will include the entire value of the property, unless the spouses acquired the property by gift or inheritance, or the surviving spouse supplied some or all of the funds to purchase the property. The estate of the first spouse to die will include only *half* the value of the jointly held property if the noncitizen surviving spouse becomes a U.S. citizen before the date on which the estate tax return is filed and if the surviving spouse meets certain residency requirements.

Spouses can leave everything they own, including property held jointly with spouses, to their spouses free of federal estate tax. (We get into this in more detail in Chapter 12, The Marital Deduction.) Remember: There is no federal estate tax on property held jointly with a spouse when the first spouse dies.

Great care and caution must be used in creating joint ownership with nonspouses. Don't forget that the jointly owned property will always belong to the surviving owners. Your estate might have to pay tax on the value of your interest in the property even though the property is going to a nonfamily member on your death. Remember that cabin owned jointly with your friend? He or she will get the cabin if you die first, and your estate may pay the federal estate tax on half its value.

There is another problem with property held jointly between spouses. It has to do with after-death income tax planning and the step-up in basis rules. These rules have always stated (except for a short interlude) that upon the death of a taxpayer, property in the estate gets a new cost basis for income tax purposes. Here is an example of this concept:

Eileen owns but one asset at her death: one share of stock. She paid $1 for it. If she sold it for $10 while alive, she would have a $9 income taxable gain. At Eileen's death, the share of stock was valued at $10 for federal estate tax purposes. If her heirs sold it after her death for $10, there would be no income tax. If Eileen sold the stock one day before her death, however, $9 would be subject to income tax. You see, her cost basis in the stock would be increased (stepped up) on her death, by operation of law, from $1 to $10, its date-of-death value. Professionals refer to this concept as step-up in basis.

In our example, if Eileen owned the stock jointly with her spouse and died, only half the stock would get a step-up in basis. If Eileen's spouse sold the stock after her death for $10, he would have a $4.50 income taxable gain. His starting cost was $0.50 (half the $1 paid). His half of the gain would be $5 ($10 price divided by 2). By subtracting his cost of $0.50 from the $5, we have a $4.50 gain. He has no gain on Eileen's half because her half got a step-up in basis to $5.

Contrast the tax problem of Eileen's spouse with this fact situation:

Eileen owns the stock in her name (not in joint names). Eileen dies and leaves it to her spouse. There would be no federal estate tax. (Remember that spouses can leave everything tax-free to surviving spouses.) The entire value of the stock gets a step-up in basis to $10. Eileen's spouse sells the stock the day after her death for $10. There is no income taxable gain to Eileen's spouse.

Joint property does not get a 100 percent step-up in basis for income tax purposes, but rather only a 50 percent step-up because only 50 percent is included in the estate of the first spouse to die. When the planning is for spouses, jointly owned property becomes unattractive in many cases. Untutored planning with jointly held property can create income tax pitfalls even when this planning appears proper.

For example, if the surviving spouse is not a U.S. citizen or if the property is not held between spouses, the step-up in basis generally will depend upon the amount each joint tenant contributed to obtain the property.

Jointly held property, at least between spouses where the surviving spouse is a U.S. citizen, is now treated much more realistically; however, many of the drawbacks of this form of ownership persist even today.

Knowledgeable individuals will continue to be sensitive to potential federal and state gift tax traps when putting property in joint names. We do not recommend the use of joint ownership to our clients to any great extent in planning their estates. In spite of the many changes in our federal estate, gift, and income tax laws, our advice remains the same: Joint ownership is a potential planning pitfall that should be avoided in most instances; but, as between spouses, the results it creates can easily be corrected. Here is a summary of the features of joint ownership:

Good Features of Joint Ownership

Easy and convenient

Psychologically pleasing

Mini estate plan

Not complicated on surface

No gift tax to U.S. citizen spouse

No death tax on the death of the first spouse, if the surviving spouse is or becomes a U.S. citizen

Bad Features of Joint Ownership

Passes property to unintended heirs

Affords no planning opportunities

No control

Excellent for creditors

Gift taxes to nonspousal owners or noncitizen spouses

Loss of complete step-up basis

4

Disability

"Living Longer Offers New Planning Challenges"

Estate planning without effective disability planning is no planning at all. Most of us have a much greater chance of becoming disabled in any one year than we do of dying. Yet disability planning is, in our experience, not given the thought and attention it deserves.

There are many types of disabilities, but not all of them require special planning. Loss of a limb, a severe illness, or even a severe injury do not usually prevent a person from being able to take care of himself or herself. However, senility, Alzheimer's disease, psychological problems, drug dependence, or other factors may make it impossible for an individual to function at a personal or financial level.

The law has long had a method for dealing with those persons who cannot take care of themselves or their financial affairs. Courts, generally the same courts that have jurisdiction over death probate, can declare a person legally incompetent in a proceeding that we call a living probate. In a living probate, the court appoints two types of agents to care for the incompetent person. The first type is called a personal guardian. A personal guardian acts as the "parent" of the incompetent person. As a surrogate parent, the guardian is charged with taking care of the day-to-day personal needs of an incompetent person. This includes making sure that they are properly fed and housed, that their health needs are met, and that they are supervised, much like a child.

The second type of agent that the court appoints is a financial guardian, sometimes called a conservator. A conservator, who may be a bank, a trust company, or an individual, is in charge of an incompetent person's financial affairs. The financial guardian handles all financial transactions normally handled by the individual. In fact, it is the financial guardian who gives the personal guardian the funds needed to care for the incompetent person. In some cases, the personal guardian and the financial guardian can be the same person; ultimately, it is up to the judge to decide who fulfills these positions.

The personal and financial guardians are appointed and supervised by the court. The personal guardian must give the court periodic reports on the person's physical and mental condition, and the financial guardian must give the court periodic reports about the condition of the person's financial affairs.

The costs of a living probate can be quite high. Attorney fees, court costs, and the costs of retaining a personal and financial guardian are all paid out of the incompetent person's assets. Of course, if for some reason the competency of an individual is in dispute, which happens more than most people realize, these costs can skyrocket. In addition, even without controversy, the costs incurred do not go away; the guardians are paid for as long as a person is incompetent, and attorneys must be paid each time a transaction requires work with the court. Even in cases where a spouse or relative is appointed as a guardian, and there are no fees charged by them, significant legal and court fees can be generated.

It has long been recognized that this court-supervised system for disabled persons is cumbersome, expensive, subject to abuse, and, above all, humiliating for the disabled person. The process is public, as are most court proceedings. Because an incompetency hearing can be brought by most anyone who has any connection with an allegedly disabled person, unhappy relatives or even creditors can begin an incompetency hearing. While the majority of these hearings are not controversial, others can be quite messy, lurid affairs.

In the past, there has been abuse reported in the incompetency system. There have been judges who appointed friends to act as financial guardians, excessive fee taking, and, unfortunately, physical and mental abuse of the disabled persons.

Obviously, it makes a great deal of sense to take all action necessary to avoid an incompetency hearing. While there is no effective method for absolutely preventing someone from bringing such a hearing, there are ways to minimize the incentive for doing so. It is one of the functions of estate planning to reduce the likelihood of court involvement when a person is incompetent. In recent decades, great strides have been made in every state to make it much easier to plan for disabled persons in ways that reduce the chance of court intervention or supervision.

There are four documents that help avoid court intervention when someone becomes disabled. They are:

Durable power of attorney

Revocable living trust

Health care power of attorney

Living will

Durable Powers of Attorney

In recent years, every state in the United States has passed legislation allowing the use of durable powers of attorney. These devices are extremely important in the scheme of estate planning, but are often misunderstood by clients.

Durable powers of attorney are special documents that allow a person who is alive and well today to appoint an agent, called an attorney-in-fact, to handle his or her financial affairs. A durable power of attorney is typically a general power of attorney that does not end if the person granting the power of attorney becomes disabled.

To understand the impact of this planning concept, a little history is necessary. Powers of attorney have long been part of the law in the United States. In a general power of attorney, a person, called a principal, grants to another person or institution (a bank or trust company, for example) the power to act in his or her place. As such, a general power of attorney states, in essence, that the attorney-in-fact can do everything the principal can do. Thus the attorney-in-fact can sign checks, borrow money, make investments, and generally have complete and absolute authority over the principal's finances without his or her consent. A general power of attorney is the ultimate granting of power to another.

General powers of attorney are subject to abuse. In the past, the attorney-in-fact was not held to a particularly high standard of conduct. The result was that some persons holding general powers of attorney were able to squander assets that they were entrusted with, but not be held liable for their errors. A person who grants another person a general power of attorney is placing a great deal of trust in that person and is relying on him or her to be honest, trustworthy, and careful. But reliance is not enough. Now, many states impose higher standards on attorneys-in-fact to reduce abuse, making it easier to sue the person who lost—or took—all the money from a trusting principal. Obviously, this is not a very effective remedy if that person squandered all the funds.

A general power of attorney terminates when a person is adjudicated as mentally incompetent. Of course, this is the time when a power of attorney is most needed.

To make planning easier, every state now has a statute that allows a power of attorney to continue even if the principal is disabled; these powers of attorney are called durable powers of attorney. Granting a durable power of attorney eliminates, at least in theory, the need to have a person adjudicated by a court as mentally incompetent, because the power of attorney survives the incompetency of the principal.

There are some drawbacks in using durable powers of attorney. First, of course, is that the general power is so broad that care must be taken in choosing whom to name as the attorney-in-fact. Remember that durable powers of attorney are in effect when signed, not upon disability. The minute you sign one, the attorney-in-fact can exercise broad powers.

Some attorneys draft "springing" durable powers of attorney. This means that when the principal becomes disabled, as defined in the power of attorney, then it becomes effective. These types of durable powers of attorney may not be effective in all states. Even if they are, third parties are reluctant to accept them without a great deal of proof that the principal is indeed disabled. This sometimes defeats the purpose of having a durable power of attorney in the first place. It may take a court hearing to determine whether the power of attorney is really in effect!

Another drawback to durable powers of attorney is that they are not universally accepted. Banks, brokerage firms, and other institutions are sometimes wary about accepting durable powers of attorney. They are concerned that the power of attorney may not be in effect because the principal revoked it or that it will be disputed. They often ask for further documentation, or refuse the power of attorney altogether. Some states require, by law, the acceptance of durable powers of attorney, but it is not uncommon for large institutions to ignore the law. They do not believe that an attorney-in-fact would initiate a lawsuit over the refusal to honor the power, and these large institutions often feel that refusal causes them less liability than complying might. Slowly, durable powers of attorney are becoming more acceptable, but they still have a way to go.

Finally, a durable power of attorney almost always does not contain any instructions as to how the attorney-in-fact is supposed to use the principal's funds. If the attorney-in-fact has no guidance, then he or she must use a lot of discretion. Does the attorney-in-fact have the power to make gifts to family members or charity? Can the attorney-in-fact amend the principal's will or trust? Can the attorney-in-fact take a fee for services rendered? These are only a few of the issues that may arise. The holder of the power either has to decide, based on his or her best judgment, how to act or, to avoid liability, must refuse to act at all. And, if a power is not specifically set forth in the power of attorney, the holder may not be able to act in any event, in spite of the principal's intent.

We have seen some durable powers of attorney with instructions included in them. They are long, sometimes complex documents. While adding instructions may be a good idea, it is not practical. It is hard enough to get someone to accept a durable power of attorney. It is exponentially more difficult when the power of attorney is long and difficult to read. Most persons then refer the document to their lawyer, and it could be weeks or months before any action is taken to allow or disallow the power of attorney.

We recommend that a special durable power of attorney be used in conjunction with a fully funded revocable living trust. A special durable power of attorney restricts the attorney-in-fact to funding the principal's living trust. It is not a general power of attorney. It is limited in scope and thus far more effective and safe than a general power of attorney. A good living trust will contain effective instructions as to how the trustee is to act on behalf of the trust maker. Also, the laws governing living trusts and their universal acceptance make using them far easier than relying solely on a power of attorney.

How a special durable power of attorney is commonly used can be demonstrated in a short example. Harry Howard had a special durable power of attorney naming his wife, Sara, as the attorney-in-fact, and he had a living trust that he thought was fully funded. Harry suffered a severe stroke, making him unable to properly manage his financial affairs. His wife found that Harry had forgotten to title his 1957 Thunderbird car in the name of his trust. Sara used her authority in the durable power of attorney to transfer the car into Harry's trust. Upon Harry's death, the car will now avoid probate and will pass under the terms of his trust.

Fully Funded Revocable Living Trusts

Using a special durable power of attorney in concert with a living trust has a number of advantages. A living trust has instructions about how its assets are to be used for the benefit of the trust's maker and his or her family. Trust law is very clear in most respects as to what the trustee can and cannot do. Under a well-drafted trust, the trustee can handle funds in the manner the maker wishes with far less administrative hassle. Almost all financial institutions will accept a trustee's authority with little more than proof of the trust's valid existence and proof that the trustee has the power to act. A short affidavit signed by the trustee and some excerpts from the trust are sufficient for its acceptance in most cases.

Courts do not, as a rule, have jurisdiction over the assets in a revocable living trust. Thus even if the maker is judged to be incompetent, the court cannot control the assets held in the living trust. Because of this feature, there is less incentive for relatives or "friends" to ask a court to declare someone incompetent; there is no money or power in it if that someone's assets are held in trust, free from court intervention under an incompetency hearing.

In our experience and that of the more than one thousand lawyers with whom we have worked, using a fully funded living trust is far more effective than using a durable power of attorney and a will for disability planning.

A durable power of attorney is not necessary if the living trust is fully funded. However, a special durable power of attorney should be an element of every estate plan as a fail-safe device, in case the maker has not fully funded his or her trust. This is a virtually risk-free approach to planning: If the trust is funded, the durable power is not needed. If the trust is not fully funded, the attorney-in-fact, usually a trustee of the trust in addition to being named in the durable special power of attorney, can transfer assets into the trust and then operate under the trust's instructions.

Health Care Powers of Attorney

A durable power of attorney addresses the financial situation of a disabled person. It does not address the personal side, which may include health care decisions, decisions as to long-term care, and other caregiving decisions. Health care powers of attorney allow you to address these very sensitive issues.

For example, if you are comatose or otherwise unable to make an informed decision as to a certain medical procedure or treatment, your attorney-in-fact under your health care power of attorney is authorized to make that decision. Or, if you need to be institutionalized in a hospital or nursing home and you are not competent to make decisions as to your care, your attorney-in-fact will make that decision consistent with your instructions in a health care power of attorney.

It is possible to add instructions to your health care power of attorney. If you prefer a particular nursing home, if you want to be taken care of at home for as long as possible, or if you prefer one hospital over another, these requests can, depending on your state's laws, be added to your health care power.

State law governs health care powers. You should fully explore with your attorney and other advisors the extent to which you want instructions included in your health care power of attorney so that you feel comfortable with the person or persons you choose to make the decisions and with the guidelines that you include in the power.

Living Wills

Living wills, which are often part of health care powers but can be separate documents, address the situation in which you are terminally ill or in a permanent vegetative state and there is no likelihood you will recover. The living will is only in effect if you physically or mentally cannot make your desires as to your treatment known.

Generally, a living will states that the maker does not want any procedures that will artificially prolong life, including intravenous feeding, hydration, or medication other than pain relievers. Sometimes, however, a living will states the opposite: that the maker wants his or her physician to take all measures to prolong life.

No matter what your feelings are in this area, a living will is a planning necessity. Not only are your wishes then known by your family, friends, and doctor, but the document also takes the pressure off the ones you love. It is a traumatic experience for a spouse, children, or even friends to be faced with making a decision as to what should be done if you are terminally ill or in a permanent vegetative state. Drafting a living will is a gesture of love that helps alleviate some of the emotional trauma when someone is dying.

Insurance

Everyone should look into the possibility of purchasing health insurance, disability income insurance, and long-term care insurance. Each of these may have a place in your planning. With the constantly rising costs of health care, it is often prudent to purchase insurance to help pay the costs and preserve more of your estate for other purposes.

Health insurance, of course, is extremely important and can be purchased through an employer or directly from a carrier through one of its agents. Disability income insurance, which is often overlooked, is especially important when there is a sole breadwinner in a family. It can be devastating to a family when the primary income earner is sick or injured and cannot provide income.

Finally, long-term care insurance may be a very important part of estate planning. There are numerous policy types and companies offering these policies. You should always include a top-notch insurance professional in your planning team so that you can make an informed and wise decision as to whether you need long-term care insurance and what kind best fits your needs.

With the ability of modern science to allow people to live longer, disability planning is even more important. One of the fastest-growing age groups in the United States is those who are over 100 years of age! As we live longer, we are not necessarily living better. We need more care, not less. That is one of the main reasons why disability planning in all aspects is so vitally important to the overall estate planning process, and why each member of the estate planning team must be intimately involved in such planning.

It is imperative that an estate plan, no matter how modest, address disability. Without disability planning, you are left purely to a legal system that, try as it might, cannot replace instructions left by you to be implemented by the people or institutions of your choosing.

To summarize, at a minimum, your basic estate plan should include:

> a special durable power of attorney,
>
> a fully funded revocable living trust,
>
> a power of attorney for health care, and
>
> a living will.

5

No Estate Plan?

"Big Brother Has One for You"

Many people die without having an estate plan. They die without leaving a will or without a legally valid will or without accomplishing complete will substitute planning. Many people simply do not take the time to plan or are intimidated by the planning process itself. Others would like to plan but do not know how to go about it. Many folks just do not get around to it. The same is true of disability planning. Some people do not plan for disability, mostly for the same reasons they do not plan for death: they just do not get around to it.

If you do not plan your estate, for either your death or disability, your state law will plan it for you. As we meet hardened nonplanners, we are tempted to say: "Worry not, plan not, if that is your choice, for Big Brother has a plan already made to dispose of your property."

Each of the fifty states has laws that prescribe in great detail what happens to a citizen's property if there is no will or will substitute. These laws are generally referred to as Statutes of Descent and Distribution or as Statutes of Intestate Succession. These Big Brother laws will distribute the property of nonplanners to the state-sanctioned heirs. The result can, at times, be most discomforting.

In order to illustrate how these laws work, let us examine the statutes of a typical state and apply them to the following family situation:

The deceased-to-be and his spouse are in their middle forties. They have one teenager and two small children. A paternal grandmother is part of the family. She has lived happily, from everyone's perspective, in their home for seven years and derives her support mainly from the deceased-to-be.

Now the unexpected happens. The deceased-to-be is deceased. A tragedy has occurred. There is no will, no plan. Wait; yes, there is. Here is Big

Brother's plan, reproduced with some fun and a little artistic license, and only a touch of exaggeration.

Big Brother's Will

Being of sound mind and disposing memory, we, the State, hereby direct the passage of the property of the departed as follows:

Paragraph I

The surviving spouse shall receive $25,000. She will receive one-half of the balance of the property.

The last half of the property will be held for the decedent's children by the probate court of the county in which the decedent resided.

Paragraph II

The surviving spouse *may* be named personal representative [administrator] of the deceased spouse's estate. If she is named [and the court may name anyone it wishes], she will be responsible for administering and managing the estate during the probate process. All her actions will be subject to the scrutiny and approval of the court and its officials [civil servants].

Paragraph III

The surviving spouse will probably be named guardian of the children by the court. If named, she will be allowed to manage the children's property as its conservator for their benefit under the scrutiny of the court and its officials [civil servants].

Paragraph IV

The court may insist, of course, that a bond [they are not inexpensive] be posted to guarantee that if the mother exercises poor judgment in the handling of the estate property and loses it, an insurance company *may* replace it.

Paragraph V

The surviving spouse will be required to render periodic accountings to the probate court about most of her actions. The court shall have the right to ask questions about what she has done, and the court's determination with regard to the answers will be final.

Paragraph VI

The paternal grandmother is of no concern to the state and has no rights under this will.

Paragraph VII

When the children reach the age of majority [18 in our State], they shall be entitled to a complete accounting from their mother as to her handling of their property [every last dime]. Should the children be displeased with that accounting, they shall have the right to sue their mother thereon.

Paragraph VIII

Each child, regardless of his or her need, may receive only one-third of the property that did not go to the mother. Each child, upon attaining age 18, shall receive the balance of the property, if any, and will be on his or her own thereafter.

Paragraph IX

Should the deceased's spouse remarry, the new spouse may be entitled to all funds previously given by us to the deceased's spouse. The new spouse shall have no obligation to use any of said funds for the benefit of the deceased's children.

Paragraph X

Should the spouse of the deceased also rely on Big Brother's will, upon her death the local probate court shall decide who will raise the children.

Paragraph XI

The state, through the probate court and through a newly appointed personal representative [administrator], shall be in total control of administering funds. All decisions may be questioned by our loyal civil servants.

Paragraph XII

All property shall be subject to the control and resulting costs of the probate court. All costs shall be paid by the children's funds.

Paragraph XIII

Significant sums may be paid to our Federal Brother as estate taxes. No attempt shall be made to reduce said taxes.

Signed,
Your Munificent Legislature

Keep in mind that the often ridiculous results of each state's legislative wills could be avoided with a little planning, if only we could convince the hardened nonplanner to take a few hours to plan.

It is a mistake to believe that a state's will gives your property directly to the state. The state ends up with property only when there are no blood relatives alive to receive it. When this occurs, the property passes (escheats) to the state.

Another problem with legislative wills is determining which state's law is going to control the assets of the deceased nonplanner. Each of our states has the right to control real property within its borders. Land and buildings are called real property. If our hardened nonplanner owns a cabin in another state, that other state's law and courts will control the disposition of the cabin. Attorneys call this *in rem jurisdiction*, a simple concept. States are jealous as to soil within their borders; their laws, taxation, and other matters apply to that soil.

Another problem our hardened nonplanner faces is determining which state's law will control his or her personal property. The state in which the nonplanner lived determines where the personal property will pass. Where did the nonplanner really live? Attorneys would ask, "Where was the person's domicile?" Domicile is the chief, number one, absolute, real residence of a citizen. There can be only one domicile, and it is sometimes hard to establish. States fight over whose laws apply if domicile is not clear. The state that wins collects death tax on that personal property. Take the estate of Howard Hughes. It seemed that any state Howard Hughes ever lived in wanted to tax the whole estate. By the way, there is precedent that indicates that more than one state may share in the tax feast if domicile is not absolutely clear.

If you become disabled, meaning you cannot take care of your person or your financial affairs because of mental or other problems, the state also has a remedy for you. You see, when you are this disabled, you cannot make personal decisions about your health or physical well-being. In addition, you cannot manage your financial affairs; it is likely you cannot sign checks, or even buy and sell assets. Someone must do that for you.

As we discussed in Chapter 4, that someone will be appointed by the local court. You will need a personal guardian and a financial guardian. The state, through its courts, will then supervise your care and your finances under its rules rather than your desires. Of course, the people or institutions that the court appoints will be assumed to be looking out for your best interests; but the system is cumbersome, crowded, and not necessarily geared to compassion and support. Just like dying without a will or other planning, experiencing an unplanned disability can result in a great deal of sadness, misunderstanding, and expense.

The point of this chapter is that a state's will and court system are always a poor substitute for your own planning and desires. These state-sponsored planning substitutes are not very personal but, when activated, they do work.

Perhaps state legislatures, in their zeal to assist their nonplanning citizens, have given false security to too many people. Maybe each state's will should say: "If you don't plan it, Big Brother will take it and put it in the general fund." With this alternative facing people, maybe they would plan.

6
Wills

"What Are They?"

Generally, a will is a set of written instructions drawn under legal formalities that directs how a person's property will be disposed of on death. "Last will and testament" is the legal label for a will. It is an old phrase meaning, "I dispose of my personal property and real estate."

Wills do not have to be written. In some states, under certain circumstances, they can be verbal; however, for purposes of this book, wills do have to be written, carefully written.

Many clients want to know if they can write their own wills. The answer is: Sure, as long as you know what you are doing and follow all the formalities required by your state's laws; that is, if you want your will to work.

Wills are a special creation of society. The law of wills is fraught with technicalities and very formal procedures. Do-it-yourselfers, as a result, should leave the drafting to professionals. Very few of the home-drawn wills we have seen actually work or accomplish what the maker intended.

Most of the law of wills that we use today is very old and steeped in tradition.

For many years common folks were unable to leave all their property to their loved ones. On their deaths, much of their property passed (escheated) to royalty. In 1540, the English Parliament passed truly progressive legislation: the Statute of Wills. Essentially, the Statute of Wills allowed common folks the right, under a body of rules, to pass all their property to others on death.

The legislation was revolutionary and vast. The rules adopted were complex. The lawsuits that followed, as a result of society's getting comfortable with the concept, made the law bigger and even more complex. Does this ring a familiar bell in terms of today's government, its rules, regulations, and growth?

A will can only control property belonging to its maker. There is, however, a noteworthy exception. If someone else left property for you to use during your lifetime and specifically gave you the right to dispose of it on your subsequent death, you have a power of appointment; you have the right to say in your will who gets that property.

A will controls the passage of property to others on its maker's death. A very small percentage of wills, in our experience, pass property left by another through a power of appointment.

Wills do not control property that goes to others by other planning devices or by operation of law. Jointly held property, for example, is not controlled by a will. Jointly held property automatically belongs to the other joint owners on death. The same is true of property owned in tenancy by the entirety. Life insurance proceeds are not controlled by a will if the owner names a beneficiary other than his or her estate. These other techniques are will substitutes and are discussed at length in other chapters.

If you would like to expand your vocabulary, try these terms:

Holographic will	A will in one's own handwriting
Nuncupative will	Oral will
Joint will	A will with two makers to dispose of their property on the death of the second maker
Mystic will	A name one author has given to filling in a cheap, preprinted will, and then signing it
Codicil	An amendment to a will

As we have stated, homemade wills usually do not work or, at best, do not work very well. Oral (nuncupative) wills hardly ever work.

Joint wills can really create planning nightmares, especially in the area of taxation. In our opinion, they should be avoided. Mystic wills may be hard to resist. Send in your $5, fill in the blanks, and sign it. "We'll get around those scoundrel lawyers." Need we say more than, "Good luck"?

A codicil is just an amendment to a will. If the desire is to alter one's will without doing the whole thing over again, one has a codicil prepared; but, and this is a big *but*, codicils must be signed with all, and not less than all, of the formalities of a regular will.

Wills are public documents. Generally, a will's contents are not made public while the maker is alive. On the death of the maker, a will *must* be filed with the local court and its contents made part of the public record; everyone and anyone can read it if they want to. Private business becomes public business. Not only is the will made public, but all assets and debts as well as the proceedings disposing of them are made public.

We do not think that taking one's family public is a very good idea. Anyone, with good intentions or bad, can know a family's intimate financial affairs. It does not seem to be a sound practice to us, but you be the judge.

Wills are not effective until the maker is dead. Most people would like a little current benefit from planning, especially in view of the energy required to plan in the first place. Wills provide no current benefits, other than peace of mind, of course.

Wills simply cannot provide for the care of their makers. What if you get sick or for a period of time lose your ability to reason or conduct your affairs? Your will cannot help you. It only controls property you own after you die. While you are alive, it has no effect whatsoever.

A will valid in the state in which it was made is valid in other states. The only problem is determining whether other states will follow their laws or the law of the state under which the will was drawn. Unfortunately, the former is often the choice.

Assume John draws a will in Florida, where he resides. Further assume that John and his family move to Montana. John does not have his will rewritten. John dies a resident (domiciliary) of Montana. Montana's law, not Florida's law, may control. The result can be disastrous at times.

We do not believe that wills are viable interstate planning tools. Clients move around. Twenty-first-century Americans are mobile; they seek opportunities and are too frequently relocated by their employers. Even deeply rooted, self-employed folks retire and are known to relocate to find that "better climate."

There is a need for interstate flexibility in estate planning. Wills do not provide it. The living trust does, but more on that later.

Wills must go through the probate process. In discussions with clients we have found that most clients have the notion that to prepare a will is to avoid the probate court. This is definitely not the case. The property that passes under your will must go through probate court.

Probate is the process of passing title from the will maker to others. With a will, the probate process will pass title the will maker's way. Without a will or will-substitute planning, the probate court will pass title to property the legislature's way. Either way, with or without a will, your property will go through probate. We discuss probate in Chapter 8. For now, please believe that probate can be a needlessly expensive and time-consuming process and that it *can* be avoided.

In our experience, clients have one universal question with regard to wills: "Now that I've got it, what do I do with it?"

First, sign only one original will. If you sign duplicates and one duplicate original is destroyed, it may, by operation of your state's law, destroy all. It is a good practice to sign only one original will.

Second, store your will in a safe place. Store your will where it can be easily found by others. Tell your family, both verbally and in writing, where that safe, easily found place is.

Many attorneys recommend that clients leave their original wills with them. We do not believe this is a good practice. A law office is not safe from vandalism, theft, or a well-intended, but fatal, housekeeping. A misplaced will among thousands of files may just be misplaced, but it is lost until found. Your will is of critical importance to you and your family, but only one will among many in your attorney's office.

Storing your will in a safe-deposit box may be prudent or not, depending upon the state in which you live. If your state has a death tax and follows the practice of sealing safe-deposit boxes until the tax examiner is present to inspect the contents, valuable time can be lost when matters must be completed under the will, but there is no will available because your civil servant has not gotten there yet.

We could write a volume or more just on wills, but others have already done that; besides, we are not all that keen on wills anyway. They are all right and they do work; they have been around for hundreds of years; but they have several features that we view as unattractive.

Wills...

Are only effective on death.

May *not* control all property.

Involve complex legal rules.

Are public.

Are not viable interstate planning tools.

Must go through probate.

Should be stored properly.

7

More on Wills

"They're Not All They're Cracked Up to Be"

In our experience, many clients and some professional advisers who do not specialize in estate planning still equate the estate planning process with the drafting of a last will and testament. They believe that estate planning is will planning, even though this is an outdated view of planning.

In the past, in countless situations when we have asked the question, "Do you have an existing estate plan?" the response has been, "Yes, I have a will, but it's out of date" or, "No, I've never had a will."

The belief that estate planning and will drafting are synonymous is unfortunate and, in most instances, not correct.

A will is but one method of disposing of property upon death. In our experience, people generally give little or no thought to other methods as they relate to the estate planning process. These methods have crept into the economic marketplace as practical and quick solutions to passing property at death.

In order to illustrate the impact of alternative methods of will planning, let us conjure up a meeting between a typical client and his adviser:

(Attorney, accountant, insurance professional, financial adviser, or trust banker: CATHERINE)

(Client: JOHN)

CATHERINE: Well, John, before we can recommend an estate plan for you and your family, we need to know what you own and how you own it.

JOHN: What do I own? Well, Liz and I own our home. The deed is in both our names as *joint owners*. I hope that's okay because that's the way the realtor said would be best.

Let's see, there're the savings accounts—four of them. One is in *both our names*, you know, jointly held, I guess. One's just *in my name*, a few dollars, that's all. The other two are with the kids, *one in my name with our son*, Robbie; the other is in our son Jamie's name, but *Liz and I are both on it* as well. The person at the bank said it would be better this way; something about our being custodians or something; but I think we're all on with the kids as joint owners.

CATHERINE: Are you sure exactly how the accounts read, John?

JOHN: (*With some irritation*) Not really, but there's not much there. We can check, I guess.

Then, we have the life insurance. There's my group plan at the office. That goes to Liz and then to the kids if she dies before I do. I've also got my G.I. insurance. That goes the same way. Oh, yes, and I also have two other policies. One's not too large, but it's permanent insurance and the other's in six figures. It's term. They go the same way.

CATHERINE: (*Patiently, but eager to get on with it*) What else do you have?

JOHN: Our checking accounts; *one's joint; one's in Liz's name*. I've got my pension and profit sharing plan at the company. I signed a card at the personnel office. I think the proceeds go to Liz and the kids.

CATHERINE: (*Sensing that the client is starting to move a little faster*) What else do you own, John?

JOHN: We have the cabin. That's in our names with my brother and his wife; *jointly*, I guess. Some stocks, some in *Liz's and my name*; some we put in the kids' names; one's with my sister and *both names are on it*. That's about it.

CATHERINE: Do you have any personal possessions, John?

JOHN: Oh, do we ever. Two cars in both names; furniture; furnishings, you know; my stamp collection, been collecting since I was a kid; clothing, you know, the usual stuff. I'll tell you, though, I don't know who owns it. I guess we both do.

CATHERINE: Thank you, John.

Now, let us backtrack. Let us go through John's assets to see how they are titled and whether or not John's new will can control them on John's death or whether they will go directly to others because John used an alternative method of planning.

Summary of John's Assets

Residence	Joint with spouse
Savings accounts:	
no. 1	Joint with spouse
no. 2	John's name
no. 3	Joint with son
no. 4	Joint with spouse and son
Life insurance	Named beneficiaries: spouse and children
Checking accounts:	
no. 1	Joint with spouse
no. 2	Spouse's name
Pension and profit sharing accounts at company	Beneficiaries: spouse and children
Cabin	Jointly between families
Personal possessions	
Cars	Joint with spouse
Other	Who knows?

As we review the summary of John's estate, we can quickly get to the bottom line. Those items that John owns solely in his name will be controlled by and pass under the terms of his will. The balance will automatically pass by contract or by operation of law:

All joint property will automatically pass to the surviving joint tenants. Those assets will be the exclusive property of the new owners.

All life insurance will go to the named beneficiaries under the terms of the policy and the beneficiary designations.

The pension and profit sharing proceeds will also transfer pursuant to the beneficiary cards John signed.

Checking account 2 is in John's spouse's name and, as such, cannot be controlled by John's will.

Our obvious point is that the only property that John's will can control is one savings account and the personal property deemed to be owned by John at his death. Wills may not control the disposition of your property as much as you think (or would like to think) they do.

We discuss the "whats" and "hows" of joint ownership or beneficiary designations in other chapters. For now, the important point to remember is this: A will is but one tool available to the client and the estate planner to dispose of property on death. *Will* planning is will planning and is only a part of estate planning. *Estate* planning envisions how those other assets will pass; how they will generate or avoid tax; to whom they will pass and how they will pass. These "other" planning techniques (we'll refer to them as will substitute techniques) are of critical importance.

A will is just one golf club in the estate planning golf bag, a club that should be used only in the appropriate situations to pull off the right shot.

8

Probate

"Red Tape That Can Be Avoided"

Probate is the legal process of passing ownership of property from a deceased person to others. Probate courts have been a part of our legal heritage for centuries.

Generally speaking, every county in every state in the United States has its own probate court. These courts are not always called probate courts; sometimes they are called surrogate or common courts. Regardless of their names, these courts all have the same purpose: passing ownership of property to the heirs of people who died with a will plan or with no plan at all.

In 1965, Norman F. Dacey, a nonlawyer, authored a national best-selling book titled *How to Avoid Probate*. The book was 349 pages long, including 50 pages of text and approximately 300 pages of tear-out "how to do it" estate planning forms. Mr. Dacey's thesis was that probate should and could be avoided. The book generated a new crisis in the relationship between attorneys and clients. It rocked the estate planning community by savagely attacking, fairly and unfairly, in our opinion, probate lawyers.

Following publication of Mr. Dacey's book, a bar-sponsored attempt to respond to his valid allegations was launched under the direction of a noted attorney and law school professor, Richard V. Wellman. Professor Wellman then authored a Uniform Probate Code that could be used in all states.

The Uniform Probate Code addressed many of the deficiencies pointed out in the Dacey book. Twenty-one states have adopted that code in one form or another. The states that have adopted either the uniform code or some of its concepts are: Alabama (used the UPC as a guide for its law), Alaska, Arizona, Colorado, Florida, Georgia (used the UPC as a guide for its law), Hawaii, Idaho, Maine, Michigan (used the UPC as a guide for its law), Minnesota, Montana, Nebraska, New Jersey (in part), New Mexico, North Dakota, South Carolina, South Dakota, Texas (in part, with significant variations), Utah, and West Virginia. Professor Wellman did a great service for the probate bar and the public; unfortunately, much of the probate bar rejected his work, as have twenty-nine states. The public was not well informed. Some magazines, such as *Reader's Digest*, did communicate Professor Wellman's work to the public. They also communicated Professor Wellman's defeat. However, it appears that as time passes, more and more states are embracing the concepts included in the Uniform Probate Code.

Please understand that if you die with a will (testate), the property your will controls goes through probate. If you die without a will (intestate) and without alternative will substitute planning, your property will go through probate.

Getting the dead citizen's property into the hands of his or her or the state's beneficiaries is but one part or function of the probate process; it is really only the end result of the probate process.

The probate agent is responsible for most of the work to be accomplished in this process. That agent reports and answers to the probate judge through the estate's attorney. The probate agent is given different names in different situations and in different states. Generally, this agent is called:

Executor (male agent named in a will)

Executrix (female agent named in a will)

Administrator (male agent named by the court when there is no will)

Administratrix (female agent named by the court when there is no will)

Personal representative (male or female agent named in those states that passed the Uniform Probate Code)

The agents, regardless of their titles, are responsible for doing the work in the probate process. They work for the court or judge. Probate is a complicated legal process; the estate or agent relies on an attorney for assistance in getting through the legal maze. At times, the attorney can and will do most, if not all, of the work, but in some probate proceedings, the attorney does very little work.

Both the probate agent and the probate attorney are entitled to compensation for serving in their prescribed roles. Their fees are usually determined by state statute, but may be reviewed and awarded by the probate judge.

Probate judges are generally nonpracticing or retired lawyers. They can be brilliant or not so brilliant. They can be industrious or lazy. They are, after all, people. Most probate judges, in our opinion, are overworked and underpaid. They preside over a red- tape system that is ancient, meticulous, and time-consuming. The probate bench attracts candidates ranging from superb attorneys who are committed and self-sacrificing individuals (they could earn a great deal more in private practice) to ne'er do well attorneys who have become involved in local politics. Probate judges can be appointed or elected, depending on the laws of the individual states.

Most practicing attorneys handle probate estates. This is particularly true in rural areas and among attorneys who conduct a general practice. In our experience, few attorneys turn away probate work. The nature of the work is time-consuming and most of the time not intellectually difficult. The economic rewards can be ample or splendid, depending upon whose point of view is being considered.

Attorneys who specialize in probate fall into one of two categories: (1) mature attorneys who harvest the will files they have built up over a lifetime of law practice and who comprise the bulk of the specialists, and (2) attorneys who restrict their practice to after-death planning. The latter are usually estate and tax attorneys who specialize in reducing costs and taxes and assist heirs in making after-death decisions. Generally, the tax specialists did not plan the estates they represent, but rather probate work is referred to them because of their expertise. These individuals, although looked upon as probate lawyers, are in reality postmortem planners.

The probate process, although complicated and confusing to most people, can be reduced to the following:

Understand the will.

Ascertain heirs.

Locate and value all property.

Pay the agent and attorney.

Ascertain and pay creditors of the estate.

Resolve all controversies between the parties.

File all tax returns.

Distribute property.

Understanding the will is usually not difficult. Homemade wills and wills drawn poorly can spell trouble, however. They usually result in will fights that generate a great deal of time and dollar expenditure.

Ascertaining or finding heirs is usually not difficult. On the other hand, when one gets into the extended family (third cousins once removed), the time and difficulty involved in locating heirs can run up the costs for probate. In fact, there are companies that provide services to attorneys strictly for the purpose of locating distant heirs.

Finding and valuing a deceased person's property is generally a total nightmare. It took the deceased a lifetime to accumulate wealth, and the records with regard to such were usually kept in his or her mind. Written records of the property, if they exist at all, are in many places. Finding the property is time-consuming and often a real detective job. Even the basic task of determining what the deceased owned, much less where it may be located, is enormous in the usual estate.

Valuing the property that is found is a major responsibility of the agent, probate lawyer, and court. The higher the value of the property, the greater the potential state and federal taxes will be. Both tax laws and estate laws require that the property be valued at its fair market value. There is no black and white in the valuation process for many assets (closely held stocks, real property, partnership interests, etc.). From the perspective of beneficiaries or heirs, property should be valued on the low side of the valuation spectrum. From the judge's perspective, it should be valued fairly. What about the attorney's perspective?

The involvement of probate attorneys in the valuation of probate and even nonprobate property has often been criticized. To whom do the attorneys owe their duty? Should they attempt to assist the probate agents in the hiring of appraisers who will come in with low valuations? Is their duty to the courts and states? Must they insist on fair market value (real value)? After all, they did take an oath to uphold the law. What about their involvement? Do attorneys have a conflict of interest? Many critics take this position: If attorneys are being paid on a fee basis and the fee is a percentage applied against the value of the estate property, there is an inherent conflict. The higher the value of the estate, the higher the fee and the higher the tax. Is there a conflict? You be the judge.

Finding, sorting out, and paying creditors of the deceased and his or her estate can be frustrating. It is important to understand that creditors get paid before beneficiaries. Problems involving creditors prevent beneficiaries from getting their money until those creditor problems are solved.

Probate agents and probate lawyers are generally, according to the laws of most states, first-class creditors. They get paid off the top. In fact, they get paid before other creditors and always before the state or federal government. All states prescribe by law how probate officials get paid. Probate agents usually get paid on a percentage of the estate's value. Some states prescribe payment on a "whatever is reasonable" basis (what is reasonable depends on the judge's determination of reasonableness). Attorneys' compensation is prescribed by law also. Attorneys are usually compensated on a percentage of the estate's value or on a whatever is reasonable basis. Some jurisdictions, in practicality, leave attorneys' fees up to the judge. Depending on the judge and his or her relationship with the attorney, fees may be very high, reasonable, or very low. Again, this depends on whose point of view is being considered.

Controversy often arises in the probate process. Potential heirs can get into some very interesting fights. The probate agent and the probate attorney can get into a dogfight with real or fake creditors. In fact, the agent and the attorney may fight with each other or even with the judge. The judge resolves all probate disputes. The estate of the deceased pays for most, if not all, of the cost of these fights. The cost of probate disputes is generally not inexpensive.

Ascertaining what taxes are due and paying them within the time periods prescribed by law would seem to be a relatively easy task. But do not forget that the assets have to be valued before the taxes can be computed. Another problem usually associated with the probate process is converting assets to cash to pay the taxes. What does and does not get sold can create probate battles among all of the probate players.

Payment of death taxes to both the state and the federal government involves, in many situations, substantial after-death tax planning. Most probate attorneys are not tax attorneys; tax attorneys, as a group, comprise a small percentage of all attorneys practicing law. Many critics of the probate process highlight this lack of professional expertise.

The distribution of probate property can be easy or difficult. If minor beneficiaries are involved and trusts have not been created for them, the court will stay involved until the minors are adults; adult beneficiaries who are mentally incompetent bring about the same result, and again the court may stay involved for a very long time.

The probate process is complex and full of red tape. Its weaknesses can be summarized as follows:

Probate is public.

Probate is time-consuming.

Probate is expensive.

Probate puts the real control in the judge's chambers.

There are several ways that you may choose to avoid probate. Commonly used methods include:

Joint tenancy with right of survivorship.

Properly designating life insurance proceeds.

Properly designating beneficiaries of employee fringe benefits.

Using payable -on- death (POD) designations for bank accounts in states that have adopted the Uniform Probate Code.

Creating and funding a living trust.

Joint Tenancy with Right of Survivorship

The survivorship feature unique to joint ownership automatically passes title to property upon the death of a joint owner. As a result, on the death of a joint owner, joint property does not go through probate. But remember, joint ownership has several drawbacks associated with its use that may outweigh the benefits of avoiding probate.

Properly Designating Life Insurance Proceeds

Life insurance proceeds made payable either to adult beneficiaries or to a living trust as beneficiary escape probate. If, however, you designate your estate as beneficiary, your insurance proceeds will go through probate. Do not make your estate the beneficiary of your insurance contracts.

Do not name minors as the beneficiaries of your life insurance proceeds. If this is done, the proceeds will end up in probate court. Minors need court supervision until they reach legal adulthood. Under state law, this can be eighteen or twenty-one years of age. Instead, leave your insurance proceeds to a living trust created for the benefit of your minor beneficiaries. If you do, your life insurance proceeds will avoid the probate swamp.

If your life insurance proceeds are left to a trust you created for your minor beneficiaries in your will (this is known as a testamentary trust), the probate court will become involved with the proceeds. Wills, and the trusts created in them, are always under the jurisdiction of the local probate court; this is particularly true when the trusts are created for minors.

Life insurance proceeds can easily avoid probate when they are properly designated.

Properly Designating Beneficiaries of Employee Fringe Benefits

Most Americans have significant sums due them or their beneficiaries resulting from employer-sponsored fringe benefits such as pension and profit sharing plans. To whom fringe-benefit funds are paid on the death of the employee participant is determined by a beneficiary designation placed on a company form. Do not forget to fill in and sign the appropriate designation forms. If you do not properly fill them out and sign them, the proceeds will go wherever the retirement plan directs. This may be your estate; if that is the case, the proceeds will go through probate. The same is true if you name your estate as beneficiary. Do not name minors as your beneficiaries because, just like life insurance proceeds, your benefits will be controlled by the probate court.

Always name adults or a living trust as your beneficiary to avoid probate. Remember to complete your company's forms properly; most companies have trained personnel to assist you.

Using POD Designations
for Bank Accounts

Earlier in this chapter we discussed Professor Wellman's work in devising a national Uniform Probate Code. Recall that twenty-one states enacted their own versions of his code:

Alabama	Montana
Alaska	Nebraska
Arizona	New Jersey
Colorado	New Mexico
Florida	North Dakota
Georgia	South Carolina
Hawaii	South Dakota
Idaho	Texas
Maine	Utah
Michigan	West Virginia
Minnesota	

If you live in one of these states, another method of avoiding probate may be available to you. This technique applies to savings and checking accounts as well as certificates of deposit. The owner, in setting up the account, instructs the bank clerk to type on the account a payable-on-death (POD) designation. The owner then names the person or persons to receive the account proceeds upon death of the owner and has those names typed on the account after the letters "POD." It is as simple as that. These accounts *by law* will not go through probate. The POD is merely a beneficiary designation for these assets. If you live in one of these states, however, do not use this technique to leave the accounts to minor beneficiaries.

Some states that have not adopted the Uniform Probate Code, such as Missouri, have adopted laws to provide for POD beneficiary designations. If you do not live in a Uniform Probate Code state, contact your attorney to determine if your state has such a law.

Creating and Funding a Living Trust

Living trusts are complete will substitutes. They have been around for hundreds of years; assets placed in a living trust have always avoided the probate process. They were created, in part, to do just that.

Using a living trust as a will substitute has certainly come of age. Traditionally, living trusts were only used by nobility. In modern times, they have been used mostly by the wealthy. Today, living trusts are used, and should be used, by just about everybody.

Property placed in a living trust is instantly available for the use and benefit of the trust maker's beneficiaries. No matter how vast and diversified your holdings may be, a living trust can accommodate all of them in avoiding the probate process.

Every probate-avoidance technique other than the living trust has potential planning disadvantages. This does not mean that the other techniques cannot or should not be used. It does mean that the living trust can be used to avoid probate for all your property and that, as a technique, it has few, if any, disadvantages compared to the other techniques we have discussed.

We include two chapters on the living trust: Chapter 17 discusses what it is and how it works. Chapter 18 describes how property can be put into a living trust (how the trust can be funded).

Planning to avoid probate involves time, some financial housekeeping, and, regardless of the methods you use, requires the following:

Collect all assets and the papers that evidence title to those assets (deeds, stock certificates, partnership agreements, etc.). This means getting your affairs organized and all the paperwork together in one place.

Review with your advisers the way ownership has been taken to your existing assets.

Change the way you own your assets in one of several ways we have discussed, so that upon your death your property will escape probate.

Probate itself, you will recall, involves the collection of assets and the passage of title to beneficiaries under the control and supervision of the probate judge. Probate your own estate while you are alive. Organize your affairs and retitle your assets so that they will not go through probate on death. Most people know what they own and can generally find the paperwork that evidences their ownership quickly. Once that is done, a professional adviser can quickly recommend the right ownership techniques to get the job done.

9

The Federal Estate Tax

"The Final Sting"

Many years ago, we had as clients a married couple who were constantly complaining about the income taxes they were paying. One day, in exasperation, they said, "Well, the only good thing about our tax situation is that our income taxes will be the most taxes that we will ever have to pay." You can imagine their consternation when we told them that the federal government's death tax is much higher than the income tax, and would, in fact, take a very substantial percentage of their lives' work. It would even tax any income left over, after it had been subject to income tax!

Federal death tax has been and continues to be serious business. However, the Taxpayer Relief Act of 1997 gave some relief to all taxpayers from our federal estate tax. It's very important for you to understand the historical perspective in order to understand and appreciate the current law.

The U.S. government's death tax is properly called federal estate tax. Like all other taxes imposed by our system of government, this one began as a rather modest tax. First imposed in 1916, it had a maximum rate of 10 percent.

It is interesting to note that by 1932 the maximum rate was 45 percent; in 1981, it was 70 percent.

In 1976, Congress made an attempt to initiate reform in the death tax area; the result was the Tax Reform Act of 1976. This legislation gave little to the taxpayer and, in fact, took away a great deal.

The Tax Reform Act of 1976 increased the size of nontaxable estate property from $60,000 in 1976 through a series of expansionary leaps to $175,625 in 1981. It attempted to simplify the rules with regard to the tax on joint property and resulted in making them more complicated, in our

45

opinion. It took away the rules that favorably taxed property after death for income tax purposes. On the last issue, because of the hue and cry of the American taxpayer and a few dedicated advocates, Congress had to backtrack and reverse itself. Enough was enough, or in this case, too much.

The Tax Reform Act of 1976 unified federal estate and federal gift taxation law. In effect, the reform act put the two together and charged identical rates. This law is still with us and is discussed in Chapter 10, The Unified System.

The Tax Reform Act of 1976 did a great deal for the coffers of the U.S. government; it did not do a great deal for its citizens.

The Economic Recovery Tax Act of 1981 (ERTA) made considerable changes to the federal estate and gift tax law. It raised the amount that was free from federal estate and gift tax considerably. It expanded the marital deduction and made planning much more flexible between spouses. Since ERTA, Congress has been busy legislating in the federal estate and gift tax arena. Between 1981 and 1999, 126 laws were passed that affected the Internal Revenue Code, most of which had some impact on federal estate and gift taxation. That is an average of seven new laws every year. It is no wonder our laws are so complex.

Federal estate tax has two distinct features. First, federal estate tax can be described as an "everything tax." Yes, Uncle Sam taxes everything, including the proverbial kitchen sink. Second, this tax is a "top tax." Uncle Sam receives his tax before your beneficiaries receive anything.

Federal estate tax is not a tax levied against a deceased person or his or her property. It is not a people or property tax at all. It is a tax levied against the "right to transfer" property on death. We could write volumes on the various property interests that Uncle Sam taxes under the federal estate tax. Fortunately, that will not be necessary. What is important to remember is that federal estate tax is an everything tax and that it is paid before beneficiaries receive their share of the proceeds.

Uncle Sam will tax all the property owned in your name at your death. Uncle Sam will tax all the life insurance proceeds owned by you on your life. Uncle Sam has attempted to tax the total value of all assets held in joint ownership. Uncle Sam has even taxed property that was given away during people's lifetimes if any of the income from that property was retained by the maker of the gift or if it was given away within three years prior to death.

We can play the game of *Uncle Sam Will Tax* until your eyes close and the book slides from your hands, but that would belabor the point. It would be easier to list what Uncle Sam does not tax. Federal estate tax does not apply to:

Money going directly to beneficiaries through an annuity purchased by your employer.

Funds passing to beneficiaries pursuant to death-benefit-only plans created by your employer.

Social Security payments to your dependents.

Insurance proceeds on your life if you did not own or have any control over those policies.

Fifty percent of the proceeds from certain sales of stock to an employee stock ownership plan if the sale occurred before 1992 for persons who died before December 20, 1989.

There are other property interests, although not many, that are not subject to federal estate tax; these other property interests are foreign to most people, and an understanding of them is not necessary to a general understanding of Uncle Sam's estate tax.

Can you believe that Uncle Sam taxes life insurance proceeds? This does not mean that Uncle Sam taxes the premiums paid for that insurance; it means that Uncle Sam taxes all the death proceeds whether they are paid in installments or in a lump sum to your designated beneficiaries. If you paid $1,000 in premiums for a $100,000 life insurance policy, the proceeds of which go to your children upon your death, all $100,000 is subject to federal estate tax but not the federal income tax. Many people believe that life insurance proceeds are not taxed on death. Some states may not have a death tax on life insurance proceeds, but the U.S. government does.

Federal estate tax rates are progressive. The more a taxpayer owns, the more tax that taxpayer is going to pay; this should be a surprise to no one. Historically, the federal estate tax has redistributed wealth; it has been a tax targeted to take from the wealthy and redistribute that wealth to the not so wealthy.

For many years (in fact, up until 1976), the first $60,000 of estate value was not taxed. As a result of the Tax Reform Act of 1976, that amount went up in stages until it peaked at $175,625 in 1981. This tax-free amount is referred to as the exemption equivalent.

Congress raised the tax-free amount to $225,000 for individuals dying in 1982, and then continued to increase the tax-free amount annually until it reached $600,000 in 1987. The Taxpayer Relief Act of 1997 (TRA 97) increased the tax-free amount for individuals dying after 1997. The increase is being phased in over nine years, with the greatest increases in the later years. The phase-in is shown in Table 9-1.

The increase in the tax-free amount, now called the applicable exclusion amount rather than the exemption equivalent (why the name was changed is

Table 9-1
The Phase-In of the Applicable Exclusion Amount under TRA 97

Tax Year	Applicable Exclusion Amount
1998	625,000
1999	650,000
2000	675,000
2001	675,000
2002	700,000
2003	700,000
2004	850,000
2005	950,000
2006	1,000,000

anybody's guess), was designed to reflect the inflation that took place between 1987 and 1997. The phase-in is allegedly another inflation hedge. However, there is no provision in the law to increase the $1,000,000 maximum amount, which goes into effect beginning in the year 2006, for inflation.

Congress has traditionally taken notice of the family unit and has made some allowances for leaving property to spouses in the federal estate tax laws. For many years, the law provided that spouses could leave one-half of their property free of federal estate tax to surviving spouses. This provision of the estate tax appeared to salve the congressional conscience. The Tax Reform Act of 1976 increased this spousal benefit to $250,000 or one-half of the estate, whichever was greater. The real change was adding a base of $250,000 that went tax-free to the surviving spouse.

The tax-saving spousal device we have been discussing is referred to as the marital deduction. Property accumulated by husband and wife that was left to the surviving spouse was taxed only when it exceeded $425,625 (the sum of $250,000 of marital deduction and the $175,625 exemption equivalent).

Whether or not this rather arbitrary marital deduction was a good deal was a matter of opinion. Former President Reagan was not of that opinion, nor was Congress. In passing ERTA, they expressed a belief that if a little was good, more would be better. Today, the marital deduction applies to all property left to a U.S. citizen spouse. Just think, a 100 percent marital deduction. But no marital deduction is available if the surviving spouse is a noncitizen spouse, unless the property passes to a qualified domestic trust, or the surviving spouse becomes a U.S. citizen within certain strict time limits and meets certain residency requirements.

A qualified domestic trust is a special trust that ensures estate assets passing for the benefit of a noncitizen spouse are available to pay any estate taxes that may be due when the noncitizen spouse dies. We discuss the qualified domestic trust in more detail in Chapter 25.

It is important to understand the rules of federal estate tax. It is equally important to understand how property is valued for purposes of applying the death tax. Understanding a tax table is not too difficult. Arriving at the value of the property prior to applying that table is very difficult.

Uncle Sam's death tax is a tax based on the fair market value of the property in an estate. It is not a tax on the value of the property when it was originally purchased. It is a tax based either on the fair market value of the property at the date of the estate owner's death or the value of that property six months after the date of the owner's death. The latter date is referred to as the alternate valuation date. Uncle Sam gives beneficiaries a valuation choice. They can value the property at its date of death value or its value six months later. Your postdeath agent can only use the alternate valuation date if it will both reduce the value of your estate and reduce the federal estate tax due. Generally, due to inflation, property goes up in value; but that does not always happen. Valuation should be computed on both dates to see if there is any decrease in the overall value of property that would result in a lower federal estate tax. Your postdeath agent must be careful, however. Your agent cannot pick and choose different dates for different assets. The date selected applies to all the assets.

If the value of property should go down after the six-month valuation date, the estate has no federal estate tax recourse; the law provides no relief for this contingency.

It is important to recognize that the fair market value of property can be astoundingly high. Most of us want to know who determines the fair market value of our property. Does the family determine the value? The attorney? The agent of the estate? Does the Internal Revenue Service determine its value? The fair market value of the property in an estate is ultimately determined by the courts if the postdeath agents and the Internal Revenue Service cannot agree on a value. The standard the courts use is the price that a willing buyer would pay a willing seller, both having no compulsion to buy or sell and each being aware of all the facts surrounding the sale.

Most assets have a spectrum of value. For example, a car that is two years old may range in value from $6,000 to $10,000, depending upon who is selling and who is buying. Its value also depends on the environment in which it is being bought and sold. This range in value is referred to as the spectrum of value. Generally speaking, postdeath agents representing an estate should always shoot for the low end of the value spectrum when submitting valuations on a federal estate tax return. At the same time, agents should not underestimate the Internal Revenue Service (IRS). The goal of the IRS is to collect revenue. In zealously seeking to achieve their objective, you can be assured that, in many cases, the IRS will go for the highest value possible within the value spectrum.

Often this difference in approach leads to heated arguments and some rather spirited negotiations between the representatives of the estate and the IRS. The result of these negotiations is usually a settlement. Sometimes, however, the two sides remain miles apart, and the courts are called upon to make the ultimate decision. Remember, the roles of the estate's agent and the Internal Revenue Service require that each lean toward a different end of the value spectrum.

Some types of property are easily valued for federal estate tax purposes. Property of this type includes:

stocks that are publicly traded,

bonds,

savings and checking accounts,

certificates of deposit,

money market accounts, and

Treasury bills.

Most property holdings are not so easily valued. Property fitting this description includes:

real estate,

closely (privately) owned business interests, including corporations, partnerships, and limited liability companies,

equipment and machinery, and

personal effects.

The best way to reduce federal estate tax is to reduce the value of the property subject to the tax. The job of the estate's agent is to keep that value down. The job of the IRS is to keep it as high as possible. It used to be that there were very effective methods for reducing the value of certain types of property by passing their future appreciation to family members on a tax-free basis. These so-called freezing techniques have been significantly curtailed. There are still some very effective techniques for reducing the value of property; we discuss them in other chapters.

Since 1976, land (real property) used in farming or ranching can be valued lower than its arguable fair market value if certain requirements are met. This exception to the general rules of fair market value resulted from intense lobbying efforts on the part of farm and ranch associations. The exceptions to the general rule apply to special interests and are covered in Chapter 38, Special Use Valuation. These legal exceptions are fair, in our opinion.

Another important aspect of federal estate tax law is that it is not a tax that can be easily deferred to a time when payment may be convenient. With few exceptions, the Internal Revenue Code says that Uncle Sam's death tax shall be paid in cash nine months from the date of death. Cash is a method of payment that does not allow for postponement. The result of not paying federal estate tax promptly unless you have special approval from the IRS is that the property will be seized by the IRS, which will be more than happy to collect what proceeds it can by means of a tax sale. The federal estate tax is a tough, no-nonsense tax.

Recent changes in our tax laws have caused the federal estate tax to become less confiscatory as to the property left by most Americans to their loved ones.

The federal estate tax can be summarized as follows:

The federal estate tax only applies to estates valued in excess of $650,000 in 1999, phased in to $1,000,000 in 2006.

The federal estate tax rates begin at 37 percent (going up to 41 percent as the applicable exclusion is being phased in) and reach 55 percent.

Spouses are able to leave property of an unlimited amount to their U.S. citizen spouses free of federal estate tax.

Prior to 1982, federal estate tax rates started at 18 percent and progressed with the size of an estate to a maximum tax rate of 70 percent. Just think, 70 percent of a citizen's estate (life's work) could have been seized by the government under the provisions of the old law; that is a lot of tax, regardless of one's political persuasion.

The old tax rates were closely patterned after the progressive income tax rates Americans lived with before TRA 1986. The concept behind these progressive rates was simple: The more successful a citizen was in accumulating property in a lifetime, the more responsibility that citizen had to share that wealth, through government, with others less fortunate. As property values increased progressively, the federal estate tax rates increased as well until that magic 70 percent bracket was achieved. There was no doubt that federal estate tax was predicated on the concept of redistribution of wealth. Our political leaders were attempting to build a great society, using as fuel the efforts of that society's most financially successful citizens.

Since 1981, the federal estate tax laws have reflected a radical departure from traditional political practices with regard to who should pay to keep the government afloat. One of the ways the law was changed was to reduce the top estate tax bracket. For those fortunate enough to have very large estates, Congress has taken a large step backward. The maximum federal estate tax rate is 60 percent for the value of an estate that is between $10,000,000 and $17,184,00.

Simple arithmetic will illustrate the impact the post-1981 brackets have on the estates of our wealthier citizens. In order to gain a perspective on these brackets, some thought should be given to inflation and the impact it has had in assisting the government in the collection of its death tax.

Traditionally, inflation has been an invaluable tool to the federal government's tax collectors. As property values have gone up, tax revenues have gone up. Inflation has forced Americans into higher income tax brackets. ERTA and the Taxpayer's Relief Act of 1997 were attempts to reverse this trend. We believe this law has been a benefit to all Americans.

Under the old law, estates were subject to federal estate tax once they exceeded $175,625. This amount was called the exemption equivalent. The exemption equivalent was raised to $225,000 in 1982 and reached $600,000 in 1987. It was raised in 1998 and is scheduled to reach $1,000,000 in 2006. (See Table 9 -1.)

The applicable exclusion amount (the old exemption equivalent) is really a deductible amount that until reached will result in no tax on the death of a property owner. If a citizen dies after 2005, that tax- free amount is $1,000,000; this amount is $400,000 more than the maximum tax-free amount under ERTA.

The increase in the applicable exclusion amount represents a benefit that has been given to all Americans. It particularly benefits those Americans whose accumulation of property does not exceed the applicable exclusion amount. A parent who left $1,000,000 to his or her children in 1997 would have lost $153,000 to federal estate tax. That same parent would lose none of the property to federal estate tax if he or she died in 2006. The comparison made in Tables 9-2 and 9-3 illustrates this point.

The cries of the traditional redistributors of wealth that these changes in the estate tax are only for the rich and superrich do not hold up. Every

Table 9 -2
Tax on a $1,000,000 Estate, 1997 through 2006

Year	Tax
1997	$153,000
1998	143,750
1999	134,500
2000	125,250
2001	125,250
2002	116,000
2003	116,000
2004	58,500
2005	19,500
2006	0

American is entitled to that \$1,000,000 benefit, and for those who do not create an estate of \$1,000,000, there will be no tax.

TRA 97 was partially designed to make up the years of inflation between 1987 and 2006. Some critics of TRA 97 believe that the applicable exclusion amount does not make up for past or future inflation. And they may be right; after 2006, the applicable exclusion amount will not grow. It is not indexed for inflation. Only time will tell whether Congress will elect to allow the applicable exclusion amount to change with inflation. Until then, the biggest concern should be whether Congress will allow the full phase-in to occur. Congress can change its mind at any time in the phase-in process, either capping the applicable exclusion amount or even lowering it.

The law continues to provide spouses with a massive benefit. Spouses can leave any portion or all of their property free of federal estate tax to their U.S. citizen surviving spouses. There is no federal estate tax on property passing between spouses on death. This is called the unlimited marital deduction, to which we devote Chapter 12, The Marital Deduction.

ERTA began this revolutionary concept of treating spouses as one economic unit. For the first time in the history of our federal estate tax law, our government recognized a plain truth: The successful accumulation of property by husband and wife is the result of the joint efforts of both spouses. Government's recognition of this plain truth had been long overdue.

The financial security that the federal estate tax now provides has helped, and will continue to help, the family unit survive economically. We believe that because of the government's recognition of spouses as true economic teams, widows and widowers are much less dependent on children and government for their economic existence. Government has given back to the family what it has taken away for years; it has allowed spouses to keep what they have earned through a lifetime of sacrifice.

Table 9-3
Tax on a \$3,000,000 Estate, 1997 through 2006

Year	Tax
1997	\$1,098,000
1998	1,088,750
1999	1,079,500
2000	1,070,250
2001	1,070,250
2002	1,061,000
2003	1,061,000
2004	1,003,500
2005	964,500
2006	945,000

In Chapter 12, The Marital Deduction, and Chapter 25, Planning for a Spouse, we delve into the ramifications of this law.

Federal Estate Tax:

Taxes the right to transfer almost all property interests.

Applies to the fair market value of property.

Is paid before beneficiaries are paid.

Is generally payable in cash nine months after the date of death.

Only applies to estates valued in excess of $1,000,000 beginning in 2006; until then the applicable exclusion amount is being phased in.

Provides rates beginning at 37 percent with a maximum rate of 55 percent (60 percent for estate values between $10,000,000 and $17, 184,000).

Allows spouses to leave unlimited amounts of property to each other free of federal estate tax.

10

The Unified System

"Robbing Peter to Pay Paul"

Prior to the Tax Reform Act of 1976, the federal tax law favored lifetime gifts over transfers upon death. The federal gift tax rates were actually 25 percent less than the federal estate tax rates.

Historically, a potential giver had a $30,000 lifetime exemption. This meant that in addition to the old $3,000 annual exclusion, an additional $30,000 was exempt from federal gift tax. Gifts in excess of the annual exclusion and lifetime exemption were then taxed on a cumulative basis. (This means that as the total value of gifts grew, the federal gift tax bracket at which they were taxed progressively increased.)

Upon death, there was a $60,000 deduction. Property in excess of $60,000 of value was taxed for federal estate tax purposes, also on a cumulative basis. The federal estate and gift tax systems were essentially separate and nonrelated. The net effect of the unrelated systems was that a gift removed property from the highest-possible estate tax rate to the lowest-possible gift tax rates.

The 1976 Tax Reform Act unified the federal estate and gift tax systems. As a result of this unification of systems, no longer was there a $30,000 lifetime exemption and a separate tax rate for gifts, nor was there a $60,000 death deduction and a separate tax rate for estates.

Under the unified system, gifts and estates were taxed the same. Instead of a gift exemption and a death deduction, a single exemption was given to taxpayers to use, at their choice, either for lifetime gifts or at death. This single exemption is called the exemption equivalent by estate planning professionals. The maximum exemption equivalent prior to ERTA was $175,625.

ERTA continued the unified system concept. Under ERTA the exemption equivalent was gradually increased to $600,000. Now, the old exemption equivalent has been replaced by the applicable exclusion amount. The applicable exclusion amount started at $600,000 and is being phased in, reaching a maximum amount of $1,000,000 in 2006. (Table 9-1 shows the scheduled phase-in of the applicable exclusion amount.)

Here is an example of how the applicable exclusion amount works:

> Ginny Monday, not married, makes $500,000 in gifts that are subject to federal gift taxation during her lifetime. Ginny dies in 2006. Ginny's taxable estate for federal estate tax purposes, before her remaining applicable exclusion amount is applied, is $800,000. Since Ginny used $500,000 of her applicable exclusion amount to make her lifetime gifts federal gift tax-free, her estate has $500,000 of remaining applicable exclusion amount (her $1,000,000 applicable exclusion less the $500,000 she used during her life). As a result, $300,000 of Ginny's property ($800,000 taxable estate less the $500,000 of remaining applicable exclusion amount) is subject to federal estate tax.

When deciding whether it is better to use the applicable exclusion amount during your life instead of at your death, the time value of money must be considered. A dollar in hand today is worth much more than receiving that same dollar in the future. You can invest a dollar today at 10 percent and next year have $1.10. But if someone promises to pay you $1 in one year, you have lost that $0.10 investment. Applying this concept to the applicable exclusion amount, if you give a highly appreciating asset away, you avoid gift tax by using your applicable exclusion amount, thereby removing both the asset and its appreciation from your estate. The value of using your applicable exclusion amount for lifetime gifts is twofold: You remove the asset and its appreciation from your estate, and do it in terms of today's dollars.

There is one other advantage to making taxable gifts rather than holding on to property until death. It has to do with how federal gifts are taxed and how the federal estate tax is imposed. Estate planning practitioners refer to the federal gift tax as exclusionary and the estate tax as inclusionary. To understand why, let's take an example of an individual, Edward, who wants to either give or leave his daughter, Carlye, $1,000,000, but wants to pay the least amount of tax. Let's further assume that Edward has used his full applicable exclusion amount and that he is in the 50 percent estate and gift tax bracket.

If Edward wants to leave Carlye $1,000,000 at his death, his estate must be at least $2,000,000. With a $2,000,000 estate, there would be $1,000,000 of federal estate tax, leaving Carlye her $1,000,000. On the other hand, if Edward gave Carlye $1,000,000 while he was still alive, the tax on the gift would be 50 percent of the value of the gift, $500,000. The reduction in Edward's estate by making a gift would be the $1,000,000 he gave Carlye and the $500,000 tax on the gift. The cost of leaving Carlye $1,000,000 at his death would be the $1,000,000 tax plus the $1,000,000 bequest, a total of $2,000,000 as opposed to the $1,500,000 cost of the gift. Now, assuming Edward made the gift, he would have a $500,000 estate at his death, generating a tax of $250,000. So, comparing the two, the gift, in total, saved $250,000.

There are other considerations when deciding whether giving a lifetime gift is better than leaving property at death. One is the time value of money. Giving a lifetime gift means that the federal government gets its money before you die. The government has the use of the money; you do not. If you live for a number of years, it is possible that the money you would have earned on the money paid in taxes would eventually leave your beneficiaries better off economically. Generally, this is not the case, but it is a consideration worthy of calculation. Another concern is that property you give away does not receive a step-up in cost basis, which it does get when you die. Step-up in basis is discussed at length in Chapter 15.

If you have a taxable estate and you want to give the maximum amount of property to your children or others, always consider making a lifetime gift. Consult with your tax advisors to see if you can benefit materially with a lifetime gift rather than leaving property at your death. You may be surprised at the results.

Many estate planning techniques involve the use of a gift program that takes current advantage of the applicable exclusion amount. With proper professional advice, you might want to consider beginning a gift program.

11

The Gift Tax

"The Manner of Giving Is Worth More Than the Gift"

Like the federal estate tax, the federal gift tax is not a tax on property. It is a tax on the privilege of transferring property. How the transfer is made determines whether a gift has been made.

A gift is defined as any transfer of property for which the giver receives less than the full property value in return. To the extent the transfer is for less than full value, a gift has been made. Intent or desire to make a gift is generally irrelevant for federal gift tax purposes. The mere act of delivering the property to its recipient is enough to create a gift subject to the federal gift tax laws. Professional estate planners call the person who makes a gift a donor and the person who receives the gift a donee.

It is apparent from the definition of a gift that an inadvertent gift can easily be made. For example, payment of someone else's expenses or debts is a gift, unless there is a legal obligation to do so. Forgiving a debt, putting property into joint tenancy, or purchasing something for the benefit of another can all be construed as making a gift.

If a gift is made, it may not necessarily be subject to federal gift tax. The Internal Revenue Code has, for many years, allowed a certain amount, called the annual exclusion, to be free of federal gift tax; that is, a giver can give certain gift amounts each year to as many individual recipients as the giver wants, all free of federal gift tax. Any amount given to a recipient in excess of the annual exclusion is subject to taxation.

For many years, the annual exclusion was $3,000 per recipient. In 1982, the annual exclusion was significantly increased, to $10,000 per recipient per year. Beginning in 1999, the annual exclusion amount is adjusted for inflation. When the cumulative inflation reaches $1,000, the annual exclusion will be bumped up by $1,000. For example, if inflation is low for several years and when applied to the current annual exclusion does not add up to $1,000, then no adjustment would be made. However, when the cumulative amount of inflation is $1,000 or more, then an adjustment will be made. The U.S. Government will announce the inflation adjustment, if any, each year.

The annual exclusion is eligible for gift splitting. Gift splitting is a method by which spouses can combine their annual exclusions and make a joint gift. For example, a mother with three children could give $30,000 with no federal gift tax to her children: $10,000 per child. However, if she decides to give an additional $30,000 to the children in the same year (a total of $20,000 per child) and her husband consents, then their combined annual exclusions can be used. All $60,000 ($20,000 per child) is free of federal gift tax because of the annual exclusion and gift splitting. The gift-splitting maximum amount is subject to the same inflation adjustment as is the annual exclusion.

It is important to remember two things about gift splitting. The first is that each spouse must consent to the gift, which is done by filing a federal gift tax return. The second is that if a spouse consents to gift splitting, each spouse will use up part or all of his or her annual exclusion as to the recipient for whom the consent was given. Thus, if an $18,000 joint gift is made to one child, each spouse uses $9,000 of his or her annual exclusion for that child. Each spouse can only give an additional $1,000 to that child in that year and have it qualify for the annual exclusion.

The annual exclusion only applies to a gift of a present interest. The annual exclusion does not apply to a gift of a future interest. A gift of a future interest is defined as a gift of property that does not give the recipient immediate use and benefit of that property. An example of a gift of a future interest is a gift to a trust in which the trustee is not required to immediately distribute the property to a beneficiary. Two exceptions to this trust rule are a 2503(c) minor's trust, discussed in Chapter 16, Trusts; and a gift of an insurance policy or money to pay its premiums to an irrevocable life insurance trust, discussed in Chapter 28, The Irrevocable Life Insurance Trust.

All gifts between spouses, when the spouse who receives the gift is a U.S. citizen, are free of federal gift tax. If the spouse who receives the gift is a noncitizen, the gifts are subject to an annual exclusion of $100,000, which is adjusted each year for inflation.

Before you start making gifts to your spouse, however, you should know that there are some drawbacks associated with them. To explain these drawbacks, we must review the rules of step-up in basis. All assets of a deceased person are valued at their fair market value upon the owner's death. The assets then receive a step-up in basis to fair market value. For example, if an individual purchased a painting for $1,000 (cost basis) and its fair market value at death was $10,000, the painting receives a new or stepped-up basis of $10,000. If the painting was sold by the estate for $11,000, only $1,000 would be subject to federal income tax.

A lifetime gift does not get a step-up in basis. Had that same individual given the painting to a spouse prior to death, the surviving spouse would receive the deceased spouse's cost basis of $1,000. If the surviving spouse sold the painting for $11,000, $10,000 would be subject to federal income tax. Thus, assets that have a low cost basis are not the kinds of assets that you should be giving to your spouse, at least from a federal income tax perspective. Remember, all assets that go to a U.S. citizen surviving spouse at death pass free of federal estate tax and receive a step-up in basis.

There are many other considerations that you should examine when making gifts. One major consideration involves the removal of highly appreciating assets from your estate. The trick is, of course, picking assets that will actually appreciate in value. However, if a highly appreciating asset is given to your spouse and you die first, the asset with all its appreciation will not be subject to federal estate tax on your death; the asset and its appreciated value will be subject to estate tax on your spouse's death. If you give highly appreciating property to someone other than your spouse, you will remove both the asset and *all* its future appreciation from your estate and your spouse's estate. If you give highly appreciating property to someone other than your spouse, you may pay federal gift tax on its value, as of the date of the gift, but neither you nor your spouse nor your respective estates will ever pay federal gift or estate tax on the appreciation of the property.

Another consideration in making lifetime gifts involves reducing federal income tax. If you own property that generates taxable income, you may wish to give the property to one or more family members who are, or will be, in lower federal income tax brackets. The current income tax rates have made this reason for making gifts less attractive, however. Because tax brackets are lower, reducing income tax has become less important. In addition, income from property and other passive sources received by children under fourteen years of age is taxed in the same bracket as that of their parents. Check with your tax adviser before attempting to use gifts to shift income to family members.

Some types of gifts are subject to a three-year pull-back rule. For example, if a person makes a gift of a life insurance policy on his or her life and dies within three years of making the gift, the value of the life insurance proceeds are pulled back into the giver's estate. If the giver makes a taxable gift of any asset, pays gift tax on the transfer, and then dies within three years, the amount of the federal gift tax paid is also pulled back into the giver's estate. However, for the vast majority of gifts made within three years of the giver's death, this pull-back rule does not apply.

Some states have their own gift tax laws. Each state's gift tax laws are unique, and a discussion of these laws is outside the scope of this book. When making gifts, be sure to consider whether or not your state has a gift tax.

Lifetime giving is as much an art as a science. *How* you give something away may be as important as *what* you give away. The making of gifts can be critical to the estate planning process and, like all other major estate planning tools, should be discussed with the members of your professional estate planning team.

Gifts, for Tax Purposes:

Can be made inadvertently.

May not be taxable because of the annual exclusion.

Can be split with a spouse.

Are tax-free when made to a U.S. citizen spouse.

Do *not* qualify for step-up in basis.

12

The Marital Deduction

"Federal Recognition
of a Spouse's Efforts"

The marital deduction is a tax concept that describes a tax-savings benefit given to spouses for purposes of federal gift and estate taxes. It is also
used by many states for purposes of their death and gift tax laws. An understanding of the marital deduction is critical when planning for a
spouse.

The Marital Deduction
and Federal Gift Tax

Before 1976, when a spouse made a gift to the other spouse, exactly one-
half of the value of the gift made was not taxed by the federal government.
This was because of the marital deduction. The marital deduction provisions of the federal gift tax law were a government-sponsored benefit made
available only for gifts between spouses. These provisions always removed
one-half of the taxable value of a gift from gift taxation. If a gift was made
to a spouse (marital), half of that gift was deducted (deduction) before gift
tax calculations were made.

Congress changed the marital deduction rules in 1976 with the enactment of the Tax Reform Act of 1976. This act made the marital deduction
more difficult to understand.

The Tax Reform Act of 1976 gave a greater marital deduction to married
citizens who made gifts of smaller amounts of property to their spouses.
This marital deduction allowed a married citizen to give up to $100,000 tax-
free to his or her spouse. This was truly a gift by the government to its married taxpayers; however, when the federal government gives, it also can take

away, and that is precisely what happened on the next $100,000 of gifts made to a spouse. Under the 1976 law, all gifts made to a spouse over $100,000 but not greater than $200,000 did not qualify for or get the benefit of the marital deduction and were subsequently fully subject to federal gift tax. For gifts over $200,000 to a spouse, the marital deduction worked just like it did before 1976: One-half of the value of the property that was given was not subject to tax.

The real change brought about by the 1976 act was to benefit only those married citizens who gave less than $200,000 to their spouses. The change in the law did not benefit spouses making gifts in excess of $200,000; for these married taxpayers, the change was no change at all.

Former President Reagan and Congress changed the marital deduction rules again with the passage of ERTA. This act took effect on January 1, 1982 and provided a 100 percent marital deduction for all gifts between spouses. The Technical and Miscellaneous Revenue Act of 1988 limited the 100 percent marital deduction to spouses who are U.S. citizens. If the spouse receiving the gift is not a U.S. citizen, the $100,000 annual gift tax exclusion applies. Any gift, regardless of its value, made to a U.S. citizen spouse is tax-free for federal gift tax purposes. This is called the 100 percent or unlimited marital deduction. Now, regardless of how much a gift to a U.S. citizen spouse is, the rules are always the same.

The unlimited marital deduction provisions of the federal gift tax law apply to married taxpayers living in all states, including the community property states (Alaska, Arizona, California, Idaho, Louisiana, Nevada, New Mexico, Texas, Washington, and Wisconsin). Prior to ERTA, married citizens residing in these states did not get the right to the federal gift tax marital deduction with respect to their community property interests. One-half of all gifts of community property between spouses was subject to federal gift tax prior to ERTA. ERTA and other recent tax acts now provide a 100 percent marital deduction for community property gifts between married taxpayers, when the spouse who receives the gift is a U.S. citizen.

The Marital Deduction and Federal Estate Tax

Prior to 1976, all spouses could leave up to one-half of their property to or for the benefit of their surviving spouses free of federal estate tax. This was because of the federal estate tax marital deduction which evidenced, in our opinion, Congress's belief that both spouses had a hand in creating the wealth in the marriage (a concept long recognized in the community property states). In order to qualify for the tax break created by the marital deduction, the following minimum rules had to be met:

The surviving spouses had to receive at least annually all the income from the property that was left for their benefit. The spouses also had the right to require that the property be invested in income-producing assets.

The surviving spouses had to be given the right to leave that property on their deaths to whomever they pleased. This right is called a general power of appointment.

In order to qualify for the marital deduction, all that spouses had to give surviving spouses was the income from the marital deduction property and the right for the surviving spouses to leave that property on their subsequent deaths to whomever they desired.

The Tax Reform Act of 1976 changed the rules with regard to the federal estate tax marital deduction. This legislation, like its federal gift tax counterpart, was designed to favor the less financially successful citizen. It provided that the marital deduction would exempt from federal estate taxation the first $250,000 left to or for the benefit of a surviving spouse. It also provided that the marital deduction would be the greater of $250,000 or one-half of the deceased spouse's adjusted gross estate (property the spouse left less debts and expenses). That $250,000 was important: An estate left to a spouse up to $250,000 was tax-free; an estate up to $500,000 still gave a surviving spouse $250,000 tax-free; an estate over $500,000 was back to the older rules under which only half of the estate would be tax-free to the surviving spouse.

ERTA and other recent tax acts dramatically changed the marital deduction rules. The law now provides for a 100 percent federal estate tax marital deduction when the surviving spouse is a U.S. citizen, and changes the rights that a surviving spouse must receive in order to qualify the property as marital deduction property.

In order to qualify for the current unlimited federal estate tax marital deduction, the following minimum rules must be met:

The surviving spouse must be a citizen of the United States.

The property interest must be included in the value of the deceased spouse's estate.

The surviving spouse must receive, at least annually, all the income from the marital deduction property for life.

The surviving spouse must have the right to require that the property be invested in income-producing assets.

No person can have the power to give any part of the marital deduction property to anyone other than the surviving spouse.

The last three requirements are called qualified income interests.

There is no longer a requirement that spouses have a general power of appointment, or the right to leave the property on their deaths according to their wishes. This represents a massive change in the federal estate tax law. There is a requirement, however, that the marital deduction property generally be left intact for the benefit of the spouse to ensure that the surviving spouse will continue to receive income for his or her life. No person can be given the power to give the marital deduction property to others during the life of the surviving spouse.

In order to qualify for the marital deduction, a surviving spouse only needs to receive a qualified income interest from that property. If income is not given for the surviving spouse's life, it is not a qualified income interest and *no* marital deduction will be allowed.

Estate planning professionals describe this marital deduction requirement as qualified terminable interest property. Most of the professional literature on the subject has nicknamed a trust used to provide the surviving spouse with income as a Q-TIP trust: **q**ualified **t**erminable **i**nterest **p**roperty trust. We believe that Q-TIPs are used for other purposes and prefer to refer to this trust as a spouse's trust or marital trust instead.

In Chapter 25, we discuss the planning opportunities available under the unlimited marital deduction. They are different—very different—from anything that has been available before.

In reviewing our discussion of the marital deduction, please remember that:

> You can give or leave all or part of your property tax-free to your U.S. citizen spouse.

> Your U.S. citizen spouse must receive, at least annually, all the income from the marital deduction property for life.

> Your U.S. citizen spouse must have the right to require that the property be invested in income-producing assets, and no person can have the power to give any part of the marital deduction property to anyone other than the surviving spouse.

13

Community Property

"Maverick Law in Maverick States"

Forty-two of our states base their laws of property ownership entirely on our English common-law heritage. Eight states base their laws of property ownership, as to property owned between a husband and wife, on a heritage of French and Spanish law. These states have community property laws with respect to the ownership of property acquired during the term of a marriage. Each of these eight states has its own brand of community property laws; but all community property laws, regardless of a state's variations, must be differentiated from the law of the forty-two non–community property law states.

Wisconsin was not a community property state initially, but changed its laws to a form of ownership that is, for most purposes, community property. Alaska also was not an original community property state, but changed its laws to allow its residents and special trusts for nonresidents to treat property as if it were community property. We consider both of these states community property states.

The community property law states are:

Alaska	Nevada
Arizona	New Mexico
California	Texas
Idaho	Washington
Louisiana	Wisconsin

In reviewing the list of community property states, you can see the historical influence of the Spanish and French tradition. The French brought the Napoleonic Code to Louisiana, and the Spanish tradition was adopted by the remaining seven states.

Community property law manifests the social and legal belief that property acquired by spouses during the marriage should be construed as one total "community" of property. Regardless of how ownership is taken in that property, it belongs to a marital partnership. Each of the spouses, as a fifty-fifty partner, owns 50 percent of the partnership or community property.

To facilitate understanding of community property, we will call the marriage the community partnership. The property that a husband and wife own before they enter into their community partnership is their separate property; it was acquired outside the community partnership and remains the separate property of each. This is also true of gifts or inheritances received by either spouse during the marriage. If that separate property is sold and the proceeds commingled with other community-partnership activities and investments, it generally becomes part of the community partnership's holdings.

Income that is generated from the community partnership's holdings is owned 50 percent by each of the community partnership's partners. From this perspective, community property should be very understandable and, in fact, very logical.

For purposes of community property laws, how property is titled is irrelevant. All property acquired during the term of a marriage is property that belongs to the community partnership, and each partner has a 50 percent ownership in that property, because the spouses are fifty-fifty partners.

In Alaska, title to property may be relevant. Alaska's laws allow residents and special trusts holding property of nonresidents to designate their property as community property. So, unlike the other nine "pure" community property states, Alaska requires affirmative actions in order for the community property rules to apply.

The federal government had to recognize the right of each of these ten states to create its own unusual form of ownership between spouses, because of the Tenth Amendment to the U.S. Constitution. As a result, the federal government had to structure its estate and gift tax laws so that they would apply fairly both to the citizens of the "normal" states and the citizens of the maverick, or community, states. Here is a historical perspective on the government's rules in this area:

> Because a community-partnership partner owned half of the marital assets, the federal government could only tax half of the marital property on the death of either partner. In order to maintain fairness, Congress was eventually persuaded in 1948 to create the marital deduction for spouses who did not reside in community property states. The marital deduction historically allowed spouses to leave half of their property tax-free to their surviving spouses. This appeared to equalize the federal estate tax treatment of marital property in all the states.

Citizens of community property states did not get the federal estate tax marital deduction except with respect to separate property; they did not need it because community property laws already gave them the same benefit.

The federal government also gave citizens of the other forty states the right to exclude from federal gift tax the value of one-half of the gifts made between spouses. This was also fair, because property acquired by community partners was acquired 50 percent by each of the partners without a gift tax.

Spouses in community property states did not get the federal gift tax marital deduction except for separate property; they already had it under their states' community property laws.

ERTA provided for an unlimited marital deduction that allows a spouse to leave all of his or her property tax-free to the surviving spouse; it also allowed a spouse to give property to a spouse during life free from all federal gift taxes. The Technical and Miscellaneous Revenue Act of 1988 restricts the unlimited marital deduction to U.S. citizen surviving spouses.

Now citizens in community property states get an unlimited marital deduction for both federal estate and gift tax purposes. This was a major change in the law. Individuals who reside in a community property state must have their estate plans reviewed by their professional advisers. The additional benefits that are afforded married taxpayers residing in community property states are enormous.

14

State Death Taxes

"States Need Revenue Too"

Every state has its own death tax in one form or another. Individual states take pride in their uniqueness, and this pride is certainly borne out in the manner in which individual states structure their death taxes.

All states' death tax laws fall into one of three general patterns: states that collect their taxes directly from the federal government (gap tax states); states that tax the estates of their citizens much like the federal government does (estate tax states); and states that base their death taxes on the value of the property that passes to certain defined beneficiaries (inheritance tax states).

To help your general understanding of state death taxes, we provide a classification of the states in terms of the three categories the states fall under.

Gap Tax States

The federal government's estate tax tables allow as a credit against federal estate tax certain dollar amounts that can be paid to the individual states instead of to the federal government. In essence, the federal estate tax system provides for a little bit of revenue sharing with those states.

The federal estate tax tables spell out what the tax will be, bracket by bracket, for different-sized estates. These same tables provide that a small percentage of the federal estate tax will be forgiven if that amount is paid to the state in which the deceased citizen resided, pursuant to that state's death tax laws.

Table 14-1
State Inheritance Tax Table

	Exemption, in $	Share in Excess of Exemption, in $	Tax, in $	Rate on Next Bracket, in %
CLASS 1 BENEFICIARIES				
a. Widow or minor child	10,000 each	0	0	2
		25,000	500	4
		50,000	1,500	6
b. Husband or adult child, grandchildren	4,000 each	100,000	4,500	8
		200,000	12,500	10
		500,000	42,500	15
CLASS 2 BENEFICIARIES				
Sisters, brothers, nieces, nephews	1,000 each	0	0	4
		25,000	1,000	6
		50,000	2,500	8
		100,000	6,500	12
		200,000	18,500	16
		500,000	68,500	20

Table 14-1 (continued)
State Inheritance Tax Table

Exemption, in $	Share in Excess of Exemption, in $	Tax, in $	Rate on Next Bracket, in %
CLASS 3 BENEFICIARIES			
Uncles, aunts, and their descendants			
500 each	0	0	6
	25,000	1,500	9
	50,000	3,750	12
	100,000	9,750	15
	200,000	24,750	20
	500,000	84,750	25
CLASS 4 BENEFICIARIES			
All others			
0	0	0	8
	25,000	2,000	14
	50,000	5,500	20
	100,000	15,500	30

Some states have structured their death tax rates so that the tax they collect is exactly the same amount as the federal government will forgive in the federal estate tax tables through the federal revenue sharing program. States whose death tax laws are structured so that the states receive funds only from the federal estate tax revenue sharing program are referred to as gap tax states by estate planning professionals.

In reality, the gap tax states only receive death tax revenues that would have gone to the federal government but for the state gap tax. A portion of the federal estate tax is paid to the gap tax state, instead of all the tax being paid to the federal government, allowing the states to collect the tax painlessly (for them).

While gap tax states used to be in the minority, now the gap tax is used by more states than any other method for collecting state death tax.

The gap tax states are:

Alabama	Maryland	Oregon
Alaska	Massachusetts	Rhode Island
Arizona	Minnesota	South Carolina
Arkansas	Mississippi*	Texas
California	Missouri	Utah
Colorado	Montana*	Vermont
Florida	Nevada	Virginia
Georgia	New Hampshire	Washington
Hawaii	New Jersey*	West Virginia
Idaho	New Mexico	Wisconsin
Illinois	New York	Wyoming
Maine	North Dakota	

*Mississippi, Montana, and New Jersey are hybrid states. They are gap tax states for property that passes to spouses and descendants. For all other heirs, they have an estate tax.

The District of Columbia also has a gap tax. Connecticut will be a gap tax state by 2005.

Estate Tax States

Some states tax the estates of their deceased citizens under death tax systems that are structured very much like the federal estate tax. These states apply their own unique tax rates and have their own unique sets of rules as to how their rates will be applied.

Estate tax states also get the benefit of the federal estate tax revenue sharing program. Unlike gap tax states, these states not only get revenues under the federal estate tax revenue sharing program, but also collect substantial additional funds as a result of their death taxes. Their death tax rates are always higher than the amount from the federal estate tax revenue sharing program.

The estate tax states are:

Michigan

Ohio

Oklahoma

Puerto Rico also has an estate tax.

Inheritance Tax States

States that fall into this category are states that apply their death tax rates against the value of the shares that pass to certain defined classes of beneficiaries. Because the state death tax is calculated on the share that *each* beneficiary will receive or inherit, it is called an inheritance tax.

Inheritance tax states have different tax rates that apply to different kinds or classes of beneficiaries. Generally, however, the closer the beneficiary's blood relationship is to the deceased, the lower the inheritance tax rate will be; spouses almost always pay inheritance taxes at the lowest tax rates. An example of an inheritance tax table is shown in Table 14-1.

The inheritance tax table illustrates how most state inheritance taxes are structured. Your review of this example should highlight the fact that the more distant a relative is to the deceased, the lower the exemption and the higher the tax will be.

Inheritance tax states also receive funds from the federal estate tax revenue sharing program. Many inheritance tax states provide that if the amount of the inheritance tax due is less than the federal estate tax revenue sharing amount allowed, then the inheritance tax due will be a minimum of the federal estate tax revenue sharing amount. This assures that they will receive the largest amount of federal funds available.

The inheritance tax states are:

Connecticut (until 2005)	Louisiana
Delaware	Nebraska
Indiana	North Carolina
Iowa	Pennsylvania
Kansas	South Dakota
Kentucky	Tennessee

A few states also have their own gift taxes. Like state death tax laws, gift tax laws are unique in each state. Connecticut, Louisiana, New York (repealed effective January 1, 2000), North Carolina, and Tennessee have some form of gift tax. Puerto Rico and the Virgin Islands have gift taxes as well.

State death and gift tax laws change from time to time, so the lists of states in this chapter may not reflect the current law in your state. A detailed discussion of individual state death and gift tax laws is outside the scope of this book. Your state's gift and death tax laws should be discussed with your professional estate planning team. The impact of your state's death and gift tax laws is important to consider when you are planning your estate.

15

Step-Up in Basis at Death

"It Almost Pays to Die"

Basis is a word developed for federal income tax purposes. Basis, or cost basis as it is sometimes known, is the amount that is generally used to compute the taxable gain for federal income tax purposes on the sale of property.

A simple example of this principle is the purchase of a family car. If you pay $5,000 for your car, $5,000 is your cost basis in the car. Upon a sale of the car for $6,000, the gain subject to federal income tax is $1,000 ($6,000 sales price less $5,000 cost basis).

The federal estate tax is an everything tax, as we discussed earlier. At death, or six months thereafter, the fair market value of all the assets owned by the deceased person is determined by the agent of the deceased person's estate. The fair market value of all the assets, less debts and expenses of the estate, is then subject to the federal estate tax. The end result of the federal estate tax is that all the appreciation in value of the assets in the estate can be taxed. Unlike the federal income tax, the cost basis is ignored.

Congress has generally recognized that there may be an inherent unfair federal income tax element of the federal estate tax. If all assets are subject to federal estate tax (everything tax) and after death the same assets are subject to federal income tax (sales price less cost basis), there is a great danger of double taxation. Appreciation (growth) of assets could be subject to the federal estate tax as well as the federal income tax. This inherent unfairness has been turned into a magnificent benefit for most estates.

Assets that are in the estate of a deceased person, whether the estate pays federal estate tax or not, take as their cost basis for federal income tax purposes the fair market value of those assets at date of death or six months after death, whichever valuation date is used. This step-up in basis means that the appreciation of assets in an estate is *not* subject to federal income tax.

For example, if the family car is purchased for $5,000 (original cost basis) by the income-earner spouse and, at that spouse's death, it has a fair market value of $6,000 (step-up in basis), the $1,000 in appreciation is not subject to federal income tax. If the estate sells the car for $6,000, there is *no* taxable gain.

The step-up in basis rules apply to *every asset in an estate,* and the rules apply whether or not any federal estate tax is paid. The step-up in basis rules, however, do not apply to lifetime gifts. A recipient of a gift has the same cost basis in the asset that the giver had. The federal gift tax is determined based on the fair market value of the asset given. Thus a gift tax may be paid on the lifetime gift, and when the recipient of the gift sells it, there may be federal income tax due. Double taxation is possible.

When lifetime gifts are contemplated, not only is the federal gift tax effect important, but the federal income tax must also be considered. For example, if an elderly taxpayer owns property with a low cost basis, making lifetime gifts may not be wise. It may be better to have the individual retain the assets so that their basis will be stepped up at death. On the other hand, if the elderly taxpayer has assets with a high cost basis, it may be good planning to use these assets for lifetime gifts.

Married residents of community property states have a distinct advantage over their non–community property counterparts when it comes to step-up in basis rules. If a community property spouse dies, *all* the community property may receive a step-up in basis, not just the interest of the deceased spouse.

There is a tax gimmick affecting step-up in basis that should be avoided because it will not work. A person with assets having a low basis could give those assets to someone who is going to die in the near future. The individual who is dying could make a will giving the property back to the original giver at death. The result was that the original giver would receive a step-up in basis on the giver's original property. This transaction will not work for any property given to the dying individual within one year of death when the property is left to the original giver.

The step-up in basis rules under our federal estate tax are of the utmost importance. Because of their far-reaching effects on estate planning, the step-up in basis rules should be discussed at great length with your professional estate planning team.

16
Trusts

"The Estate Planner's Golf Clubs"

A significant number of estate planning techniques are implemented in the form of a trust. Trusts can be designed to accomplish a host of planning alternatives. Most professionals use a panoply of trust documents in accomplishing the objectives of their clients. An estate planner uses trusts like a professional golfer uses clubs. In our experience, however, very few clients we initially meet understand what trusts do, what they involve, and how they are structured. The subject of trusts and how they are used is apparently seldom taught outside of the professional domain.

Many people believe that trusts are on the government hit list, and this is understandable. They read in their daily papers or favorite magazines about antitrust lawsuits between government and big business. Before we explain what trusts are, how they work, and what they accomplish, let us make some sense out of this antitrust nonsense.

We start with John D. Rockefeller, Sr. Toward the end of the nineteenth century, Mr. Rockefeller was engaged in the capitalist pursuit of controlling the petroleum marketplace. Regardless of your politics, Mr. Rockefeller made a pretty good job of it. One of the problems he faced, however, was that different states had different laws, and these legal impediments threatened to curtail his interstate growth.

With the help of his chief legal mogul, Mr. Dodd, Mr. Rockefeller signed a document called the Standard Oil Trust. He transferred all his Standard Oil stock to his trust, and he then named trustees to run that trust. Using a bold common-law form of title holding, Mr. Rockefeller set the world of finance on its ears. Through the use of the Standard Oil Trust, Mr. Rockefeller crossed state lines with impunity and an empire was established.

A monopoly resulted from the Standard Oil Trust because Mr. Rockefeller indeed controlled the petroleum marketplace. Government stepped in and passed antitrust laws. These laws were passed to curtail and regulate

Mr. Rockefeller's monopoly and other monopolies throughout the American marketplace.

These laws were antimonopoly laws, not really antitrust laws; but because Mr. Rockefeller's legal genius, Mr. Dodd, chose to use an old form of ownership to effectuate his client's industrial dominance, trust became synonymous with and a symbol of monopoly. Even the *World Book Encyclopedia* defines trust as a "term used in economics to describe a large industrial monopoly." Estate planners have inherited a public that, too often, equates a trust with its Rockefellerian usage.

In Appendix D, we have included a short history of estate planning. It explains the ancient roots of trusts and why they survive today. This history will give you a perspective on how trusts have been adapted to our laws in the United States and other countries that are based on English common law.

In estate planning, trusts enable people to pass title to their property to others either during lifetime or at death. When a person creates a trust and places property in a trust, the trust maker, in effect, makes a gift. Trusts enable their makers to make gifts to their beneficiaries and allow the trust maker to exercise significant control, on a prearranged basis, over the disposition of the trust property. In effect, trusts allow property to pass to others with strings attached.

All trusts have the following characteristics:

A trust is created by a trust maker. Attorneys call the maker a settlor, trustor, creator, or grantor.

The person responsible for following the maker's instructions is called the trustee.

Trustees can be individuals or licensed institutions. The maker can also be his or her own trustee.

Trusts can be created by more than one maker. Joint makers are called joint makers or comakers. Trusts can be operated by more than one trustee, called cotrustees.

Trusts can be created for the benefit of the maker or for the benefit of other people. The people for whose benefit a trust is created are called beneficiaries.

Trusts can accomplish just about any objective of the maker as long as it is not illegal or against public policy.

Trusts cannot last forever unless the beneficiary is a legally recognized charity or unless state law allows them to last forever.

The beneficiaries who have the first rights to the trust property are called primary beneficiaries. If the primary beneficiaries die or become disqualified, and according to the instructions given to the trustee by the trust maker, then the property will go to other named beneficiaries called contingent beneficiaries.

Trusts, to be effective, must be in writing. They must be signed by the maker, and if a living trust is used, it should be signed by the trustee, although the trustee's signature is not necessary to make a trust valid. If the trust document is not signed by a trustee, the trust is not void; it still exists.

The law has always stated that "No trust shall fail for lack of a trustee." The local court having jurisdiction over trusts will name a trustee if one is not named in the trust document.

The trust document is often referred to as an indenture or a trust indenture (historically, a deed to which two or more persons are parties).

Trust beneficiaries do not have to sign the trust document or will containing a trust.

Any number of separate trusts can be created in a single trust document.

When the maker puts property in a trust, the maker funds the trust.

Trust makers can be primary or contingent beneficiaries of their own trusts.

There are several different kinds of trusts that accomplish a host of estate planning objectives. (Please refer to Figure 16-1.) All trusts can be categorized in one of two ways. A trust is either a living trust or a death trust. Living trusts are often referred to as *inter vivos* (Latin for living) trusts. Death trusts are called testamentary (from the Latin *testamentum*) trusts and are created in a person's will. They do not come into existence until the death of the will maker.

A living trust is always created during the lifetime of the trust maker. A living trust usually provides that the maker is to be his or her own primary beneficiary. Living trusts can also pass the trust property to the maker's beneficiaries on the maker's death. Because living trusts can pass property on the death of the maker, they are often referred to as will substitutes. We discuss the living trust in greater detail in Chapters 17 and 18.

A death, or testamentary, trust can only be created in a valid will. These trusts are never created to benefit the maker. Death trusts are created by a will maker, and although they are created or drafted during the will maker's life, they are not operative until the maker's death. Death trusts have no life until the death of the maker.

Because a will goes through the probate process, the trusts created in that will also go through the probate process. Testamentary trusts are involved in the probate process and are subject to the local probate court's direction and control (jurisdiction).

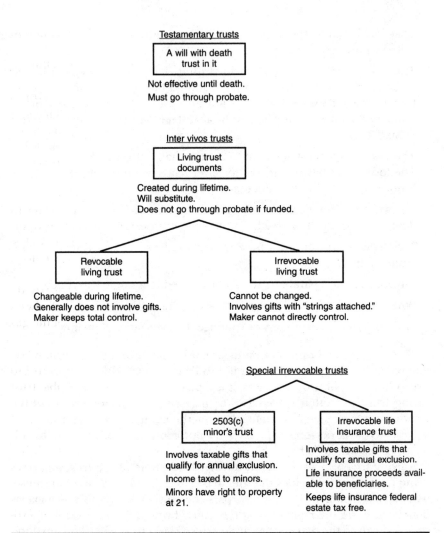

Figure 16-1. Different kinds of trusts.

Both living trusts and death trusts are important tools to estate planning professionals. They allow professionals to accomplish their clients' estate planning objectives. You may recall from our discussion in Chapter 1, What Is Estate Planning?, that estate planning involves more than the outright passing of property from one person to another. People want to give what they have, to whom they want, in the way and at the time they want. They wish to reduce taxes, attorneys' fees, and court costs to the greatest extent possible. These objectives are almost always accomplished by using various trust formats. Remember that trusts are gifts with strings attached: instructions and conditions given to the trustee as to the who, how, and when of distribution of property.

Death trusts can always be canceled or changed by the maker, as long as the maker is competent, up until the maker's death.

Living trusts can be structured so that the maker can retain the right to change or terminate the trust while the maker is alive. Living trusts that give the maker the right to change his or her mind are called revocable living trusts. Living trusts that cannot be changed are called irrevocable living trusts; trusts created under this format can be altered only by court action. Neither the maker nor anyone else, for that matter, may alter these trusts.

When a trust maker creates a revocable living trust, a gift is not made. Because the maker has the right to change his or her mind about all the terms of the trust document, there can be no gift for federal or state gift tax purposes. If, however, property does pass to others while the maker is alive (even though the trust is revocable), there may be a gift for both federal and state gift tax purposes.

It is important to remember that whether a person gives property directly to others or gives property to others through a trust, a gift will always result. Whether that gift will be taxed depends upon the amount of the gift and the circumstances surrounding how the gift was made.

When a trust maker funds an irrevocable living trust, a gift will always result. By creating an irrevocable trust, a trust maker gives up all control to the trust property *and* to the terms of the trust. Once the irrevocable trust is signed, a maker cannot change his or her mind or alter the terms of the trust.

By creating an irrevocable living trust, a trust maker makes a gift with strings attached. That is usually why these trusts are used. Irrevocable living trusts allow a person to give the use of property to others on a living basis pursuant to the maker's wishes and instructions to the trustee as to its use. Without the use of such a vehicle, gifts could not be made with instructions that would guarantee and control their use. Without the use of an irrevocable trust, a gift made is a gift completed; the recipient can do anything with the property received.

Irrevocable trusts are used in many situations, including:

To own life insurance policies on the life of the trust maker. These trusts are designed to keep the insurance proceeds federal estate tax-free on death and are discussed in Chapter 28, The Irrevocable Life Insurance Trust.

To hold title to property given to minors so that the gift maker can exercise control over the property.

When a person wishes to make a gift to minors but wants to control the use of the property, a minor's trust can be created. A minor's trust is often called a 2503(c), or accumulation, trust. It is named after the Internal Revenue Code provision that gives the trust its existence.

When a minor's trust is created and property is given to the trustee to manage and distribute to the minor beneficiaries according to the written instructions of the trust maker, the trust must be irrevocable. The income from the trust will be taxed for income tax purposes to the minor beneficiaries. Under prior law, this was an advantage because parents could give their children income-producing property and control the property by putting it into a minor's trust. This income would be taxed in the children's lower income tax brackets.

Unearned income, including income from trusts, received by minors under fourteen years of age is now taxed in the same income tax bracket as their parents' income. For minors who are fourteen years of age or older, income tax can be reduced by having it taxed in a minor's bracket. Minor's trusts are used as devices to control gifts made to minors and to tax income at lower brackets.

It should be noted that for these trusts to be effective, the trust maker should not be the trustee; the minor must have the right to the trust principal on attaining the age of twenty-one; and the income from the trust cannot be used to discharge a support obligation the maker of the trust owes to the minor beneficiary.

Trusts created under section 2503(c) of the Internal Revenue Code are often used to pass property to children or grandchildren subject to controls provided by the maker in the trust document. Minors' trusts should be drafted carefully by an estate planning professional.

Other trusts include special short-term trusts, called grantor retained income trusts. In Chapter 31, we describe how these trusts are used to discount gifts while allowing the trust maker to retain income from the assets placed in these trusts. There are also trusts used to give personal residences and vacation homes to children or others. These personal residence trusts, discussed more fully in Chapter 36, are very effective in lowering the value of an estate and also allowing the giver to use the home.

There are many different kinds of trusts that professional estate planners use to accomplish the objectives of their clients. Estate-planning trusts are designed to allow people to pass title to their property to others either during lifetime or at death. In the chapters that follow, we demonstrate how some of these trusts can be utilized to meet most estate planning goals.

17

The Revocable Living Trust

"The Foundation of Estate Planning"

When this book was originally written in 1981, the living trust was a little-known but highly controversial, estate planning concept. Living trusts had been used for years by a small group of professionals who recognized the great value of trusts, but who were considered to be out of the mainstream because of their "avoid probate" theme. At that time, the probate process was almost a sacrosanct pillar of the estate planning bar.

Since then, there has been a living trust revolution. As the public became more aware of the often unnecessary costs and time delays associated with wills and probate, many lawyers and other advisors began to realize that living trusts were in virtually every way superior to will-based planning.

We tried very hard to educate both the professions and the public about the benefits of living trusts. In 1988, we wrote *Loving Trust*, a book detailing the wonderful planning opportunities available in using living trusts for estate planning. In 1992, we wrote *The Living Trust Revolution*, which compared living trusts and will planning with probate in detail. It presented an overwhelming factual case for living trust planning and sounded the death knell for those practitioners who still clung to wills as superior planning vehicles. Finally, in 1996, we wrote *The Living Trust Workbook*. It is an owner's manual for living trusts that allows individuals and families to work closely with their attorneys, accountants, and financial planners to design, create, and implement proper living trust planning.

Today, living trusts are not the "new kids on the block." They have replaced wills and probate planning as the foundation for all planning. While there are still some diehard professionals who cling to the will and probate notion, they have mostly fallen by the wayside. At one time, these professionals called for wills in every situation. Now, they admit that living trusts are certainly viable, but are not for everyone. This is another myth that will disappear over time.

Even Congress, through the Internal Revenue Code, recognizes living trusts as a tremendous force in estate planning. For years, probate estates had certain after-death income tax advantages that trusts did not. In the last fifteen years, Congress has changed the laws so that now probate estates and living trusts are offered identical after-death income tax benefits. While the income tax advantages of probate estates were not significant, especially after 1986, this recognition by Congress really announced the death of will planning and probate as the planning of choice.

We have always, in our professional careers, strongly believed that estate planning professionals should use the revocable living trust as the main or foundation document to accomplish the majority of their clients' estate planning objectives. The revocable living trust is a most attractive estate planning device. It can be used instead of a will to accomplish the bulk of your estate planning goals. Revocable living trusts have been used successfully for centuries. In our opinion and that of virtually all our colleagues, they should be used by just about everybody.

Living trusts can be revocable or irrevocable (we discussed the difference in Chapter 16, Trusts); this chapter discusses the former, a trust that you can create and change at your whim while alive.

Here's a preview of the benefits that can be derived from the use of this very attractive estate planning vehicle:

You can give what you own to whom you want and when you want subsequent to your death through the use of a revocable living trust. As the trust maker, you can spell out all the distribution terms and requirements as to how your property passes after your death.

Your revocable living trust can provide one receptacle to receive and distribute all your assets on your death.

A revocable living trust can control, coordinate, and distribute all your property interests while you are alive, if you become disabled, and on your death. By using a revocable living trust, you can arrange for your well-being under your terms as you advance in years, become ill, or become mentally incompetent.

The use of a revocable living trust assures that your plans and affairs will remain private, rather than being made public, on your death or incapacity.

Revocable living trusts are easy to create and maintain during your lifetime.

It is not difficult for you to change or amend your revocable living trust at any time during your lifetime.

There are no adverse lifetime income tax consequences that result from the use of a revocable living trust.

Property that has been placed in a revocable living trust during your lifetime is not subject to and does not pass through the probate process on your death; it is probate-free.

Continuity of cash flow and investments in your portfolio is not interrupted by your death.

All opportunities of death tax planning available through will planning are equally available through the use of a revocable living trust.

Revocable living trusts are legal in every state. Your trust can easily be moved with you as you cross state lines.

By using a revocable living trust, you can measure your postdeath trustees' abilities to manage your assets while you are alive.

Revocable living trusts are more difficult to attack, and usually less successfully attacked, by disgruntled beneficiaries than are wills.

If you choose to use a revocable living trust, you can avail yourself of all the benefits we have highlighted above. A detailed discussion of each of these benefits follows.

Property Distribution
after Your Death

On and after your death, all property in your trust and the income that property generates will be distributed by the trustee according to your precise written instructions. Anything that can be accomplished through the use of a trust created by a will (testamentary trust) can be accomplished identically through the use of a revocable living trust.

Property in a revocable living trust can be left to the beneficiaries outright on your death, or it can remain in trust and be distributed over a certain period of time to your beneficiaries. Several trusts can be created within a revocable living trust, which will become operative for designated beneficiaries on your death. In fact, there is no limit to the number of separate trusts that can be created in a single revocable living trust. Each trust that is created within the trust document can spell out its individual terms with regard to the amounts to be distributed and the timing under which those amounts are to pass to your beneficiaries. Each of the trusts that are created in the trust document may have different terms and conditions as to the distribution of income and principal to your selected beneficiaries.

If you are married, you and your spouse can create a joint revocable living trust. In this single trust for the two of you, you can make all the distributions that each of you want. By creating subtrusts, there are unlimited possibilities for making after-death distributions.

One Receptacle to Receive and Distribute All Property

Through the use of a revocable living trust, you can control the distribution of all your property. This is true not only for the property you put in your trust while alive, but also for other property that flows into your trust on your death. Proceeds from life insurance can be left to your trust if you name your trust as the beneficiary; the same is true with respect to proceeds from pension and profit sharing plans. For that matter, any proceeds from third-party beneficiary contracts can be left to your trust if you simply make the trust the beneficiary of those contracts.

Property that is not placed in the trust during your lifetime can still be put in the trust after your death through the use of a short, well-drafted will that attorneys call a pour-over will. The provisions of a pour-over will simply state that any property you neglected to put in your trust will, nevertheless, pass to your trust (pour over to it) after your death. The pour-over will should always be used in conjunction with a revocable living trust. We often refer to these special wills as fail-safe wills; their use assures that any forgotten property will ultimately be placed in the planning pot to be controlled pursuant to your master plan.

It is important to understand, however, that property owned jointly cannot be put into a trust on your death. We have discussed this in several other chapters, but we say it again: Beware of owning jointly held property; you cannot control it on your death, and it may go to unintended heirs.

Take Care of Yourself Too

A revocable living trust can be designed so that it can provide for your care during your lifetime. In your revocable living trust, you can spell out in as much detail as you like how you wish to be taken care of with *your own* trust property in case of your incapacity, which could result from senility, accident, or illness. You can specify who your trustees will be if you become incompetent. You can also provide for the care of your loved ones should you lose control of your mental faculties.

The ability to provide for your care as well as the care of your loved ones during your lifetime is, in our opinion, one of the greatest attributes of a revocable living trust. We illustrate our point by asking you to recall Groucho Marx's last years.

Groucho, you will recall, like other older people, lost control of his mental faculties. Friends and family members, through attorneys and court proceedings, litigated who should take care of Groucho and his property. The sad plight of a great entertainer's final days was made public. Many of the costs that resulted were paid out of Groucho's estate. The entire affair could have been avoided if Groucho had planned for the contingency of his illness through the use of a revocable living trust.

A revocable living trust can avoid all the confusion and publicity occasioned by court proceedings that would otherwise come about upon your incapacity. Our point takes on even greater significance in light of the ability of modern medicine to keep people alive under almost unbelievable circumstances.

All fifty states and the District of Columbia allow the use of a durable special power of attorney. This document allows you to give the right to someone you trust to place your property in your revocable living trust if you are unable to do so. It is durable in that, unlike general powers of attorney, its legality continues even if you are incompetent. By using a durable power of attorney as an addition to your revocable living trust, you can assure yourself that your property will be placed in your trust and used pursuant to your directions for your and your loved ones' benefit without costly court interference and publicity.

Trusts Are Private

Unlike a will, revocable living trusts are private documents. They are not made public either while you are alive, at your death, or subsequent to your death. By using a revocable living trust, you can be assured that you will not be taking your affairs and your family's affairs public. We have read too many books that have exposed the affairs of great people to the public's scrutiny. The authors of these books had at their fingertips the probate court's records as to all the affairs of these people, because they elected to use wills rather than revocable living trusts.

Some professionals take the position from time to time that living trusts are not private because third parties such as banks and financial brokerage firms ask to see the full trust. The reason that they want to see the trust is to make sure that the correct trustees have the authority to act and that the trust is in effect. There is usually no reason for anyone to see the full trust, especially those private provisions as to how you leave your property. The only parts of a trust that have to be disclosed are the provisions relating to who the trustees are, the powers given to the trustees under the trust document, and evidence that the trust is in existence. Generally, all of this information can be put into an Affidavit of Trust, which is then signed by the trustees. Before you disclose anything, consult your attorney to find out what you do need to let others see and what you do not.

Revocable living trusts, their provisions, and the property they control remain the exclusive business of the beneficiaries for whom they were created; other than the trustee, the trusts are nobody else's business.

Trusts Are Easy to Create and Maintain

Revocable living trusts are easy to create. In our opinion, you should always seek out an attorney who knows estate planning, convey your wishes, and set a time for a future meeting to review your trust.

We do not believe that you should fill in preprinted forms sold in books. We do believe very strongly that you should be knowledgeable but that you should always seek the assistance of estate planning professionals.

Once the attorney completes your plan, sign it if it meets your objectives. Unlike a will, the formalities of signing a trust are almost nonexistent. That is all there is to it. Of course, the trust should be funded. That, too, is not difficult and is discussed at length in Chapter 18.

After creating your revocable living trust, you should check back with your attorney from time to time to make sure your trust has kept current with your objectives and with new legal developments. Keeping current is important and can be accomplished through the use of a revocable living trust.

It is a good idea to set a schedule with your attorney and other advisors to periodically review your living trust and your estate and financial planning. In our complex world, changes seem to occur more frequently than ever. By forming a team of trusted advisors and periodically meeting with them, you can exchange ideas and make changes so that your planning will maintain its relevance and stay technically on the cutting edge of planning.

Trusts Can Be Changed without Formality

In Chapters 6 and 7 on wills, we discussed that wills have to be signed and executed, with a great deal of legal formality, and that codicils (will amendments) have the same formal requirements. This is not the case with revocable living trusts. These trusts need only your signature to infuse life into them. Likewise, trust amendments, regardless of their scope, require only your signature. Witnesses are generally not required, nor is the signature of the trustee (each state's laws are different in this area). There can be no doubt that you must know what you are signing when signing your trust or an amendment to it. Most states' laws are very clear on this subject. The point is that signing a trust amendment does not require a great deal of time or effort, and it can be accomplished with few legal formalities.

Avoid Adverse Lifetime Income Tax Consequences

There are no adverse income tax consequences associated with the use of a revocable living trust during your life. Because the trust is revocable, the income generated by the property that is in the name of the trust is taxed to you and is reported on your personal income tax returns. A revocable living trust for which you are the trustee is not required to have a separate federal identification number or file a separate tax return. If you are married, as long as either you or your spouse is a trustee, a separate identification number or tax return is not required. Thus, income generated by the property that is in the name of the revocable living trust requires little extra effort by its maker.

Trusts Are Probate-Free

Property that is in a revocable living trust will not, on your death, go through the probate process. Probate is a process that passes title to assets. Because the title to your property is already in your trust and the trust does not die with you, there is no passing of title required; title has already passed during your life. The probate process is not applicable to trust property.

Total avoidance of probate is an enormous benefit to you and your beneficiaries. It represents significant savings in costs, time, and court interference with respect to your affairs. Mr. Dacey wrote his national best-seller on this single benefit. Funded revocable living trusts avoid the probate process.

Please understand that there are still some administrative expenses for most trusts upon the death of their maker. These fees are substantially less than the standard fees charged for probate and administration. Based on our many years in the practice and our interaction with over a thousand attorneys who are part of the National Network of Estate Planning Attorneys, we estimate that trust administration fees are about one-third of those charged for probate and administration.

Continuity in the Handling
of Your Affairs

Because there is no probate associated with revocable living trust property, you can be assured that a smooth and uneventful transition will occur with respect to your affairs on your death. Your beneficiaries automatically begin to receive income and principal on your death, pursuant to the terms written in your trust document. This fluidity with regard to your affairs is of major importance because it reduces cost and does not create unnecessary change or crisis for your survivors.

Death Tax Planning
Opportunities

A host of techniques are used to reduce federal estate taxes by professional estate planners. In the main, these techniques have traditionally been implemented by planners through the use of trusts created by the client's will (testamentary trusts). A significant percentage of estate planning professionals have used, and continue to use, the will as the vehicle within which they plan to reduce federal estate taxes.

Remember, every technique of federal estate tax savings that can be implemented in a will can also be implemented in a revocable living trust.

Good in Every State

Every state's laws recognize the validity of a revocable living trust. A truly beneficial feature attributed to these estate planning instruments is that they can cross state lines with their makers without any need to redraft their terms to comply with local law.

You may change your domicile; many people do. They move around the country with increasing regularity. Their moves are usually associated with career opportunities or a better place to live after retirement. With each move the question is generally asked, "Do I have to redo my estate plan?" If a revocable living trust has been used, the answer is no. The state law under which that trust was prepared will still be the law that is used with respect to its legal validity. Most well-written revocable living trusts provide that the law with respect to the administration of the trust will be the law of the state in which the maker and trust reside from time to time.

Revocable living trusts can cross state lines much more easily than their will counterparts. This flexibility gives you the security and knowledge that you will not have to redo your estate plan every time you are transferred or move to another state. Any time you do move to another state, however, you should have your estate plan reviewed by an estate planner in that state, because additional planning opportunities may be available to you with regard to your new state's law. Remember, each state has its own system with respect to death taxes.

Measuring Trustees during Life

Most trust makers elect to be their own trustees during their lives. Many of our clients elect to be their own trustees and name their spouses or close family members or friends as cotrustees. The advantage of the cotrusteeship is that on the incapacity or death of the trust maker, the cotrustee can continue the operation of the trust without the need to seek court assistance.

You may elect, however, to name the persons or professional institutions who will be handling your trust after your death on a current, or living, basis. If you decide to name your death trustees on a current basis, you will be able to observe their performance and abilities as they manage the trust property for your benefit. By using a revocable living trust, you are able to measure the performance of your after-death trustees while you are alive.

Difficult for Disgruntled Heirs to Attack

Most of you are aware of the horror stories associated with unhappy heirs attacking the will of a maker who did not leave those unhappy folks what they thought they had coming. Attacking a will is called a will contest by attorneys. Will contests occur too frequently. Wills are usually contested by family members who were cut out or who received less than their anticipated share of the maker's property.

Revocable living trusts are much more difficult for disgruntled heirs to attack than are their will counterparts. Revocable living trusts are private documents that are not involved in the probate process. They are not placed in a public forum that encourages debate and advocacy, as are their will counterparts. They are not subject to all the legal formalities that are associated with wills. Because there are fewer legal rules with regard to their creation, there are fewer legal opportunities to invalidate them. Our experience has driven this point home most convincingly. Our firm has prepared several thousand revocable living trusts over the years, and to the best of our knowledge, not one has ever been attacked, much less attacked successfully.

Criticisms of Revocable Living Trusts

The revocable living trust has so many attractive features unique to it that we cannot understand why it is not used more frequently as a will substitute by more professionals. Many professionals are suspicious of it because they do not understand it. Other professionals are critical of it and allege the following negatives with regard to its use:

It is difficult to establish and maintain.

It is expensive.

It is less effective in limiting creditors' claims after death.

Gifts from a trust may still be included in the maker's estate for federal estate tax purposes.

Significant savings on after-death income tax are lost because of its use.

Revocable living trusts are not difficult to establish. A professional estate planner can create them, at times, more easily than their will counterparts.

In our experience, they are not difficult to maintain. It is true that if you do create a revocable living trust, you will have to take time to organize your affairs and keep them organized within your trust's parameters. We believe that this is a positive feature that should encourage their use. Remember, what you do not do while alive, the probate court and your beneficiaries must do after you are gone. Please reread Chapter 8, Probate, if you doubt our conclusion.

Revocable living trusts can cost more to create than their will counterparts. The increase in cost is due to an increase in work that is required of the planning professionals. When an attorney draws a will, that is all that is done, which is only a small part of the total estate planning job. The attorney will finish that job when the will is taken through the probate process.

The attorney who utilizes a revocable living trust as an estate planning vehicle charges one fee. That fee may be for both drafting the document and funding the document so there will be no probate process. Some attorneys charge separately for funding and some work with other advisors who assume the responsibility of funding the trust.

Common sense and our experience would indicate a huge difference in cost between wills and fully funded revocable living trusts. Generally, the fee for a will coupled with the cost of probate is enormous when compared to the cost of preparing and funding a revocable living trust.

Some attorneys believe that a revocable living trust is not as effective as a will in cutting off the claims of creditors against the assets of a deceased trust maker. In all but a few states, however, a revocable living trust is actually a better device than a will for limiting creditors' claims after a trust maker's death. In the few states in which a will has an advantage in limiting creditors' claims, a living trust can be used in conjunction with a will to effectively and promptly settle the claims of creditors.

Prior to TRA 1986, critics of the revocable living trust charged that its use reduced income tax planning opportunities after death. This criticism had some validity then, but has none now. Beginning in 1998, wills and trusts have exactly the same income tax consequences. Neither one has an advantage over the other. Given the many other advantages that living trusts have over wills, this income tax equality makes the living trust even more attractive.

It is our belief that a revocable living trust should be used as a will substitute whenever *any* of its benefits are desired; the size of one's estate should not dictate its use.

Benefits of Revocable Living Trusts

Distribute property after your death.

Create one receptacle for all your property.

Take care of you.

Offer privacy.

Easy to create and maintain.

Easily changed.

No adverse lifetime or after-death income tax consequences.

Probate-free.

Continuity in your affairs.

Planning for death tax.

Good in every state.

Can measure trustees during your life.

Difficult to attack.

18

Funding a Revocable Living Trust

"Placing All Your Eggs in One Basket"

A revocable living trust can be unfunded, partially funded, or totally funded during the lifetime of its maker; it can also be funded on its maker's death. When estate planning professionals refer to funding, they are referring to property that has actually been placed in a living trust or, more accurately, in the name of the trustees of the trust.

The advantages that result from funding a revocable living trust during the lifetime of the maker are profound:

Property that is in a revocable living trust does not go through the probate process on the death of the trust maker.

Property that is in a revocable living trust can be used to care for the trust maker and loved ones in the event of the trust maker's incapacity, without the intervention and control of a court.

To understand the funded revocable living trust, it is important to contrast it with its unfunded counterpart.

The Unfunded Revocable
Living Trust

A living trust that has no assets in it is called an unfunded revocable living trust. Sometimes, an unfunded revocable living trust is referred to as an unfunded life insurance trust. It gets this nickname because there is no property placed in the trust when it is created except the *right* of the trust to receive the death proceeds of life insurance on the life of the trust maker. The trust is funded with only the expectancy of receiving those insurance proceeds. The expectancy of receiving insurance proceeds legally funds the revocable living trust in many states even though, in reality, nothing is in the trust at all.

In those states that require something more than a mere expectancy to establish the trust, professionals generally instruct their clients to place a nominal amount of cash in the trust, such as $10.

Either technique or both techniques used together still result in an unfunded living trust. Why are either of these techniques required? Because in many states a trust must have some type of property in it to be valid. Both of these techniques can do the job. A number of states do not require either of these techniques in order for an unfunded revocable living trust to be valid under state law. In those states, the mere creation of the trust establishes its legal validity.

Advocates of the unfunded revocable living trust make the following points in defense of its use:

The trust can receive all life insurance proceeds as well as all other third-party beneficiary contract property. These include pension and profit sharing proceeds paid on the death of the maker.

The revocable living trust can be funded at a later time if the trust maker gives a durable special power of attorney to others. Durable special powers of attorney are discussed later in this chapter.

Because relatively few deaths result from accidental causes, most trust makers can generally predict or have notice of their impending demise, and as a result, trust makers can fund their trusts at that time.

In addition, a pour-over will can transfer property into the trust after the death of the trust maker.

There can be no doubt that an unfunded revocable living trust is far better than its will counterpart; however, when it is contrasted with its funded counterpart, it leaves much to be desired.

There are several problems usually associated with unfunded living trusts.

If the trust maker dies accidentally or unexpectedly, his or her property will have to go through the probate process before it can ultimately end up in the trust. Thus, a pour-over will guarantees probate on the assets it passes to the unfunded trust. Because most people set up a revocable living trust to avoid probate, not funding the trust pretty much defeats one of its primary purposes.

In our experience, if a trust is not funded from the outset, it does not get funded properly later. If funding is accomplished from the outset, the maker is much more likely to continue funding the trust as new assets are acquired. This new habit assures that at least a great many of a maker's assets will be in the trust upon the maker's disability or death.

A problem that we see much more of is the selling of revocable living trusts at a low cost by living trust companies rather than skilled attorneys. Not only are the trusts themselves woefully inadequate, but they are not funded. Thus a maker ends up with an inferior document that does not avoid probate. However, these trusts are sold as if they were fully funded. The maker and his or her family are misled and probate is not avoided. Consumers should avoid these types of fraudulent schemes.

Funded Revocable Living Trusts

A funded revocable living trust, as its name implies, is a revocable living trust that has within it property owned by the maker. You may be wondering, "How can the trust have the property when the trust maker still owns it?" The answer is that the property is titled in the trust's name, but the maker owns the right to use, possess, and enjoy the property. The maker owns the trust and is the beneficiary of the trust and, therefore, really owns the property.

Another way to explain this legal phenomenon is to say that the trust maker owns equitable title and the trust owns bare legal title. Equitable title is greater than legal title. Regardless of the explanation used, a revocable living trust that is properly funded leaves the ownership and control of the trust property in the hands of its maker.

Funded revocable living trusts have these advantages:

All property in the trust totally avoids the probate process on the death of its maker.

The trust assets are instantly available to the maker's beneficiaries pursuant to written instructions.

Should the maker become incapacitated or be adjudicated mentally incompetent, the trust property can be used to care for the trust maker and loved ones without the delays, expenses, and publicity associated with court proceedings.

Funded revocable living trusts take the guesswork out of probate avoidance and avoid the Groucho Marx problem. By funding a revocable living trust, the maker can be assured that trust assets are put to their highest and best use.

Estate planning professionals use different techniques to fund revocable living trusts, but generally there are two major approaches:

Retitling all the trust maker's property in the name of the trust, for example, "Karen Smith as Trustee of the Karen Smith Trust."

Retitling all the trust maker's property in the name of an entity, called a nominee partnership, which is a holding device for the trust.

Titling Property Directly in the Trust

In order to place property directly in the name of a trust, the property must be retitled in the name of the trustees of that trust, such as "Karen Smith as Trustee of the Karen Smith Trust." This form of trust funding certainly appears simple and, to most people, is very understandable. It does, however, create some problems.

1. If real estate is transferred directly into the name of the trust, the entire trust agreement may have to be recorded under the laws of some states. This recording requirement can abrogate the privacy feature of the trust. Because of the growing acceptance of trusts, these filing requirements are becoming much less stringent. In any case, there are several alternatives available that avoid the necessity to record the full trust document.

2. Publicly traded stocks and bonds that are titled directly in the name of a trust sometimes present logistical problems. When the stock or bond is sold, the transfer agent may require that it be provided with a complete and certified copy of the trust. The privacy feature of the trust can then be lost. Just as in real estate, there is much less likelihood of this happening today than even a few short years ago. Generally, only certain provisions of the trust will have to be disclosed, none of which deal with how the trust assets are ultimately to be disposed of.

3. Safe-deposit boxes taken directly in the name of the trust have the same problem; a complete, certified copy of the trust may have to be kept on

file in the institution where the box is located. This obstacle usually can be overcome by giving successor trustees signature authority on the box.

4. Titling property directly in the name of a trust can present some problems when the trust maker attempts to dispose of trust property. It is easy to put property directly in the name of a trust, but may be somewhat more difficult to get that property out of the trust. Some of the people with whom the trustees deal with regard to the trust property will want to assure themselves that the trustees do indeed have the right to dispose of the property.

5. People who deal with trustees may get sweaty palms because without a complete review of the trust document, they can never be sure that the trustee has the power to properly pass title to the trust property. Most trusts are written in legal jargon, and that means that the wary buyer or transfer agent may want to seek the services of an attorney prior to completing any transaction involving trust property.

One technique that is used to reduce or eliminate problems associated with titling property directly in the trust is called an Affidavit of Trust or a Trust Certification. This is a short document signed by the trustees, and sometimes signed by the attorney who prepared the trust, stating that the trust is in existence and that the trustees have the power to transact business on behalf of the trust. Certain provisions of the trust document may be attached to the Affidavit or Certification, including who the trustees are, their powers, and the signature pages of the trust itself.

Over the years, revocable living trusts have been criticized because of the expense and time that it takes to fund them. While this may have been partially true at one time, it is certainly not true now. For the most part, revocable living trusts have been accepted as the estate planning vehicle of choice by a majority of attorneys and other estate planning experts. Banks, stock brokerages, and other financial institutions are set up to expedite transfers into living trusts. Rarely will an individual run into a reputable business or financial institution that will not be willing and able to help fund a living trust. In fact, many financial institutions encourage the funding of revocable living trusts by advertising their expertise in helping to fund the trusts.

Even with the acceptance of living trusts, sometimes it may be more difficult to do business with assets that are titled in the trust name than if they were titled in the name of individual owners or a business. This fact of life should not deter most people from titling property directly in the names of their trusts. More and more, dealing with trusts and trustees is becoming common in the business world. If problems are encountered, there are usually alternate methods of funding that are effective and less likely to cause problems.

Using the Nominee Partnership
to Fund the Trust

This is a method that we recommend to many of our clients in order to facilitate funding their trusts. It is a method that is easily accomplished and facilitates commerce as trust makers buy and sell property during their lifetimes. It protects the privacy of the trust document and results in little additional expense to the trust maker or trustees. Most corporate fiduciaries have used this technique for years in dealing with property in their various trust accounts. Its simplicity in expediting the buying and selling of trust assets both within the home state and across state lines has fostered its use.

The concept of a nominee partnership is simple: Rather than put the assets directly in the trust's name, they are put in a holding vehicle created expressly for dealing with trust property. This holding vehicle is called a nominee partnership. The partnership holds bare legal title to the assets for the trustees of the trust. The nominee partnership generally does not own any property in its own right. Its terms provide that the partners deal with the trust property to expedite the buying and selling of trust assets.

The partners of the nominee partnership are totally responsible to the trustees and usually are the trustees. In fact, the partners of the nominee partnership and the trustees enter into a short agreement that makes it clear that the trust is the owner of the property and that the partners must abide by the trust's terms. Here is an example that will assist you in understanding this device:

> Bill Wagner makes a trust. Bill and his wife Diana are the trustees. Bill and Diana Wagner are also partners in Bill and Diana Company, a nominee partnership. Bill funds his trust by retitling all his assets in the name of Bill and Diana Company. Bill and Diana, as partners in Bill and Diana Company, report to Bill and Diana, as trustees of Bill's trust. Bill and Diana, as trustees of Bill's trust, report to Bill, the maker of the trust. What a paper tiger!

> But look what happened: Bill, as a partner in Bill and Diana Company, can buy and sell assets without saying, "Look at us, we're trustees."

In our example, the fact that Bill is buying and selling property as a partner in Bill and Diana Company, a nominee for the Bill Wagner Trust, is of major consequence. Buyers and sellers are used to doing business with partners of partnerships; they may not be used to doing business with trustees.

The benefits of a nominee partnership can be summarized as follows:

Trust documents stay private because the only document that needs to be recorded is the partnership agreement or a substitute agreement called a trade name affidavit. It is generally short and does not divulge any private matters.

Property can be bought and sold for the trust in the partnership name without buyers, sellers, and transfer agents getting sweaty palms.

Subsequent to the death of the trust maker, successor trustees can become successor partners so that the buying and selling of trust property continues to be commercially expedient.

Nominee partnerships provide an excellent solution to the trust funding problem. The only thing that a trust maker who uses this technique will have to learn to do is to sign his name "Bill Wagner, Partner," instead of "Bill Wagner, Owner." In the eyes of the world, Bill and Diana Company, a partnership, owns the property. In reality, Bill Wagner owns the property.

As we discussed in Chapter 17, there are no income tax consequences with respect to the use of a revocable living trust. If the nominee partnership method of funding is used, the partnership simply files an information tax return that says, in essence, "See Bill Wagner's tax return." This practice presents no problems. In our experience, the Internal Revenue Service does not raise an eyebrow when presented with these returns. It understands them and sees them frequently.

Other Methods of Funding a Trust

In some states, estate planning professionals have additional techniques available to them to fund a revocable living trust. These techniques are generally used in addition to the nominee partnership and are used on a frequent basis. The four techniques are: durable special powers of attorney, unrecorded deeds, after-death assignments, and POD designations.

Durable Special Powers of Attorney

A trust maker can give others the power to place the maker's assets into the maker's living trust. This power is given by using a durable special power of attorney. Unlike most powers of attorney, a durable special power of attorney continues even if the maker is incapacitated because of illness or injury. The durable power of attorney is "special" because it limits the power to this single function.

Unrecorded Deeds

In using this technique, the trust maker deeds real estate to the trustee or successor trustee of the trust, but the deed is not recorded until after the death of the trust maker. If the trust maker disposes of the deeded property during lifetime, the unrecorded deed is reclaimed and destroyed. If the trustee at death is a bank or nominee, the existence of the trust does not have to be revealed for title to the deeded property to pass to the trust. Some states have title standards specifically creating presumptions in favor of the validity of such transfers. The disadvantage of this form of funding is that it may be argued that no effective transfer took place when the deed was signed; however, if the trust maker's heirs and unsecured creditors are adequately provided for, it is unlikely that anyone would raise an objection. This is an excellent funding technique that can be used in the states that allow it.

After Death (Postmortem) Assignments

Most of the Uniform Probate Code states provide that many property interests, with the exception of real estate, can be assigned by an owner to a revocable living trust but that the transfer will not take effect until after the owner's death. This technique, where permitted, allows a property owner to retain the use and control of property during lifetime and pass that property automatically to a revocable living trust on death. These assignments are not made public.

From a practical perspective, publicly traded stocks and bonds are not suited to this technique. The New York Stock Transfer Association apparently does not and will not recognize this approach under its rules. As a result, individual stock transfer agents will not transfer the stock or bond that was assigned by use of this technique. The Stock Transfer Association is, in effect, ignoring the laws of the states that allow this technique. We believe that the New York Stock Transfer Association should change its rules, but until it does, we recommend that our clients put their publicly traded stocks and bonds in a nominee partnership or directly in the name of their trusts.

Postmortem assignments, where allowed, are extremely effective in transferring closely held (private company) stock certificates and partnership interests into a property owner's revocable living trust.

POD designations

Generally, Uniform Probate Code states allow the use of payable-on-death (POD) designations with respect to savings accounts, checking accounts, and certificates of deposit. In creating such an account, the owner simply designates a revocable living trust as the entity that will receive the account proceeds on death. When the owner dies, the account proceeds pass automatically to the trust without the intervention of the probate court.

Funding a revocable living trust is an important aspect of the estate planning process. As you can see, there are many techniques available to fund your trust. Please understand that assets that are not in your trust at your death will be subject to the probate process. Assets that are not in the trust if you become incapacitated can be titled in the name of your trust by a durable power of attorney. However, there is no assurance that this method of funding will be effective. Funding your trust when it is set up and as you acquire new property assures you that your trust will work as intended.

19
Trustees
"Modern Superagents"

The trust relationship necessitates three types of players: a trust maker; trust beneficiaries; and the person who runs the trust, the trustee.

A good synonym for trustee is agent, or better yet, superagent. Our law refers to superagents as fiduciaries. The word *fiduciary* is used interchangeably with *trustee*. Trustee is a word meaning "a person who runs a trust." Fiduciary comes from Roman law and means a person who has the same duties and responsibilities as a trustee.

Trustees in General

When a trustee is named, that trustee is given, both by the maker and by operation of law, massive rights and powers to be exercised on behalf of the trust's beneficiaries.

Trustees can be individuals or properly licensed state and federal institutions. Individual trustees are usually family members, friends, or advisers of the trust maker. Institutional trustees are either trust companies or trust departments of commercial banks. Institutional trustees are often referred to as corporate fiduciaries.

Trustees, whether individual or institutional, must act in a fiduciary capacity. When acting in that capacity, trustees have the ultimate duty imposed by law as to relationships between people. When trustees make mistakes and those mistakes are proven, they are liable to the beneficiaries for those mistakes. For a long time, trustees' actions and liability for their actions have been measured by what attorneys refer to as the reasonable person rule. This rule asks the question, "Would a similar, reasonably prudent person acting in the same capacity, in the same or similar circumstances, have made the same judgment?" If the answer is no, trustees will be liable for the consequences of their actions.

The trend today is to apply even tougher standards in the measurement of trustee's actions. Since 1991, nearly forty states have adopted the Prudent Investor Rule, or some version thereof. Under the Prudent Investor Rule, trustees must minimize the risk at any given level of return on trust assets. Therefore, in effect, the prudent-person rule has quickly become the prudent-expert rule. Clearly, a prudent expert makes no mistakes—or so it would seem. Philosophically, we take no position on this trend. Knowing it exists and is being amplified is enough.

Becoming or naming a trustee is serious business. Trustees are fiduciaries; fiduciaries are superagents; and superagents are superliable for acts or failures to act that are not superbeneficial to beneficiaries.

Knowledge of the trustee's role and the consequences of poor performance in that role should dissuade kind but ill-prepared folks from acting as trustees. One does not accommodate a family member, friend, or client by accepting a trusteeship without opening one's eyes about what a trustee is and does. If you have volunteered to be a trustee, please reexamine your decision.

The trustee's role can be a confusing one. Trustees are totally responsible for expert performance and judgment while following the written instructions of a trust maker for the benefit of that maker's beneficiaries. Trustees are responsible, as experts, for the preservation of the maker's property (principal), its growth with respect to income and capital appreciation, and its application to the beneficiaries.

People create relationships. Each relationship involves different expectations, duties, and results. Most relationships are not fiduciary relationships; they are business or personal relationships. Laws have been created to govern these relationships, and all of them fall short of the excellence required under fiduciary law.

In terms of practicality, however, trustees have only two major responsibilities: (1) Trustees have an absolute mandate, by operation of law, to follow precisely the written instructions of a trust maker. (2) Trustees have absolute responsibility to read between the lines and make judgment calls when there is no clear-cut alternative. If trustees are called upon to make decisions that are too tough for them, they ask a court to assist them. This is particularly true in a controversial environment.

Most clients view the trustee's role as primarily financial. After all, trustees are financial advisers; but not all trustees' decisions are financial. People decisions may affect financial decisions; thus our superagent needs to be supersensitive, indeed.

It is difficult to find competent and willing trustees on both a personal and an institutional basis because trustees must work superhard and are always held superaccountable for their actions.

In discussing the selection of an appropriate trustee with our clients, concerns center in the area of the trustee's knowledge of their families' affairs, investment performance, and the empathy that will potentially be accorded their beneficiaries.

A trustee's knowledge of the affairs of most trust makers is usually deficient. Our experience would suggest that people carry most of their affairs in their heads. Most spouses and children know too little about the family's economic affairs. We believe that you should fully brief your loved ones as to your financial affairs when possible and start now to communicate your affairs to your ultimate trustee.

As to investment performance, we often hear, "He's no good, he can't even handle his own money," or, "She's made a bundle for herself; she'll do all right for me." "What rate of return can he get?" "How effective will she be in making my principal grow?" "What guarantees do I get?" There are no easy answers to these questions.

Trustees cannot speculate with principal or the income it generates. This does not mean that assets cannot be sold or traded, nor does it mean that trustees cannot invest in assets that may go down in value, such as real estate, stocks, bonds, and so on. It does mean that trustees must invest in proven investment areas on a conservative and cautious basis. It also means that they diversify, using good judgment in all cases, or not diversify if the assets they are given are profitable on a proven basis. It does mean that they must exercise prudent judgment.

Trustees should not knowingly (if they are aware of their liability) attempt to achieve a return predicated on speculative investment. Trustee speculators are liable for their losses. Speculation with regard to one's own funds may be all right; if losses are incurred, they may be earned back through labor and industry. If trustees speculate and lose, that is *not* all right; if trustees cannot pay back what they have lost, it probably cannot be replaced.

The trustee's investment approach should always be cautious. It should be prudent and relatively risk-free. There is little room for speculation in the trustee's portfolio.

Conversely, trustees have been known, on an all-too-frequent basis, to be too conservative in their investment strategies. The investment of funds at a below-market yield, in terms of both income and capital appreciation, can result in trustees being liable for lost opportunities. Safe investment is not necessarily prudent investment.

The accountability of trustees as to the empathy shown to beneficiaries is difficult to ascertain and difficult to measure. Regardless of whether individual or institutional trustees are selected, there are no guarantees that sound overall performance will result or that the beneficiaries will be satisfied with the trustees.

The point to remember is that trustees have awesome power, accountability, and liability, all wrapped together in their roles as superagents.

Institutional Trustees

Now that we have discussed trustees in general, let's take a closer look at the role of the institutional trustee. Institutional trustees, often called corporate fiduciaries, fall into two separate categories: the full-time trust company and the trust department or trust division of a commercial bank. A number of financial brokerage firms have formed or purchased separate trust companies. For our purposes, these are the same as full-time trust companies.

Both the full-time trust company and the trust division of a commercial bank do precisely the same thing. They function as professional trustees. To discuss one is to discuss the other. How can they be the same if one is a separate professional trust company and the other is just part of a bank? The answer is fairly simple.

Originally, banks were banks and trust companies were trust companies. Both existed side by side. Commercial banks accepted depositors' money and lent the majority of that money back to the public. Trust companies have historically managed trust assets for a fee. They were separate entities, both serving the public in a different way. Each had its own building, ownership, and board of directors; each served the same local population.

A trend developed that resulted in the merging of the two institutions. The opportunity was taken to consolidate and reduce the overhead of the surviving institution and provide full-service banking. To a certain extent, this has taken place in the major stock brokerage firms. They too have consolidated, to a great extent, their function as financial advisors and investment managers with the option to manage money under a separate trust company.

This has been the trend for many years. Look around you. Many banks still have the title "and Trust Company" at the end of their names. At some point in time they acquired or created a trust company and brought it within the umbrella of the concept of a full-service bank.

Today, however, there are still trust companies that have elected not to merge with or be acquired by a commercial bank. Nevertheless, trust companies and bank trust departments function the same way.

The first question every client asks when we discuss the institutional trustee is, "Does the bank lend my trust funds to bank customers?" The answer is, "Absolutely not." That is a bank function conducted with the money of the bank's commercial depositors. It does not occur with trust assets.

The trust division of the typical commercial bank is an entirely separate entity. Literally it is the successor of the historical trust company. Within a bank's trust division, assets are managed for beneficiaries of individual trusts. The same is true for the trust company that is part of a stock brokerage firm; it is a separate entity in which assets are managed for beneficiaries of trusts.

An interesting note with regard to the dual relationship of a bank and trust company is that the commercial sector of the bank is 100 percent liable in terms of the fiduciary liability of its trust division. On the other hand, individual trusts are never liable for the acts or omissions of the bank with respect to the bank's banking function. This means that if the trust division makes a mistake, the beneficiaries can go against all the bank's assets. On the other hand, if the commercial sector of the bank makes a mistake, the bank's creditors cannot go against individual trust assets.

The institutional or corporate fiduciary is basically no different from any other trustee. It has the same duties, the same responsibilities, and the same opportunities to fail or succeed as any other trustee. As a practical consideration, however, it should be noted that the corporate fiduciary appears to have a higher duty or standard of care in administering and investing trust assets than a personal trustee. A judge or jury is more likely to measure the prudent person standard on a tougher basis against the professional fiduciary than against a personal, nonprofessional trustee.

Trust divisions or companies are basically organized into distinct and separate areas. The first we will call the administrative section. It contains the trust department's hand-holders, the people who work directly with the beneficiaries to accomplish their goals and objectives as well as those set forth by the maker of the trust. These men and women are usually attorneys, although there are many excellent trust officers who are not. They are people who tend to be public relations oriented and who are extremely patient with beneficiaries.

In addition, most trust departments have an investment area. The people in this area assist the hand-holders in fulfilling investment objectives. They are usually trained in investing in stocks and bonds.

Many trust departments are large enough to have an additional investment function called the real estate area or the special asset section. The individuals in this section obviously specialize in the managing, purchasing, and selling of real estate and other not-so-easy-to-manage assets to meet investment objectives.

Apart from the account management and investment functions, most trust entities have a taxation section. The function of this area, as its name implies, is to consider all tax ramifications of investment decisions. Any time an asset is purchased or sold, the tax implications of the transaction should be analyzed.

Depending upon the sophistication of the institution in question, additional services may be available to assist beneficiaries. Figure 19-1 illustrates a typical bank's organization.

When looking at these functions—administration, investment, and tax—one may wonder how anything gets done. The answer is that all final decisions are made by committee. Corporate fiduciaries work almost exclusively through the committee approach to problem solving. The advocates of this approach say every decision is examined and reexamined, questioned and requestioned, before it is made. This process, although lengthy, is supposed to be in the best interests of the beneficiaries. Conceptually, it should result in little or no error.

The opponents of institutional trustees cite the committee approach as the horse-and-camel approach (referring to the committee that decided to design the horse and ended up with a camel instead). The criticism may or may not be fair, depending on the institution and the types of decisions to be made.

A sound critique of institutional trustees attacks their speed and timeliness, not necessarily their ultimate conclusions.

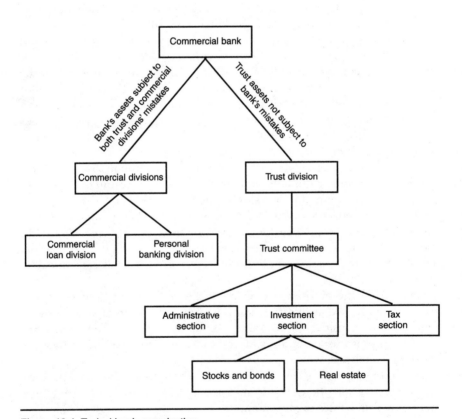

Figure 19-1. Typical bank organization.

One of the claims made by most financial institutions offering trust services is that they provide professional advice. Opponents of institutional trustees state that this is so much baloney, that what they provide is nothing but cautious investment in stocks and bonds. Regardless of what assets are left in trust, these critics assert it will not be long before the institution will have sold the original assets and invested all the proceeds in a stock and bond portfolio. Critics also attack, with frequent justification, the investment abilities of these institutions.

These traditional claims may have some validity, although in the great bull market of the 1990s this complaint seems to have disappeared. Financial institutions offering trust services have primarily centered their investment portfolios in stocks and bonds. They have done this in one of two ways. They either purchase stocks and bonds especially suited to a particular trust's objectives and held exclusively for that account, or purchase and hold stocks and bonds through common trust funds. These are funds created within the trust department to meet a broad range of investment objectives. These funds may be equity funds (funds that are supposed to grow over the years by way of capital appreciation) or they can be fixed-income funds (funds invested to provide current income). Another common trust fund that is frequently used is a tax-free fund. This fund is invested in securities, primarily municipal bonds, that will produce tax-free income. Some trust companies also use certain mutual funds for the same purposes.

By creating common trust funds, institutional trustees have attempted to offer diversification and lower management costs for many of their trusts that have common investment objectives.

Because one trust may be able to own relatively few securities due to the size of its principal, that principal can be pooled with the principal of other trusts by using a common trust fund. Each trust owns units in a common pool or fund that owns a diversified portfolio of stocks or bonds. This, proponents of professional trustees claim, provides a benefit for individual trusts at no additional fee and provides sound diversification.

Opponents of professional trustees assert that these common trust funds, as well as directly invested accounts, are nothing more than studies in carefully planned mediocrity—that, in fact, all investments are made in the same static pool of stocks and bonds selected by the institutions. Opponents claim that trust department employees are underpaid and that their collective investment decisions generally result in substandard performance.

Without taking sides, let us examine the reasons for using a corporate fiduciary. First and foremost, a corporate fiduciary is generally always collectible. A corporate fiduciary is backed by the entire institution's resources, so if a mistake is made, there is a good likelihood that recovery will be made. This can be very comforting. If the institutional trustee makes a mistake, you can, with some security, rest assured that if proven wrong, the institution will return what was lost as a result of its error. Most do have money. Also, keep in mind that the money that is being returned is not coming from other trusts, but from that institution's shareholders.

Another reason that a corporate fiduciary is often selected is that it will not die or become mentally incompetent, sick, or senile. It is there day after day, year after year. The institution generally does not change. This is an important attribute of the institutional trustee. Even in this climate of bank takeovers and mergers, there is continuity. Trust departments have been consolidated in the same manner as the banks. Like the banks, the trust departments have continued in spite of name changes and new ownership.

Talk to the opponents of corporate fiduciaries, and you will find they believe most, if not all, corporate fiduciaries have a high turnover rate among their personnel. Opponents claim there is no continuity in the management of a trust account because of the high turnover, and that turnover is high because institutions pay too little. Institutional trustees have been accused of underpaying talented people, which, in effect, makes them training grounds for talented young professionals and havens for others less blessed.

There is more than a little truth on both sides. The important thing to keep in mind is this: A trust instrument names the institution as trustee, not its employees. It is the institution that can boast when a good job has been done, and it is the institution that will pay if it is proven in error. Collectibility is of utmost importance. That, in our opinion, is the ultimate justification for naming an institutional trustee.

Another factor emphasized by proponents of institutional trustees is that institutions are capable of objective, third-party decision making. There is another side to this coin. Opponents of institutional trustees argue that third-party institutional objectivity does not exist. They claim that decisions are usually made by one or two employees who do not really care about the beneficiaries. Critics claim that relationships are distant at best and accountability for poor results is relatively nonexistent.

Institutional versus Individual Trustees

How do institutional trustees measure up against individual trustees? Before discussing this question, we would first like to outline the pros and cons of personal trustees.

Personal trustees are people. They have all the human strengths and weaknesses we all have. A personal trustee can be you or others you are close to.

Tables 19-1 and 19-2 outline pros and cons attributed to different types of personal and institutional trustees. The outlines of the relative pros and

Table 19 -1
Personal Trustees

Pros	Cons
FAMILY MEMBERS	
Family knowledge	Indecisive and insecure
Personal	No track record or experience
Investment	Too emotionally involved
Business	Unskilled at business
Empathetic, loving	People-prejudiced
Bright	Uncollectible as to mistakes
Good common sense	
Personally involved	
FRIEND OR BUSINESS ASSOCIATE	
Family knowledge:	Human:
Personal	May embezzle
Investment	May speculate poorly
Business	May die
Empathetic	Not enough time; a burden
Good businessperson	May play favorites
Good investor personally	Probably not collectible
Good common sense	
Tough, honest, hardworking	
PROFESSIONAL ADVISERS **(Attorney, CPA, Investment Adviser)**	
Family knowledge:	Human:
Personal	May embezzle
Investment	May speculate
Business	May be too conservative
Tough, honest, hardworking	May die
Trained professional	Not enough time
	May not be collectible
	Conflicts of interest
	Limited investment knowledge

Table 19-2
The Institutional Trustee

Pros	Cons
Professional	Dispassionate
Experienced	Ignorant of family affairs
Established track record	High turnover among staff
Collectible	Hard to reach
Will always be there	Too conservative
Not emotionally involved	Slow to act
Objective	
Regulated	

cons of individual trustees are obviously not all-inclusive. We are sure that you can add to each and we encourage you to do so. Our outlines contain the essence of what clients and professionals have communicated to us about individual trustees over the years. They contrast the pros and cons of an individual trustee with the pros and cons of an institutional trustee.

Practical Advice on Your Trustees

Our advice is that you should not pick a single trustee, whether an individual or an institution. Create combinations of trustees in your trust and provide a pattern for trustee succession. Planning for trustee succession involves stating which trustees you want to take over in the event previous trustees quit, die, or are fired. Providing for trustee succession is good business. It can provide for the use of both personal and institutional trustees.

In your trust document, always spell out who has the authority to terminate a trustee. Trustees who are not doing the job to the satisfaction of the beneficiaries should be terminated. Many trusts we have reviewed do not provide for trustee termination. We believe this is a mistake. Poorly performing trustees who continue as trustees become a burden to beneficiaries. They are not easy to get rid of unless the document provides for their termination.

To remove a trustee without termination rights in the trust itself requires review and approval by a court of law. Generally, that court is the probate court. In our experience, using the court as a planning alternative is poor planning. There is no guarantee that the court will agree with the unhappy beneficiaries. The legal process can be slow, expensive, and disappointing in its results.

The trust maker should always stipulate which beneficiaries may exercise the right to terminate trustees. For example, the termination rights may be given as follows:

> My spouse can fire the trustee at any time for any reason. After my spouse's death, a majority of the children may do so. If they are minors, then their guardian or a majority of their guardians can fire the trustee.

Another might say:

> My spouse and my sister, if they agree, can fire the trustee at any time for any reason. If either dies, then the survivor along with my attorney can fire any trustee. If everyone is deceased, then a majority of my living beneficiaries can fire the trustee.

The important point to understand is that you should communicate your list of those individuals, in succession, who are to have the power to fire the trustee at any time and see that your instructions are placed in your trust.

Another major, and in our opinion mandatory, planning tool is for you to set forth whom you want to take over as trustee when a trustee is fired, quits, or dies. For example:

> If my sister is fired, quits, or dies, she shall be replaced by my friend, Fred. Likewise, if Fred is fired, quits, or dies, then he shall be replaced by First National Bank.

You can also provide for the appointment of trustees by giving others the right to select those trustees. For example:

> If my spouse quits or dies, my attorney, Ellen, may select a new trustee, either personal or corporate, but my attorney is not to serve as trustee. Should Ellen not be living, a majority of my children may select a trustee to replace my spouse, as long as their choice is made among institutional trustees with a capital and surplus of not less than $5 million.

There is no limit to the personal and creative choices you can make; just make sure that you think your choices out and see to it that your estate planner accomplishes your goals in this area.

When naming trustees for your trust, a good general rule is not to name your spouse as sole trustee. Give your spouse some help. If you desire, name an adult child of yours or, if you prefer, all your adult children. Perhaps you are close to another family member, business associate, or adviser. If you are, and feel good about that person, name one or more as trustee with your spouse; just remember to provide for their termination and replacement.

If your planning situation dictates that there are no personal trustee candidates to assist your spouse, select an institutional trustee. There is nothing wrong with naming an institution as cotrustee with your spouse. In fact, our experience suggests that some clients prefer this approach. If you use this approach, always give your spouse the power to fire the institution and replace it according to your instructions.

You might want to combine the strengths of a personal trustee with the strengths of an institutional trustee. You may get the best of both worlds. You should choose your trustees based on your beliefs, prejudices, and particular situation.

Trustees' Fees

"Does a trustee get paid?" "How much do they charge?" These are questions clients commonly ask. Trustees are compensated. There is no such thing as a free lunch in the trust business.

Historically, trustees, especially professional trustees, charged an annual fee calculated as a percentage of the income earned by the trust property over the course of a year. This method is rarely used today.

Today most, if not all, institutional trustees charge and are paid pursuant to published fee schedules. These fee schedules generally are a percentage of the dollar value of the assets managed by the trustee. They are published to avoid any confusion that might otherwise arise between the trustee and the beneficiaries. The value that trustees apply their percentage fees to is the fair market value of the trust property as determined by the trustee. Institutional trustees almost always have a minimum fee that will be charged regardless of the value of the trust property. The minimum fee is not based on a percentage of the assets, but is a fixed amount.

Each institution, although independent, closely follows the fee structure of its competitors. Competition in the marketplace dictates this.

Institutional trustees generally apply their percentage fees on a sliding scale of asset value; for example, 1 percent on the first $100,000, three-quarters of 1 percent on the next $400,000, and one-half of 1 percent on the balance. It is common in the institutional fiduciary world to reduce the fee as the value of the trust assets increases in size.

Institutional trustees vary in the amounts they charge if extraordinary management services are provided. For example, managing a closely held business interest may necessitate a special or negotiated fee. Many institutional trustees do not publish special fees for managing special property in their fee schedules.

Our review of several published fee schedules of institutional trustees suggests that:

Fee schedules are all pretty much the same. Shopping for trustees' fees may not be very productive.

Most, if not all, have a minimum fee.

Most use the percentage-of-value approach.

Most have sliding scales rather than escalating schedules.

The larger the institution, the more likely it is to charge differently for extraordinary services.

Some have termination fees.

The last entry in our synopsis suggests that some institutions charge termination fees; that is, they have language in their fee schedules setting forth additional charges that will be levied against the trust assets if the institution is fired or quits. These additional charges can involve hourly billing, percentage billing, or flat fee billing to cover the costs of terminating the trust.

We strongly disagree with the institutional practice of charging termination fees. We do not accept the institutional arguments offered in their defense. If the trust is run properly, a great deal of time should not be required to turn over trust assets and records to another trustee. The time that is involved should be minimal and, in most cases, should have been covered by the ongoing fee.

Termination charges become a rear-end load. They might dissuade unhappy beneficiaries from terminating the trustee, but usually only result in bitter feelings, fee disputes, and arguments. These charges should be discussed with the institution from the outset and eliminated if at all possible.

On the other hand, we believe that most institutional trustees do not charge enough. Most fee schedules hover at around 1 percent. That is not significant when compared with the trustees' duties and responsibilities.

We would prefer that institutional trustees raise their fees if that would result in increased competence and service to those of our clients who have elected to name them as their trustees. Put bluntly, we believe that institutional trustees do not charge enough to enable them to render the expert advice expected of them. It is difficult to provide top-notch advice without spending top-notch dollars on top-notch people.

Many of our clients question the fees of institutional trustees. Clients are too shrewd to believe that in the commercial marketplace they get a lot for little cost. Low rates generate suspicion as to promised results. There are, however, some institutions that are well operated and provide sound investment results. They provide some of the great bargains still around.

Personal or individual trustees are not sophisticated in the manner in which they charge fees. Many negotiate their fees. Many provide their services on a gratuitous or quasi-gratuitous basis. Some overcharge; but most do not charge enough.

Some states set fee schedules in their laws. Many trustees' fees are set by the court having jurisdiction over trusts. These courts are generally, but not always, probate courts. Fee disputes are ultimately settled by the judge of that court.

Trustees' fees are not, in general, a major concern to most of our clients. A trustee's performance is the major concern of all of our clients. Your knowledge of trustees' fees, how they work, and what they are will assist you in selecting your trustees.

20

Giving Property to Minors

"Young Ones Are Tough to Give To"

If ever an estate planning professional were to make a generalized statement, it would be, "Most people want their property to ultimately end up in the hands of their children and grandchildren."

Almost every simple will we have reviewed over the years has said, "I leave my property to my spouse. If my spouse does not survive me, I leave it equally to my children. If a child of mine dies leaving children, I want his or her share to go to his or her children, my grandchildren."

Almost every life insurance contract we have reviewed has named beneficiaries precisely like the simple will does: a spouse, children, and grandchildren, in that order.

The purpose of this chapter is to discuss the problems associated with giving or leaving property to minor children and grandchildren. Under our system of laws, giving your property to minor beneficiaries is not easy.

Most states' laws define minors as persons who have not attained the age of eighteen. Some states have retained the age of twenty-one, which was the common age of majority for many years.

Can you make an outright gift of property to your minor children or grandchildren? The answer is yes and no: Yes, in that you can do anything you want; no, unless you follow the legal formalities under your state's law for the making of that gift. Under most states' laws, in order to make a gift of more than a nominal amount to a minor, you must take one of five steps.

1. Set Up a Uniform Gifts to Minors Act Account or a Uniform Transfers to Minors Act Account.

These custodial accounts are generally used to make a gift of stock, but in many states, they can be used to hold cash, securities, and annuity contracts. An adult custodian must be named on the account with the minor. The custodian manages the account until the minor becomes an adult. A newer version of the Uniform Gifts to Minors Act, called the Uniform Transfers to Minors Act, has been enacted in many states. Under this newer version of the law, nearly all types of property, including real estate, can be titled in the name of a custodian on behalf of a minor.

2. Create a Savings Account Trust.

The savings and loan association law provides liberalized handling of accounts created in the name of a minor. These accounts can be established in the name of a minor, and the minor is entitled to make deposits or withdrawals in the same manner as an adult without any liability to the savings and loan association.

3. Establish a Totten Trust.

An account called a Totten trust can be established with a commercial bank or savings and loan association. An account of this kind is created by registering the account in a form such as, "John Jones in trust for Mary Jones." In states that recognize this technique, it is usually presumed that the account belongs to the adult person named as trustee, unless it can be shown that the trust was intended to be irrevocable. On the death of the adult trustee, the account proceeds belong to the minor beneficiary but are controlled by the local probate court on behalf of the minor until he or she reaches adulthood.

4. Fund a Living Trust Created for the Benefit of the Minor Beneficiary.

A living trust that is used to give property to minors is called a 2503(c) trust. It is named after the Internal Revenue Code section that allows the income from the trust to be taxed to the minor beneficiaries. The lower tax brackets make the potential savings attractive in some cases. There is no income tax benefit at all for children under fourteen years of age under the so called Kiddie Tax provisions introduced by TRA 1986.

5. Petition the Local Court, Usually the Probate Court, to Authorize a Custodial Relationship.

The court will name an adult custodian who will manage the property under the court's direction and supervision until the minor becomes an adult.

The techniques that we have discussed represent, in the main, the alternatives available to you when you want to give property to your minor children and grandchildren. If you think these living techniques are complex, can you imagine how difficult it is to get your property into the hands of these minors on your death?

If your will leaves property directly to minors or if your insurance proceeds are to be paid directly to minors, we can assure you that your minor beneficiaries will not directly receive anything. Every state in our country will require that those funds receive the supervision of a court-directed custodianship. The court that will supervise all matters relating to these funds will generally be the local probate court.

If you did not name a guardian for your minor children in your will, the probate court will select a guardian on its terms—not yours. If you have more than one child, the court could name a separate guardian for each child. Each court-appointed guardian will be totally responsible for all his or her actions to an already overburdened and extremely busy probate judge.

If you were prudent and named your choice of guardian in your will but, nevertheless, left property directly to minor children, the court will have to supervise the distribution of that property. The probate judge will appoint a custodian to administer your children's property. The custodian who is selected may be an adult person or a licensed institutional trustee. The person whom the judge selects will be responsible to the judge on an ongoing basis for all acts with respect to the children's property. The custodian may or may not be the same person who has been named as the children's guardian.

A court-imposed conservatorship that results from leaving property directly to minors on death has, in our opinion, the following drawbacks:

All your property and all the conservator's actions with respect to it are made public.

The court will require that a bond be posted for each year of the conservatorship and that it be paid for from the children's funds. The cost will be approximately 1 percent of the fund value each year.

The conservator will have to keep detailed records of his or her transactions and will have to show those records to the court. This takes time and costs money.

The conservator will be paid out of the children's funds.

The conservator is usually required to use the services of an attorney in working with the court; attorneys' fees will be paid out of the children's funds.

The conservator whom the court appoints may not be experienced in the investment of funds and may not have the best interests of the children at heart.

Leaving property directly to minors on death involves a great deal of red tape; it depersonalizes the planning process and can create confusion and insecurity in your loved ones. It can also generate substantial expenses and unreasonable delays.

In talking with both parents and grandparents, we are convinced that they have very definite feelings with respect to how they want their children and grandchildren raised and provided for economically after their deaths; and yet so many people leave most of what they have directly to their minor children and grandchildren in the belief that somehow their property will miraculously be used to care for the children. This assumption is a mistaken one.

Any parent or grandparent who wishes to leave property to minor beneficiaries should always seek out a professional estate planner to accomplish those wishes through the creation of a properly drawn trust. Through the use of such a trust, the following are accomplished:

Parents and grandparents can give what they have to minor beneficiaries in the way they want and when they want those beneficiaries to receive it; they can control the disposition of their estates and create unique planning solutions to accommodate unique planning objectives.

They can select the children's guardians and the person or persons who will invest and control the purse strings with respect to their property.

They can avoid the active control and intervention of the probate court and keep their affairs and those of their beneficiaries out of the public eye.

All expenses that result through a conservatorship are avoided; the only expense is the trustees' fees.

Chapters 21, 22, and 23 on trusts and planning for children should offer more than a glimmer of hope to parents and grandparents who want to plan properly for loved ones who are underage.

21

Planning
for Children

"Beliefs and Caring
Can Survive Death"

In discussing estate planning with our clients who have minor children, we have learned that most parents have very strong and definite ideas as to how their children should be raised and provided for. Our clients express significant concern with respect to who would raise their minor children and how the children would be economically provided for if neither parent were alive. Their fears and insecurities with respect to the reality that would follow a catastrophe have, in the main, been well-founded.

The responsibility of a professional estate planner includes helping parents to plan for their children in the event that the unspeakable occurs. Planning in this area involves far more than mere economics. Planning for minor children involves creating an environment that will allow underaged loved ones to experience love and the care that goes with it, as well as the economic security that will provide more than the necessities of life as they grow to adulthood. The thought and sensitivity required to plan properly for potential orphans should not be taken lightly by any parent or professional adviser.

In this chapter, we discuss the techniques you can use to provide a substitute lifestyle for your minor loved ones should a catastrophe occur. It is important to understand that your wishes can become reality after your death if you take the time to plan properly.

Selecting the Guardian

It is mandatory that you take the time to select and name the person or persons whom you wish to raise your children in your absence; these persons are called guardians of the person. Under the laws of most states, guardians are named in a will. When a revocable living trust is used, the guardians should be named in the pour-over will that accompanies it.

Many of our clients become exasperated when asked, "Who do you want to raise and care for your children in your absence?" In attempting to respond, they can generally think of no one who, as a replacement parent, would do as good a job as they. Several names are usually discussed, and all are usually discarded because of one deficiency or another. Often the result of this process is no result at all. The parents, in frustration, come to this conclusion: "We don't know anyone who could raise our children as well as we would."

Our advice is always, "We understand, but please, after giving it much thought and after discussing it together, give us the best of the worst." You must select your children's guardian because, regardless of its drawbacks, your choice will, in all likelihood, be far better than the choice of the probate judge. If you do not name a guardian, the court will. The selection of a guardian is a painful process, but it must be done. In going through the process, you should always:

Provide for a succession of guardians in your will. There is no guarantee that any guardian will be alive when needed or that your chosen guardian will agree to serve. Always spell out your first, second, and, if important to you, third choice of guardians in your will.

Always discuss the situation with the guardians you would like to name before you name them. Be sure that they will, in fact, serve if named.

Share your estate plan with the guardians you have named so they will know and understand what they may be getting into.

Select your guardians on the basis of their beliefs, morality, and lifestyle, not on their ability to manage a financial portfolio. Management of the children's funds will not necessarily be the responsibility of the guardians. Others can be named to manage the children's property as trustees. If you choose, however, the guardians and the trustees can be the same.

If you elect to name a married couple as guardians, use both of their full names in describing them in your will. If you use a "Mr. and Mrs." designation, there could be a different "Mrs." at the time they are needed.

In most states, the guardians who are selected and named in a will do not serve automatically. The probate court judge must, after independent inquiry, approve and name the guardian who will ultimately serve. In some states, the parents' choice is presumptive; in others, it is not. Regardless of the laws of the state in which you reside, always include your choices in your will to give the judge some help and direction.

Leaving Property to Children

Do not leave your property or insurance proceeds directly to your minor children. We have discussed the problems that occur when this is attempted in Chapter 20, Giving Property to Minors.

Always use a trust vehicle to leave your property to minor loved ones. As we discuss in the chapters on trusts, you may elect to use either a trust in your will (testamentary trust) or a revocable living trust. We believe that a revocable living trust should be used, for all the reasons we have already discussed.

By using a trust, you can spell out in great detail precisely how you wish your children to be taken care of and when you wish them to receive the balance of your property. You can also name the individuals or institutions you would like to have manage the property for the benefit of your children. The trustees or financial guardians can and will work closely with the personal guardians in following your instructions to provide for your children's well-being. The rest of this chapter describes many of the techniques that are used in a trust by professional estate planners to care for minor children.

When the Property Is Divided among the Children

Many wills and trusts we have reviewed on behalf of our clients divide the property up into equal, but separate, shares for each child immediately upon the death of the maker. This technique reflects the maker's intent to treat the children equally, and as a result, each child has a separate trust share that can only be used for that child's benefit.

We believe that planning of this sort is ill-conceived and does not accomplish what the parent had in mind. What happens if one or more of the children have extraordinary needs for funds because of sickness or other unforeseen emergencies? The answer is that, under this technique, once their individual trusts are depleted, they will become wards of the state.

This would be true even though their brothers or sisters still have significant sums remaining in their trusts that they do not need.

A better technique, in our opinion, is to leave all your property in a common trust for the benefit of all your children for their health, support, maintenance, education, and general welfare. Once all your children become adults, whatever is left can be divided equally among them and given to them or placed in a separate trust for each of them to be distributed in accordance with your wishes.

The statement that "There is nothing so unequal as the equal treatment of unequals" certainly applies here. In reality, most parents, while they are alive, care for their children based on need rather than on a basis of equal shares. The resources of the parents are used to care for all the children based on the needs of the children, not on a dollar-for-dollar accounting parity; after death, this reality should be no different.

When the common trust for the children will be divided into shares is a matter of individual preference. Many of our clients believe that it should be divided when the youngest child attains the age of twenty-three or even twenty-five years of age. One technique that we find particularly intriguing divides the common trust into separate shares when the youngest child attains the age of twenty-three or, in the alternative, upon graduation from college, whichever happens first. When you choose to divide the common trust is your decision. The important consideration in your estate plan is to make sure that all your children are provided for while they are minors and that they are provided for from all your resources.

One of the questions that this technique frequently raises is, "Do my older children have to wait until their youngest brother or sister reaches that magic age before my adult children can get some of their money to invest in a business or for any other good purpose?" The answer is no, if the trust document is carefully written. Instructions can be given to the trustee to advance money to any older child for the purposes that are enumerated in the trust instructions. In advancing the money, the trustee should be instructed to first be sure that enough common trust funds will be left to feed, clothe, educate, and care for the minor brothers and sisters. A provision can also be included in the trust document to provide that upon ultimate division of the common trust into separate and equal shares for each of the children, any amounts advanced to adult children will reduce the amount of the shares those adult children actually receive.

The choices that are available to you are limited only by your imagination. If we have spurred your thinking, we have accomplished our purpose.

When the Property Is Distributed to Children

Many of our clients believe that when all their children have reached adulthood, the property in the common trust should be given or distributed to them outright. This approach is all right, but it may not be as sound as some other alternatives that can be used.

Wealth is a strange phenomenon; it is a concept that is relative to the perception of the wealth holder. Whether one's wealth is acquired quickly or over a long period of time appears to be relevant when a person makes the judgment as to whether or not one is indeed wealthy. Most of our clients are wealthy when measured against world or national averages; yet with few exceptions, they do not view themselves as financially secure and are prudent and relatively conservative in their lifestyles. They are concerned with the need to always have enough for the tomorrows in their lives.

Whether a young adult will exercise good judgment with regard to inherited property is always uncertain; most young adults do not have the experience or maturity to handle what are to them large sums of money. People do make mistakes, and generally the frequency of their mistakes is tied directly to their experience or lack of it. Property that is left to a young adult all at one time is frequently lost through poor investment or spent as if there would be no tomorrow. Parents know too well what tomorrow may bring and are generally very concerned about when and how their children receive their funds.

Parents who are concerned about when their children will receive their funds usually provide for a pattern of distribution in their trust documents. They provide that when the youngest child attains a certain age, the common trust property will be divided equally among their children. Rather than giving it to them outright, however, it is placed in each child's separate trust to be distributed in accordance with the parents' wishes. How that property is distributed and when it is distributed always depends on the wishes, beliefs, and prejudices of the parents. While the property is in the child's trust, however, the trustee will always be instructed to care for the child with both the income and principal of the trust in accordance with the written instructions of the parents. Here are some distribution techniques that are selected with regularity by many of our clients.

The first technique is to distribute the trust proceeds in two distributions, such as:

> The child will receive the trust proceeds in two distributions. These distributions will be half at twenty-one and half at twenty-five; or half at twenty-five and half at thirty; or half at thirty and half at thirty-five.

Regardless of the ages used, the concept is to ease the child into the money, to provide that if a mistake is made with the first half, time and experience will be on the child's side when the second half is received. This technique also manifests the belief that there is a certain age below which the child should not have the opportunity to exercise judgment with regard to the inherited funds. The advantage of this technique is that there will always be two or more distributions. This distribution method should enable the child to learn from previous mistakes.

The problem with the multiple-age technique is that if the child is already over the last distribution age specified by the parent, the funds will be received at one time. Many people believe that age does not a wise person make, but rather, experience does. These people obviously would not use this approach.

Parents who do not like a distribution pattern predicated strictly on age could use a pattern of distribution similar to this:

> The child will receive half the funds upon attaining a minimum age or, if over that age, immediately on the death of the parents. The balance of the trust fund will be distributed five, ten, or fifteen years later.

Many of our clients prefer that their children receive their property in three or more distributions, which may be tied to certain ages or time intervals. Some parents like a plan of distribution that uses both time intervals and attained ages. These parents reason that if the distributions are spread out, each child will gain more experience and wisdom with every additional distribution. The disadvantage to this approach is that the child will have to wait to receive the funds and might think that the deceased parent was not confident of the child's abilities or was trying to exercise control from the grave. An example of this distribution pattern is:

> One-fourth at twenty-five or one-fourth immediately if the child is over twenty-five on the death of the parent, with additional equal distributions every five years thereafter until all the trust principal has been distributed.

Some of our clients create uneven distribution, patterns such as one-third of the property at twenty-five and the balance at age forty.

A few of our clients elect not to make outright distributions of property to their children. These parents usually instruct the trustee to care for their children from their respective separate shares of both the income and principal of their trusts in accordance with the terms of the trust, and provide that on the child's death the balance of the trust principal will go to that child's children. If that child has no children, the balance will go to the trusts created for the child's brothers and sisters.

The important point to recognize is that you can control how you wish your property to pass to your children. When you think about your preferences for distribution, remember that you can also create different patterns of distribution for each of your children. For example:

> To my sons, one-half of their share at twenty-five or immediately on my death if they are over twenty-five, and the balance five years later. To my daughters, one-fourth of their share at twenty-five or immediately on my death if they are over twenty-five, another fourth five years later, and the balance of the trust property is in trust for the lifetimes of each of my daughters.

Parents who select this pattern of distribution believe that a daughter may need more protection in our society than a son. If that is their belief, this pattern might suit them. Obviously, this concern could be directed at sons and, if so, the pattern is reversed.

Please understand that you can leave your property equally to your children and, through the use of trusts, create different patterns of distribution with regard to each child's individual share. This technique is of major importance when planning for handicapped or disadvantaged children. Disadvantaged children may never have the ability to handle their own affairs; they may require lifetime care with respect to the property in their trusts. Trusts can be tailored to fit the needs of any child.

Most parents know their children, and all parents know their own minds; they should plan accordingly.

Planning for Children

Select a guardian for your minor children.

Leave your property in a trust for your children, not as an outright bequest.

Use a common trust for minor children.

Divide your property when all your children are adults.

Make several distributions to your children.

22

Per Stirpes versus Per Capita

"Serious Latin"

In reviewing estate plans with clients over the years, many of our clients have asked, "What does *per stirpes* mean?" or "What does *per capita* mean?" For years we have vowed that if we ever wrote a book on estate planning, we would explain these important words to our readers.

Per stirpes and per capita are Latin phrases, either of which can almost always be found in a will or trust. The use of the terms *per stirpes* and *per capita* by an attorney provides a precise way to create a property distribution pattern. In using them, an attorney can cut the use of words considerably.

Per stirpes means "by roots or stocks; by representation." This distribution pattern means that beneficiaries get what their immediate ancestors had, or were to receive. Some professionals use its English name, "by representation."

Per capita means "by the head or polls; according to the number of individuals; share and share alike." This distribution pattern means that all beneficiaries are counted, irrespective of generation, and their number divided into the property at hand, with each beneficiary receiving a resulting equal percentage interest in the property. Some professionals use its English name, "share and share alike."

Please look at Figure 22-1. Notice that we have created the same family tree twice. If the father, Jim, and his son, John, were both dead, notice how differently Jim's property would be distributed under each method.

Under the plan that used a per stirpes pattern of distribution, Jim's son, Herb, received one-half of his father's property, and Herb's nephew, Dick, and niece, Jane, each received equal shares of the half that was to pass to

John; Dick and Jane each received one-half of what was supposed to pass to their father, John.

Under the plan that used a per capita pattern of distribution, Herb, Dick, and Jane each received the same distribution, one-third of Jim's estate.

If Dick died in the same accident that took his father John's life, and Dick had no children, the result under both distribution plans would be the same; Jim's son, Herb, would receive half of Jim's property and Jim's granddaughter, Jane, would receive half of Jim's property.

If Dick died in the same accident that took his father John's life and left two living children, each plan would provide a dramatically different result.

Under the per stirpes plan, Herb would receive one-half of his father's, Jim's, property, or $50,000. Herb's niece, Jane, would receive one-half of the property that was to pass to her father, John, or $25,000. Herb's great-nephews, Chip and Dale, would each receive one-half of the $25,000 that was supposed to pass to their father, Dick, or $12,500 each.

Under the per capita plan, Jim's son, Herb, would receive one-quarter of his father's property as would Herb's niece, Jane, and greatnephews, Chip and Dale. Under the per capita method, they each would receive the same amount, $25,000.

These results are illustrated in Figure 22-2.

It is absolutely critical that you understand these distribution concepts and that you understand what Latin and English words go with each. If your attorney does not use the right words to accomplish your desires and you do not catch the mistake, your property will go in the wrong amounts to your beneficiaries.

People involved in planning their estates should understand the results that each distribution pattern creates. Other than your review, there may be no checkpoint that will ensure that the right words have been used. Mistakes in their use cannot be corrected after death.

We have listened to clients describe how they wish to distribute their property on death. We have also reviewed the existing wills and trusts of these same clients and have discovered that the wrong words were used. This does not happen often, but it can and does happen. Know your Latin, or at least four words of it.

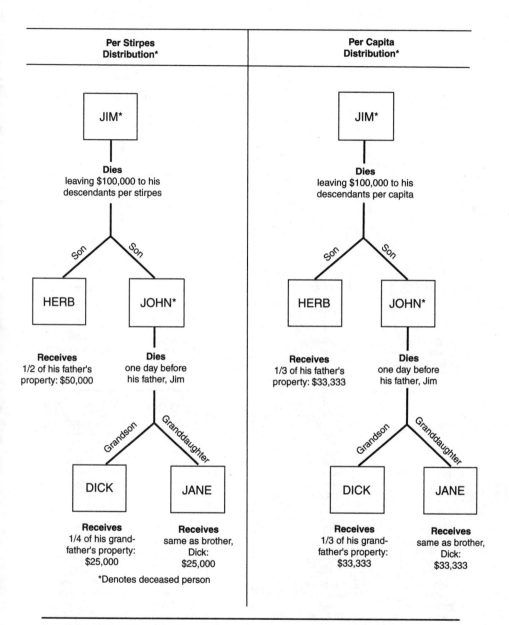

Figure 22-1. Per stirpes distribution and per capita distribution (illustrated through grandchildren).

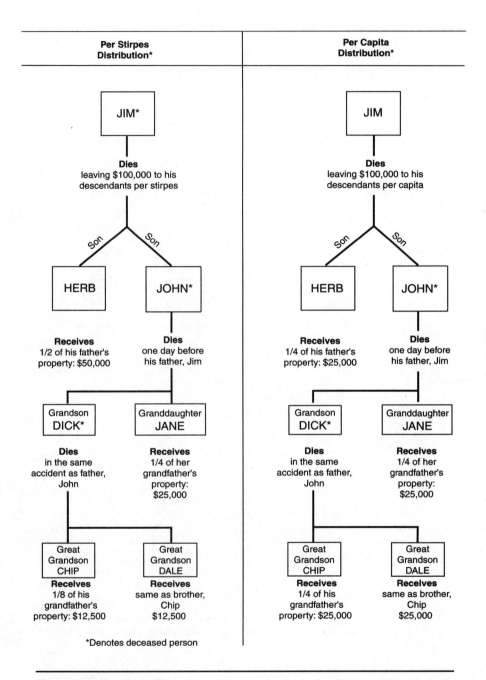

Figure 22-2. Per stirpes distribution and per capita distribution (illustrated through great-grandchildren).

23

Generation Skipping

"Geometrically Increasing Your Estate"

As property passes from one generation to the next, it is subject to the federal estate tax. Before 1976, it was possible to avoid the federal estate tax when property passed to subsequent generations. The avoidance of federal estate tax was usually accomplished by the use of a generation-skipping trust.

A generation-skipping trust allows the maker of the trust to skip federal estate tax as property passes from generation to generation. Here is how it works:

The maker of the trust creates a trust, which receives the assets at the maker's death.

The trust provides that the maker's spouse receives all income from the trust. The spouse receives principal from the trust if needed.

At the death of the trust maker's spouse, the trust maker's children receive all the trust income. They, too, can receive principal from the trust if they need it.

Upon the deaths of the trust maker's children, the principal of the trust passes to the maker's grandchildren.

Alternatively, the trust maker could, at the death of the trust maker's spouse, provide that the trust property go directly to the trust maker's grandchildren, bypassing the trust maker's children completely.

Generation-skipping trusts have historically accomplished three basic objectives:

Provide support for the maker's spouse, if any, and children, if the maker so chooses.

Prevent the maker's spouse and children from "wasting" the maker's property by having the property controlled by a trustee.

Limit federal estate tax payments to one on the maker's death and one on the death(s) of the grandchild(ren). (The maker's spouse and children paid *no* federal estate tax on the generation-skipping property on their deaths.)

While generation-skipping was not restricted to the use of a trust or for the benefit of family members, generation skipping became very popular, especially among the very wealthy. The federal estate tax savings from generation to generation were significant. Because generation skipping was considered a tax loophole for the rich, its use was severely restricted by the Tax Reform Act of 1976.

The Tax Reform Act of 1976 subjected generation-skipping assets to federal estate tax on the deaths of the beneficiaries of the generation-skipping trust. For example, upon the deaths of a trust maker's children, the trust assets would be added to their federally taxable estates. The 1976 act treated generation skipping just as if the property had passed through each generation's estate.

Because the generation-skipping provisions of the Tax Reform Act of 1976 were so complex, they were virtually unenforceable. TRA 1986 repealed the 1976 law and replaced it with an only slightly less complex law. This new generation-skipping law generally became effective on October 22, 1986. It provided special rules that make generation-skipping taxes paid under the Tax Reform Act of 1976 subject to refund.

The current generation-skipping transfer tax subjects to tax almost all transfers of property from an individual in one generation to a person or persons at least two generations below the transferring individual's generation. The simplest example of a generation-skip is a gift made by a grandparent to a grandchild. The generation-skipping tax can apply whether this gift is made during the grandparent's lifetime, at death, or by a trust or other method that delays the gift until some future time. Thus not only are the traditional generation-skipping methods covered by this tax, but so are all other methods that have the effect of skipping the federal estate tax in one or more generations.

Under the generation-skipping tax, everyone has $1,000,000 with which to generation-skip. This base amount of $1,000,000 is indexed for inflation and can go up in $10,000 increments. In this chapter, because of the ease of using $1,000,000, that is the amount our examples are based on. You should always find out from your estate planning professionals the current amount of generation-skipping transfer tax exemption that is in effect.

Because a husband and a wife each have a $1,000,000 exemption, they can, if they so choose, treat a generation-skipping transfer by one of them as being made one-half by each of them. Combined, then, they have at least $2,000,000 to work with.

The $1,000,000 exemption applies to lifetime generation skips or those occurring at the death of the trust maker. The $1,000,000 can be allocated to one generation-skipping transfer, or it can be allocated in any manner the trust maker chooses among several generation-skipping transfers.

If a child of a trust maker dies before a generation-skipping transfer is made, then any transfers to that child's children by the trust maker are *not* considered to be generation-skipping transfers. This is called the predeceased ancestor exception.

The generation-skipping tax is due when the recipient of the generation-skipping property receives property, when the recipient has the right to the property (even when it is in a trust), or when a direct gift is made from a grandparent to a grandchild. The applicable tax rate is the highest federal estate tax rate: 55 percent. As you can see, this tax is extremely high.

There is a common misconception about the generation-skipping transfer tax exemption. Many people think that they can leave the $1,000,000 exemption amount to their grandchildren entirely free from tax. However, the property is also subject to federal estate tax. Here is how the federal estate tax and the generation-skipping transfer tax work in tandem:

> Bill Anderson is not married; his wife died several years ago. Bill's only son, Ed, has one child, Andrea. Ed is wealthy in his own right, so Bill wants to leave his $1,500,000 taxable estate to Andrea. On Bill's death, the applicable exclusion amount is $700,000. Because Bill's estate is $1,500,000 and his applicable exclusion is $700,000, his taxable estate is $800,000. The tax is $326,000. That means that there is $1,174,000 left to pass to Andrea. But, let's assume that the generation-skipping exemption is $1,000,000. That means that $174,000 is subject to the generation-skipping tax. The tax is imposed at a 55 percent rate, meaning an additional tax of $95,700. Andrea will end up with $1,078,300; part of her inheritance was subject to both the federal estate tax and the generation-skipping tax.

A similar result occurs if Bill makes a direct lifetime gift to Andrea. The gift tax is imposed and the generation-skipping tax is imposed, making the gift much more expensive.

The amount of the actual tax assessed will vary based on the year of death and the amount of the estate. The generation-skipping exclusion amount is

$1,000,000, and is increased for inflation after 1998. The applicable exclusion amount will be phased in to $1,000,000 in 2006, so the two amounts will never be the same. If a full generation-skipping gift is made, it will almost always create some type of generation-skipping tax. Of course, the larger one's estate, the greater the tax will be as a percentage of that estate.

For those who want to pass more than $1,000,000 to their grandchildren, or $2,000,000 if they are married, some planning techniques are available that avoid the gift tax, the federal estate tax, and the generation-skipping tax. For example, certain gifts of life insurance allow the generation-skipping tax to be leveraged. By making gifts of life insurance premiums, at worst, the amount of the premiums reduces the $1,000,000 exemption. At best, the premiums do not even reduce the $1,000,000 exemption. The following example shows how this leveraging can work:

> Charlotte McCarthy's grandchildren buy a $1,500,000 life insurance policy on her life, naming themselves as the beneficiaries. Each year, Charlotte gives her grandchildren enough money to pay the premiums on the life insurance, but does not require them to pay the premiums. Because the gifts to the grandchildren are gifts of a present interest and are in amounts less than $10,000 per year, there are no adverse federal gift tax consequences. The gifts do not reduce Charlotte's $1,000,000 generation-skipping exemption because they are direct gifts to Charlotte's grandchildren. On Charlotte's death, the $1,500,000 in life insurance proceeds that passes to her grandchildren is not included in her estate for federal estate tax purposes. In addition, *none* of the $1,500,000 counts toward her $1,000,000 generation-skipping exemption. Therefore, she still can leave another $1,000,000 to her grandchildren free from the generation-skipping tax.

The generation-skipping tax is aimed at wealthy individuals who want to pass a substantial amount of property to younger family members without paying federal estate tax when intervening generations of family members die. While this tax has made it more difficult to generation-skip, some methods still exist to maximize the amount that can pass from grandparents to grandchildren or greatgrandchildren.

To illustrate the importance of using the generation-skipping exemption amount, Table 23-1 presents estate tax numbers for an estate that passes through three generations. It assumes that the family has used its applicable exclusion amount and that the estate is taxed at 55 percent. We use $1,000,000 to make our point. After three generations, over 90 percent of the value of the estate has gone to federal estate tax. We know this is an oversimplified example, but in larger estates, even taking into account that the inherited money is invested, each generation's estate will diminish by about 55 percent.

Table 23-1
Federal Estate Tax Over Three Generations at 55 percent on $1,000,000

Generation	Beginning Estate	Estate Tax	Remaining Estate
Grandparents	$1,000,000	$550,000	$450,000
Children	450,000	247,500	202,500
Grandchildren	202,500	113,375	89,125

Table 23-2 demonstrates the results of simple generation-skipping planning. If children are skipped, much more goes to the grandchildren and greatgrandchildren.

Table 23-2
Generation-Skipping Over Three Generations at 55 percent on $1,000,000

Generation	Beginning Estate	Estate Tax	Remaining Estate
Grandparents	$1,000,000	$550,000	$450,000
Children	-0-	-0-	-0-
Grandchildren	450,000	247,500	202,500

Planning can be done that will theoretically leave property free from any gift, estate, or generation-skipping tax for as long as the grandparent would like. It is called dynasty trust planning. Since the inception of the United States, every state has adopted a rule that we inherited from England called the Rule against Perpetuities. Many legal treatises have been written about this rule, but in essence it says that you cannot leave your property in trust forever. Eight states have now repealed this rule: Alaska, Delaware, Idaho, Illinois, New Jersey, Rhode Island, South Dakota, and Wisconsin. By creating a trust in one of these states, it is possible to allow all of your succeeding generations to use your wealth and, at the same time, avoid any gift, estate, and generation-skipping tax on it. You do not have to live in one of these states to create a trust that falls within its law.

If you have a large estate, you should explore dynasty trust planning. Over time, it can save literally millions of dollars in taxes, and can also be used to help all of those family members who come after you.

Generation-skipping transfer tax affects only those taxpayers who have large estates. However, if used properly and coupled with sophisticated planning, the generation-skipping exemption can be used to geometrically increase the amount of property passing to other generations.

24

Disinheriting
a Spouse

"Spouses Have Rights Too"

In planning estates over the years, we have often been asked, "What happens after my death if I disinherit my spouse?" "If I disinherit my spouse, can my spouse contest my will or trust, and get my property?" The answer to both questions is that in all states, with the exception of Georgia, disinherited spouses have the right to receive some of the property that was not left to them.

We must stress that each state has its own unique laws with respect to a surviving spouse's rights in the property of a deceased spouse. Most states give a surviving spouse the right to receive far less than half of the deceased spouse's property.

The name ownership to property is taken in can become of critical importance on the death of a spouse, because ownership rights not established during life will not be meaningfully restored on death under the laws of most states. Even in states with liberal laws in bestowing rights to a surviving spouse, the rights are usually limited to a spouse's receiving a maximum of one-half of the deceased spouse's property.

Prior to 1982, many husbands and wives were persuaded to leave up to one-half of their property to their spouses in order to maximize federal estate tax savings. In order to qualify for the marital deduction, a surviving spouse had to be given at least the income from half the deceased spouse's property and the right to leave that property to anyone he or she chose. The requirements that a spouse had to be given the right to dispose of half the estate on his or her subsequent death brought about many a tear and much anger. Every spouse wanted to reduce federal estate tax by qualifying his or her planning for the marital deduction. But many spouses sacrificed the great tax benefits of the marital deduction because they knew or suspected that half their property would pass to their spouses' loved ones on the spouses' subsequent deaths. This was particularly true when each spouse had children from a prior marriage or when there were no children.

Under current laws, your spouse no longer has to be given the right to leave half your property to whomever your spouse wants. The marital deduction requirements now absolutely remove this planning impediment.

If you are getting excited about the potential opportunity to disinherit your spouse and still obtain the federal estate tax savings resulting from the marital deduction provisions of the federal estate tax law, *be careful.* After your death, your spouse will still have all the rights given under your state law to elect against your will and perhaps even your trust.

If you choose to disinherit your spouse totally or partially, your estate planning needs can be determined only after you are aware of the rights your state gives your spouse after your death. After you finish this chapter, read the introduction to Appendix C and then read about your state's law with respect to your and your spouse's rights. It is important that you read the introduction to the appendix because it will familiarize you with the terms you will need to understand as you read your state's law. A knowledge of your state's law will also enable you to better apply the techniques of spousal planning that we discuss in Chapter 25, Planning for a Spouse.

Two techniques are generally used to assure persons that their spouses will not successfully elect against their wills or trusts. The first technique is called a premarriage contract. Attorneys refer to this contract as a premarital, or antenuptial, contract. The second technique is called an after-marriage contract and is referred to by attorneys as a postnuptial agreement.

A premarriage contract is used by persons who wish to marry but who also wish to establish their right to leave property to their loved ones prior to taking their marriage vows. The right of potential spouses to enter into premarriage contracts is recognized in every state. Premarriage contracts have been in use for centuries and are used more than ever today, particularly in second marriages. In order for these agreements to be valid, the following requirements usually must be met:

Each party must be bound to the agreement and consent to it.

Each party must totally disclose all assets.

The agreement must be in writing.

Both parties must understand what they are signing.

Premarriage contracts make it possible for spouses to protect the inheritance rights of their respective children by prior marriages and, as a result, prevent strife over the disposition of their estates. The laws of all states favor these contracts if they are properly prepared.

After-marriage contracts can also be used to set forth the spouses' inheritance wishes. They are not legally recognized to the extent that premarriage contracts are. The laws of each state are unique as they apply to the after marriage contract. Most states that recognize these contracts require that:

They be negotiated in good faith and reduced to writing.

There is complete and frank disclosure of all the economic facts of each party.

The provisions are fair and reasonable.

The circumstances leading up to the signed agreement are free of fraud, duress, and undue influence of any kind.

After-marriage contracts are looked upon with suspicion by courts and, as a result, must be entered into very carefully. Because of this suspicion, the requirements for an after marriage contract, where permitted, are much more complicated and rigorous than for a premarriage contract.

Given a choice between signing a premarriage contract or an after-marriage contract, always opt for the former; they are valid and binding if fair and fairly made and have always been favored by the laws of most states.

Second marriages offer the most troublesome of estate planning challenges. The trouble arises because many people have children from their first marriages and want to assure that all or most of their estates go to those children. Alternatively, if there are children from one, two, or more marriages, making sure the children and the current spouse are all taken care of can be very difficult. Mickey Rooneys and Elizabeth Taylors are hard to plan for.

The best way to plan for a second marriage is through the use of a premarriage contract. Most problems concerning who gets what can be solved. If a premarriage contract was overlooked, an after-marriage contract may solve the problem.

What happens if neither premarriage nor after-marriage contracts can be used? Spouses in a second marriage have rights too. As a matter of fact, absent those contracts, their rights are exactly the same as a first spouse's rights given under your state's law. Please refer to Appendix C for your state's law with respect to your spouse's rights.

When you are planning your affairs, whether you are married or are contemplating marriage, remember: Spouses have rights too!

25

Planning
for a Spouse

"An Incredible Number of Choices"

Planning for a spouse under the old federal estate tax law was fairly simple. The maximum marital deduction was the greater of $250,000 or half the value of the estate of the deceased spouse. It is important that we illustrate the planning basics under the old federal estate tax law so that you can truly understand the planning alternatives available to you now. For purposes of comparing different planning techniques, we will assume an estate of $1,200,000.

Before 1982, a $1,200,000 estate left outright to a surviving spouse resulted in $145,800 of federal estate tax on the death of the first spouse. On the death of the second spouse (assuming for simplicity's sake no appreciation in the value of the property left to that spouse), there would have been an additional $321,022 federal estate tax. This is diagrammed in Figure 25-1.

In making federal estate tax calculations, the applicable exclusion amount must be used. In our calculations it is included.

Before 1982, that same $1,200,000 estate could have been planned so that the total federal estate tax resulting from both spouses' deaths would have been reduced from $466,822 to $291,600, a saving of $175,222.

The typical planning strategy that accomplished this massive tax saving was to create two separate trusts that came into existence within the overall master trust document on the death of the trust maker. The first separate trust received the maximum marital deduction amount ($600,000); it was called the marital trust. The marital trust was only for the surviving spouse. The terms of this trust had to provide the surviving spouse with all the income and the right to leave the trust property on death to whomev-

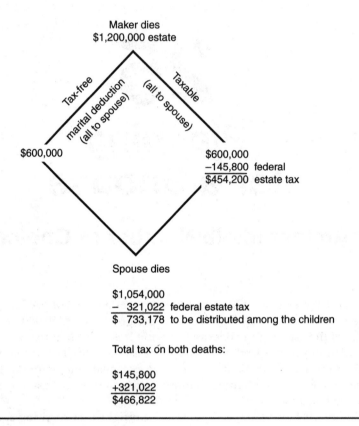

Figure 25-1. Outright to spouse, pre–1982.

er that spouse desired (general power of appointment). The principal of that trust could be used by the surviving spouse either whenever the spouse desired or only in the discretion of the trustee of the marital trust. The principal of the marital trust did not have to be distributed at all. The maker of the trust had the right to give as much or as little of the principal of the marital trust to the spouse as the maker desired.

The family trust, or second trust, was created to receive the balance of the estate funds (in our example, $600,000 as well). The income and principal of the family trust generally were left in trust for the benefit of the surviving spouse and the children of the trust maker. The trustees were instructed to care for the needs of the spouse first and, after those needs were met, then the children. Many times, the spouse and a close friend or adult family member were named as cotrustees of the trusts, and the spouse was given the right to fire the other trustee as long as a replacement trustee was named.

The proceeds that went into the family trust were subject to federal estate tax on the death of the first spouse. In our case, the family trust would have incurred $145,800 in federal estate tax, the same amount of federal estate tax as in Figure 25-1. On the death of the surviving spouse, however, the family trust proceeds would not have been subject to federal estate tax and would have passed tax-free directly to the beneficiaries of the family trust. In our situation, the beneficiaries were the maker's children. Because the surviving spouse did not own the family trust property under the rules of the federal estate tax law, the family trust proceeds were not included in the surviving spouse's estate.

On the death of the surviving spouse, the proceeds of the marital trust would have been subject to federal estate tax in the amount of $145,800. As a result of this two-trust planning, the total federal estate tax that would have to have been paid on both spouses' deaths was $291,600. This result is illustrated in Figure 25-2.

Professional advisers call this two-trust planning the marital deduction trust planning. Before 1982, it was generally used to save federal estate taxes when the estate of a married couple exceeded $425,000, as discussed in Chapter 9 on federal estate tax.

By using this planning approach, the trust maker could reduce the federal estate tax that would result from both spouses' deaths. The marital deduction trust technique both saved tax and allowed the trust maker to determine how one-half of the property ultimately passed. It also created substantial after-death income planning opportunities for the maker's beneficiaries. Under the old law, the maximum income tax on trust income paid to a beneficiary was 70 percent. If all of a spouse's property were left to a surviving spouse, as illustrated in Figure 25-1, the surviving spouse would have received all the income from the property, potentially placing that spouse into the 70 percent income tax bracket.

Under the two-trust plan, the income from the family trust could be distributed by the surviving spouse as trustee, with the approval of the cotrustee, directly to the other beneficiaries. When the children and grandchildren received the income, they were more likely to be in an income tax bracket that was far lower than the surviving spouse's bracket. Because of this difference in income tax brackets, substantial income tax could have been saved in caring for the family's needs. Two-trust plans were the tax-saving vehicles to use because they saved both federal estate tax and income tax.

Before we discuss how these techniques are used, let us spend a little more time on how they were structured for the maker's spouse and children under the old law. This will help you to understand how effective marital deduction planning is when used under our current law.

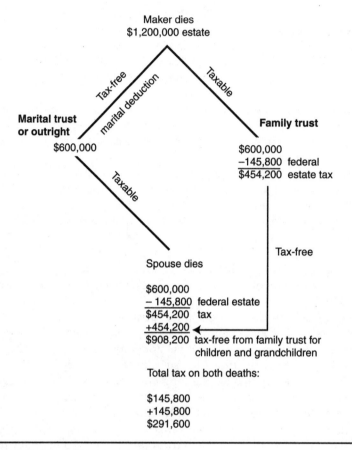

Maker dies
$1,200,000 estate

Tax-free
marital deduction

Taxable

**Marital trust
or outright**

$600,000

Family trust

$600,000
−145,800 federal
$454,200 estate tax

Taxable

Tax-free

Spouse dies

$600,000
− 145,800 federal estate
$454,200 tax
+454,200
$908,200 tax-free from family trust for
children and grandchildren

Total tax on both deaths:

$145,800
+145,800
$291,600

Figure 25-2. Two-trust planning, pre–1982.

Time, space, and your understanding do not require that we discuss all the historical variations that were possible under the two-trust plans. In order to illustrate these concepts, we will discuss two planning alternatives. The first alternative assumes that a trust maker wants to save federal estate tax, but in so doing wants to benefit children and grandchildren rather than the spouse with the family trust (Figure 25-3). The second alternative is to save federal estate tax and give the spouse as much control and use of the family trust as possible (Figure 25-4).

In Figure 25-3, the first alternative, you can see that the surviving spouse would only receive income from the marital trust and the right to leave the principal of the marital trust to that spouse's chosen beneficiaries. A potential problem resulting from this technique is that the surviving spouse might

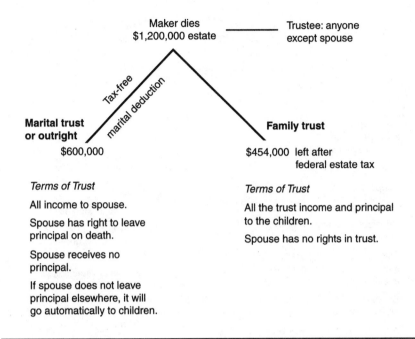

Maker dies
$1,200,000 estate

Trustee: anyone
except spouse

Tax-free
marital deduction

**Marital trust
or outright**
$600,000

Family trust

$454,000 left after
federal estate tax

Terms of Trust

All income to spouse.

Spouse has right to leave
principal on death.

Spouse receives no
principal.

If spouse does not leave
principal elsewhere, it will
go automatically to children.

Terms of Trust

All the trust income and principal
to the children.

Spouse has no rights in trust.

Figure 25-3. Minimum to spouse, pre–1982.

be able to use state spousal rights to elect against the entire estate. (See Chapter 24, Disinheriting a Spouse. This concept is of critical importance to the discussion of the planning opportunities now available.)

In order for the trust maker to prevent the spouse from electing against the two-trust plan, the maker generally modified the terms of the marital trust to give the surviving spouse the minimum benefits that the surviving spouse would receive under the state's law.

Figure 25-4 illustrates the maximum amounts and benefits a trust maker could leave to a surviving spouse under the pre-1982 two-trust plan.

Here, the surviving spouse certainly controls and benefits from the property in both trusts. In a marital trust, the spouse can use principal for any purpose. The family trust principal is primarily for the benefit of the surviving spouse if needed, as determined by the spouse in the cotrustee's role. If the cotrustee disagrees with the spouse about the spouse's determination of need, the spouse can fire the cotrustee and select a more willing cotrustee. The children can also be taken care of by the spouse as cotrustee under the same terms.

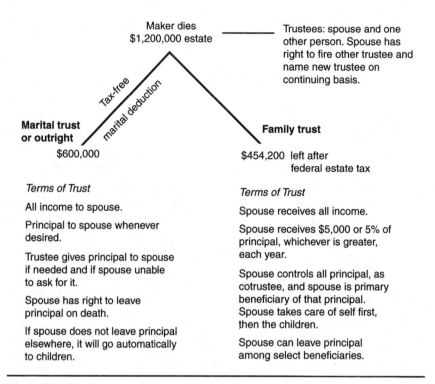

Figure 25-4. Maximum to spouse, pre–1982.

In our opinion, when a trust maker wishes to maximize the benefits for a surviving spouse, the family trust should always provide for the distribution of income from the family trust according to the trustees' discretion. If the surviving spouse does not have to receive the income from the family trust, it can be given to the children, who may be in lower income tax brackets; however, the family trust can provide that the spouse could always pay the income to the spouse if needed.

The two-trust planning format continues to be used by professional estate planners to reduce federal estate taxes on the deaths of both marriage partners. It is also used, in some cases, to provide for after-death income tax planning.

When discussing the planning alternatives available to you, we assume, for purposes of our illustrations, that death occurs after 2005. You may recall from Chapter 9, The Federal Estate Tax, that the applicable exclusion amount (formerly called the exemption equivalent) increases each year until it reaches its maximum of $1,000,000 in 2006. The applicable exclusion amount represents the amount that can be left free of federal estate tax to nonspouses and noncitizen spouses.

Before we discuss the planning opportunities available, it is important that you understand that the marital deduction is unlimited when property is left to U.S. citizen spouses. There are special rules for property that passes to spouses who are not U.S. citizens. These rules are discussed later in this chapter. For purposes of the figures that follow, all references to spouses are to surviving spouses who are U.S. citizens.

You could, if you desired, leave all your property outright to your spouse and be assured that your estate would pay no federal estate tax on your death. The discussion that follows is directed to those who desire to reduce federal estate tax for both spouses.

Figure 25-5 illustrates the federal estate tax consequences of leaving all your property directly to your spouse.

The result, in our illustration, of leaving your entire $1,200,000 estate to your spouse is the payment of $82,000 of federal estate tax when your spouse dies. Contrast this with the result that would occur under the traditional two-trust plan, illustrated in Figure 25-6. This plan assumes that you want to leave one-half of your estate to your spouse outright or in a marital trust for the benefit of your spouse and one-half of your estate for the benefit of your spouse and children in a family trust.

If you used a traditional two-trust plan, there would be absolutely no federal estate tax on the death of either you or your spouse on a $1,200,000

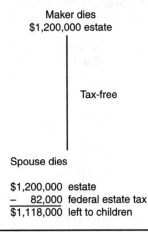

Figure 25-5. Outright to spouse.

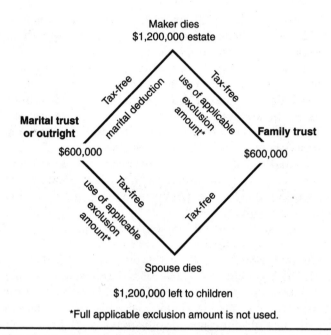

Figure 25-6. Traditional two-trust plan, one-half to spouse and one-half to a family trust.

estate. The two-trust plan would save $82,000 of federal estate tax. If your estate is $2,000,000, the results are even more impressive. If you left your full $2,000,000 estate to your spouse, it would pass to him or her tax-free because of the unlimited marital deduction. On your spouse's death, there would be a tax of $435,000 (Figure 25-7). By using a traditional two-trust

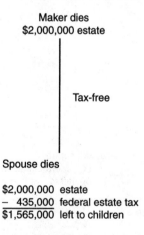

Figure 25-7. Outright to spouse, $2,000,000 estate.

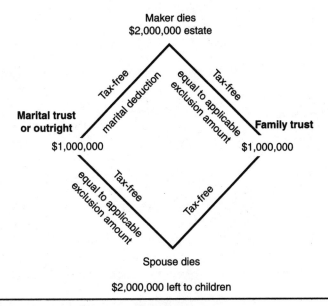

Figure 25-8. Traditional two-trust plan, $2,000,000 estate.

plan, the taxes can be reduced to zero! This dramatic tax reduction is accomplished by fully using your applicable exclusion amount at your death and your spouse's applicable exclusion amount at his or her death. Figure 25-8 illustrates this point.

Right now you may be asking yourself, "What should I do if I do not want to leave one-half of my estate to my spouse?" The answer depends on whether your planning motive is to give your spouse the maximum benefits from and control over your estate (Figure 25-9) or whether your motive is to give your spouse the least benefit from and control over your estate (Figure 25-10). Figures 25-9 and 25-10 illustrate how you can accomplish either of these aims and still reduce federal estate tax.

You can see the dramatic difference in the results for the surviving spouse between the two scenarios. In either illustration, there will be no federal estate tax on the death of either you or your spouse, unless the marital share grows to exceed the applicable exclusion amount ($1,000,000) or if your spouse has assets of his or her own.

In Figure 25-10, our minimum-to-spouse diagram, the only right your spouse has is the right to the income from the $200,000 in the marital trust. Do not forget, however, that under state law your spouse may have the right to elect against your plan. Good planning for estates when a spouse is to receive minimal benefits is to create a marital trust that would equal but not exceed the spousal rights accorded that spouse under state law. For exam-

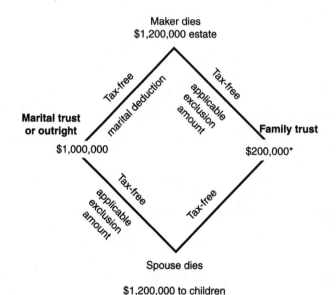

Figure 25-9. Maximum-to-spouse motive.

Maker dies
$1,200,000 estate

Tax-free marital deduction

Tax-free applicable exclusion amount

Marital trust or outright
$1,000,000

Family trust
$200,000*

Tax-free applicable exclusion amount

Tax-free

Spouse dies

$1,200,000 to children
(no tax)

Terms of Trust

All income to spouse.

Principal to spouse whenever desired.

Trustee gives principal to spouse if needed and spouse unable to ask for it.

Spouse has right to leave principal on death.

If spouse does not leave principal elsewhere, it will go automatically to children.

Terms of Trust

Spouse receives all income.

Spouse receives $5,000 or 5% of principal, whichever is greater, each year.

Spouse controls all principal as costrustee, and spouse is primary beneficiary of principal. Spouse takes care of self first, then children.

Spouse can leave principal among select beneficiaries.

*Here the full applicable exclusion amount is not used.

Figure 25-9. Maximum-to-spouse motive.

ple, assume you died a citizen of a state that provides that if your spouse and children survive you, your spouse is entitled to one-third of your estate. A plan that would accomplish your objectives and not be inconsistent with state law is illustrated in Figure 25-11.

For estates of $2,000,000 or less, the planning variations are almost endless. If your estate is under $2,000,000, you can accomplish your planning motives and always keep your estate free of federal estate tax on the deaths

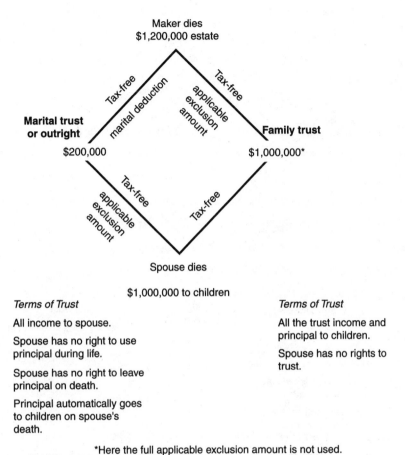

Figure 25-10. Minimum-to-spouse motive.

of both you and your spouse. How your objectives will be accomplished can be determined through the advice and counsel of your estate planning professionals.

If your estate is less than $1,000,000, you may be tempted to do nothing with respect to planning your estate. This may not be a wise decision. In addition to the many nontax reasons for estate planning, you should not ignore inflation and what it may do to the value of your estate. It is important to remember the impact that growth may have on the value of your property.

If your estate has a value in excess of $2,000,000, the planning opportunities that are available to you are staggering. Planning your estate in order to minimize federal estate tax on your death and the death of your spouse

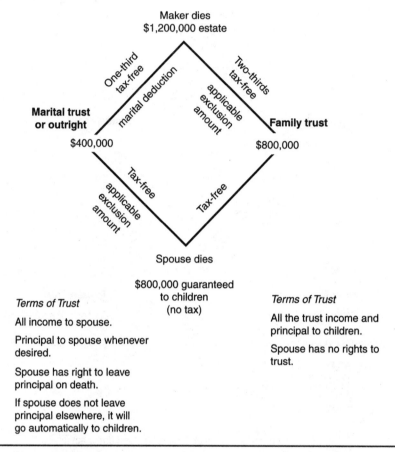

Figure 25-11. Minimum to spouse under state law.

will always depend on your planning objectives. Let us first compare a traditional two-trust plan with a new two-trust plan. The traditional plan puts half of your property in a marital trust and the balance in a family trust. If we use a hypothetical estate value of $3 million, the traditional two-trust approach generates a total federal estate tax of $420,000, $210,000 on the death of the first spouse and an additional $210,000 when the second spouse dies. This is illustrated in Figure 25-12. Contrast the traditional plan with a typical two-trust plan that would first put the applicable exclusion amount ($1,000,000 for our purposes) in the family trust and the balance in the marital trust, shown in Figure 25-13. If you used the typical plan, the children would have lost an additional $15,000 to federal estate tax on the death of your spouse over what they would have lost had the traditional two-trust plan been used.

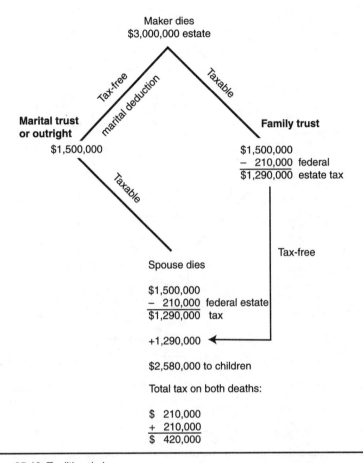

Figure 25-12. Traditional plan.

The old plan may look better at first. Under the old plan, $210,000 of the total federal estate tax was paid on the maker's death. Under the typical plan, no federal estate tax is due until the maker's spouse dies. Therefore, under the typical plan, there is $210,000 available to invest until the second spouse dies. The value of deferring the federal estate tax until the second death could be significant.

Whether one should use the deferral technique as opposed to staying with the traditional two-trust approach depends on a host of economic considerations, such as:

The life expectancy of the surviving spouse.

The projected inflation and real growth rates.

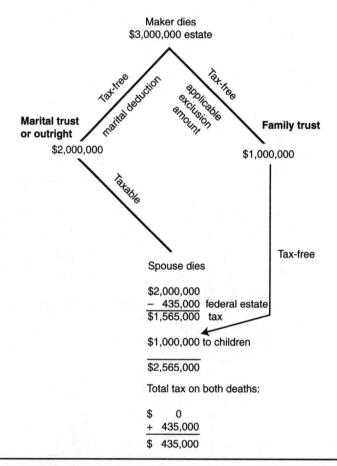

Figure 25-13. Typical two-trust plan, deferring tax until the second spouse dies.

The liquidity of the estate.

The projected income tax brackets of all beneficiaries.

The asset mix of the estate.

The projected reduction of the estate for the needs of the beneficiaries after the maker's death.

Given the relatively small difference in taxes between the two methods, it is almost always economically better to defer the taxes until the second spouse dies. Having the tax money to invest rather than giving it to the government immediately pays off over any period of time.

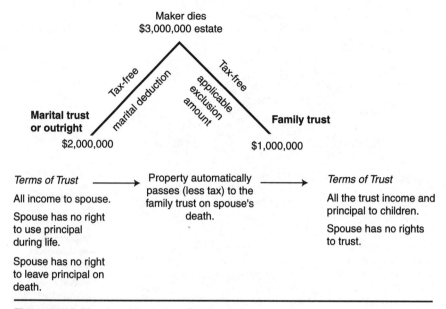

Figure 25-14. Plan 1—minimum benefit to spouse.

Because of the unlimited marital deduction, there is no requirement that you give your spouse the right to leave your property to anyone else on your spouse's death. This feature of the unlimited marital deduction offers a number of planning possibilities. Three major planning formats come readily to mind. They can best be explained through the illustrations in Figures 25-14, 25-15, and 25-16.

You have probably noticed that the federal estate tax for each plan is not shown. The federal estate tax on each is identical. A total tax of $435,000 is due on the death of the second spouse in each example.

In reviewing the three alternatives set forth in Figures 25-14, 25-15, and 25-16, we believe that Figure 25-16 reflects the planning desires of most of our clients. It is an ideal alternative that maximizes the benefits a spouse will receive but, at the same time, assures the maker that at least half of the estate will go directly to the children on the second spouse's death.

In Figures 25-14, 25-15, and 25-16, for non-community-property states, the total value of the estate, $3,000,000, represents the value of the property owned by one spouse in his or her name. In Figures 25-14 and 25-15, in a community property state, the $3,000,000 is one spouse's share of the community property plus any sole and separate property owned by that spouse. In Figure 25-16, in community property states, the $3,000,000 is the total value of the community property. The $1,500,000 allocated to marital trust 1 is the surviving spouse's share of the community property.

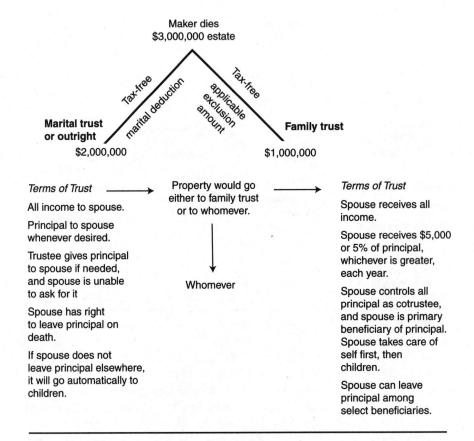

Figure 25-15. Plan 2—maximum benefit to spouse.

For those of you who are concerned about your state law and the rights your spouse has under it, the plan shown in Figure 25-17 should be of interest.

In a non-community-property state, when a married couple owns most or all of their property in the name of only one spouse, or in a community property state when a spouse owns the majority of his or her property as sole and separate property, another technique can be used to reduce federal estate tax. In using this technique, the asset-owner spouse gives property free of federal gift tax to the other spouse, who must be a U.S. citizen. The value of the gift should equal $1,000,000, the full applicable exclusion amount. If the spouse already has $1,000,000 worth of property, a gift is not necessary. If the spouse then dies first, an amount up to the $1,000,000 applicable exclusion amount will not generate federal estate tax. If this property is left in a family trust for the benefit of the asset-owner spouse and

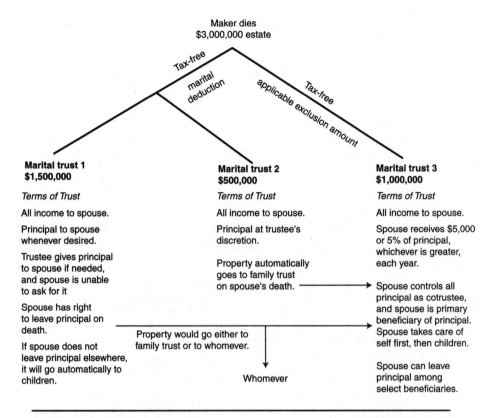

Maker dies
$3,000,000 estate

Tax-free marital deduction

applicable exclusion amount Tax-free

Marital trust 1
$1,500,000

Terms of Trust

All income to spouse.

Principal to spouse whenever desired.

Trustee gives principal to spouse if needed, and spouse is unable to ask for it

Spouse has right to leave principal on death.

If spouse does not leave principal elsewhere, it will go automatically to children.

Marital trust 2
$500,000

Terms of Trust

All income to spouse.

Principal at trustee's discretion.

Property automatically goes to family trust on spouse's death.

Property would go either to family trust or to whomever.

Whomever

Marital trust 3
$1,000,000

Terms of Trust

All income to spouse.

Spouse receives $5,000 or 5% of principal, whichever is greater, each year.

Spouse controls all principal as cotrustee, and spouse is primary beneficiary of principal. Spouse takes care of self first, then children.

Spouse can leave principal among select beneficiaries.

Figure 25-16. Plan 3—maximum benefit to spouse with children guaranteed at least half your property.

children, there will be no federal estate tax on the death of the asset-owner spouse. If this technique is not used and the non-asset-owner spouse dies first, that non-asset-owner spouse's exemption equivalent is lost. The loss of the applicable exclusion amount could cost as much as $510,000 in additional federal estate tax on the death of the asset-owner spouse. The bypass trust technique is used when both spouses own property at least equal to the applicable exclusion amount. This technique is illustrated in Figure 25-18.

Now that the gift-to-spouse technique has been illustrated, we compare the federal estate tax result when it is not used and when it is used. Please refer to Figures 25-19 and 25-20.

Without using the gift technique, federal estate tax is $945,000. Using the gift technique generates only $435,000 of federal estate tax. The difference is a whopping $510,000!

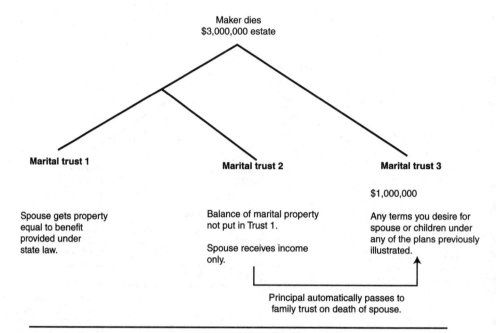

Figure 25-17. A compromise under state law.

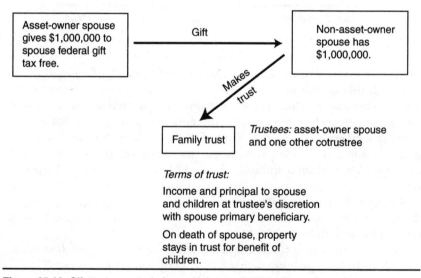

Figure 25-18. Gift-to-spouse technique with bypass trust.

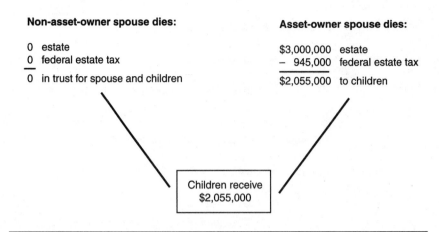

Figure 25-19. Without gift technique.

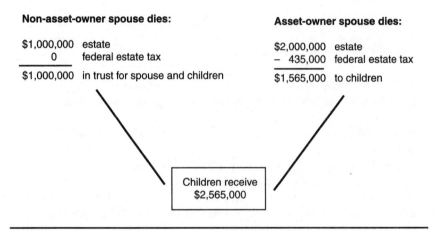

Figure 25-20. With gift technique.

The gift technique that we have illustrated uses a bypass family trust. Not only does it save federal estate tax on the second spouse's death, but the bypass trust also gives substantial control of the property to the asset-owner spouse as a trustee. As a trustee, the asset-owner spouse can control both the income and the principal of the bypass family trust. By naming a cotrustee serving with the asset-owner spouse, the income from the trust principal can be paid to both the asset-owner spouse and children for income tax savings, as we discussed earlier. In using this planning technique, the asset-owner spouse should always be given the right to terminate and replace the cotrustee.

Spouse 1 has $1,200,000 and dies first:

Family trust

$ 1,200,000	estate
− 1,000,000	applicable exclusion amount
$ 200,000	taxable estate*
$ 82,000	federal estate tax

Spouse 2 has $1,200,000 and dies second
(remember, all of Spouse 1's property went
to the family trust):

Family trust

$ 1,200,000	estate
− 1,000,000	applicable exclusion amount
$ 200,000	taxable estate
$ 82,000	federal estate tax*

*The total federal estate tax on both deaths is

Figure 25-21. Bypass trust when over applicable exclusion amount.

When using the bypass trust technique, remember that the applicable exclusion amount is $1,000,000 beginning in 2006. Prior to that date, the applicable exclusion amount is being phased in. Table 9-1 in Chapter 9, The Federal Estate Tax, is a schedule of the phase-in of the applicable exclusion amount.

What if each spouse has assets in excess of the exemption equivalent? If bypass trust planning is used, federal estate tax will be generated.

For example, if each spouse has an estate of $1,200,000 and the first spouse to die has a bypass trust, the results shown in Figure 25-21 occur.

What is the result if the first spouse to die uses two-trust planning in such a way as to maximize tax benefits? Figure 25-22 will show you.

Under the two-trust plan, a total federal estate tax of $167,000 was generated. Under the bypass family trust, $164,000 of federal estate tax was generated. The two-trust plan *increased* the total federal estate tax by $3,000 ($167,000 minus $164,000).

Remember, though, that the two-trust plan actually defers the federal estate tax until the second death. As we discussed earlier, this deferral may be significant. Also, be aware that under our two-trust example, the minimum-to-spouse motive was used. If it is not used, the second spouse to die has a higher estate for federal estate tax purposes, and taxes increase significantly. You can see that as estates increase in size and assets are owned in each spouse's name, the estate planning possibilities and variables increase significantly.

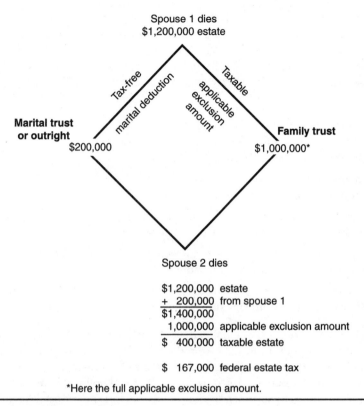

Spouse 1 dies
$1,200,000 estate

Tax-free
marital deduction

Taxable
applicable
exclusion
amount

**Marital trust
or outright**
$200,000

Family trust
$1,000,000*

Spouse 2 dies

$1,200,000	estate
+ 200,000	from spouse 1
$1,400,000	
1,000,000	applicable exclusion amount
$ 400,000	taxable estate
$ 167,000	federal estate tax

*Here the full applicable exclusion amount.

Figure 25-22. Two-trust approach.

Planning for a Spouse Who Is Not a U.S. Citizen

If your spouse is not a U.S. citizen, some significant marital deduction planning advantages are lost. First and foremost is the unlimited marital deduction for gifts. Gifts between spouses who are U.S. citizens qualify for the unlimited marital deduction. For these spouses, there is no limit on the amount of tax-free gifts. Gifts from a spouse to a noncitizen spouse are tax-free up to $100,000 annually. If gifts exceed this amount in any one year, the excess is a taxable gift. The $100,000 amount does change with inflation, so check with your estate planning professional for the current allowable amount.

Sometimes, unintended gifts are made that cause gift taxation. For example, if one spouse purchases a home using his or her own funds and titles the property in joint tenancy with rights of survivorship, a gift of one-half of the value of the property has been made. If the amount paid is in excess of $200,000, then a gift has been made. It is very important to consult a competent estate planning advisor if either your spouse or you are not a citizen and you want to make interspousal gifts.

There are a number of restrictions on the marital deduction when a spouse dies and leaves property to a noncitizen spouse. To qualify for the unlimited marital deduction, the following rules must be followed:

Property must be left in a marital deduction trust requiring income to be paid to the spouse for life, and paid at least annually; this trust is called a Qualified Domestic Trust (QDOT).

Principal distributions are subject to estate taxes when made to the spouse, unless made for hardship reasons.

At least one trustee of the marital deduction trust must be a U.S. citizen or a domestic corporation with trust powers.

No principal distributions are allowed unless the U.S. trustee has the right to withhold any tax imposed on distribution.

The trust must have a security arrangement to insure payment of death taxes when the beneficiary spouse dies.

It is difficult to get principal out of the marital trust without taxation. The only way to get it out tax-free, other than for the spouse to become a U.S. citizen, is for hardship reasons. Hardship is defined as an immediate and substantial financial need relating to the spouse's health, maintenance, education, or support, or that of any person the spouse is legally obligated to support. Any other distributions are taxable at the highest marginal rate applicable to the estate of the spouse who created the marital trust.

If you do not set up a trust that qualifies as a QDOT, there are methods to have the trust reformed to qualify. It is better by far to have your attorney create a QDOT trust to avoid costly and stressful action after the death of a spouse. In addition, if the surviving spouse becomes a U.S. citizen after the death of his or her spouse and prior to the date the federal estate tax return is due (nine months after date of death), a QDOT is not necessary.

We must reiterate the importance of seeking proper planning if your spouse or you are not a U.S. citizen. The penalties for not planning can be costly, so seeking out experts is a real necessity.

In this chapter, we have highlighted some basic planning techniques that you should be familiar with when planning for your family. This discussion of techniques is not exhaustive, however. The number of planning alternatives that are available to you and your professional advisers is staggering. It is critical that you seek out professional estate planners to assist you in planning your estate.

26

Life Insurance

"Estate Planning Fuel"

Finding a discussion of life insurance in a book on estate planning should not surprise anyone. Life insurance and estate planning go hand in hand. Life insurance very often represents a major building block in the estate planning process. We devote three chapters to the relationship between life insurance and the planning process. Here and in Chapter 27, we discuss the basics of the role life insurance plays in the estate planning process. In Chapter 28 we discuss the all-important irrevocable life insurance trust.

A majority of our clients have expressed a desire to know more about life insurance and how its proper purchase facilitates the accomplishment of their estate planning objectives. Many of our clients have been and continue to be confused as to the amount of life insurance they should purchase. They also do not know what type should be purchased. They do not understand its pricing and have a very difficult time comparing product costs between companies and even between products offered by the same company. They do understand that life insurance costs money and does not represent a current benefit to them or their families. They are often reluctant to make a purchasing decision and are concerned that they may be overinsured. They then turn to the noninsurance estate planning professionals for guidance and information.

Within the estate planning process, life insurance should be purchased for one of two reasons: to create an estate that does not exist or to protect an existing estate from losses that will be sustained through death taxes and the probate and administration process.

Life insurance purchased to create an estate should be looked upon as casualty insurance—insurance purchased to replace economic loss resulting from the death of the family wage earner. The problem resulting from a wage earner's death is lost income over a period of years. The solution that life insurance provides is to create a fund of cash dollars that can be used to sustain family members who do not have an alternative source of income for a projected period of time.

Life insurance is also used to replace the monetary value of the non-wage-earner's contribution to a marriage. There are substantial costs involved in replacing the parent who cares for the children and the home. Loss of a marriage partner or significant other can cause a significant hardship if there are not sufficient discretionary funds available to hire someone to replace his or her functions.

The amount of life insurance purchased should be tailored to the family's lifestyle as it existed before the death of the wage earner and his or her spouse. The amount of insurance that is purchased should be tempered with the income the proceeds will generate after death to living beneficiaries. The income that will be generated from prudent investment of life insurance proceeds should be calculated by using a conservative interest factor. Unreasonably high estimates of income resulting from the investment of insurance proceeds generally result in inadequate insurance portfolios.

In our experience, most clients who need casualty or estate-creation (income-replacement) life insurance are significantly underinsured. They do not realize the value of their income contribution to their dependents. They do not consider the present dollar value of their income over the period of years required to care for those dependents. They do not consider inflation and they place too much emphasis on a Social Security system they do not understand. Many of our clients who do understand Social Security benefits believe them to be too little for too much cost. They are concerned that our Social Security system will not survive, and if it somehow does survive, they are pessimistic about the amounts that will be derived by their family members. Many of our clients believe that the Social Security system is bankrupt and that prudent planning dictates that it be ignored.

Life insurance is not affordable in the minds of many people. These people are trying to build their estates and, at the same time, are trying to maintain a reasonable standard of living—a standard, we might add, that appears difficult to sustain, much less improve upon. Most clients we have talked to prefer to maintain their lifestyles at the expense of realistic insurance portfolios. They are betting that they will survive, at least for the foreseeable future. They reason, "I'll buy it when I can afford it" or, "I'll go without it and use my surplus funds to create an estate that will care for my family after my death."

Good estate planning dictates that all reasonably foreseeable needs must be planned for on a current basis. Clients who bet that they will survive are betting against themselves, in our opinion. Fortunately, most of our clients who find themselves in the situation we have been discussing do have life insurance, but it is often the wrong kind. These clients usually have two or three small policies that augment an employer-sponsored group policy. In our experience, most clients have insurance programs that represent, in sum total, less than five years' gross income.

We strongly believe that maximizing life insurance coverage should be the goal of clients who need estate-creation life insurance. This belief dictates that the clients buy as much coverage as possible within their premium budgets.

Life insurance that is purchased to protect an estate from losses sustained as a result of death taxes or probate requires a planning process unique to the economics of that specific situation. In this area, insurance should not be purchased before first calculating what the death costs are likely to be. The calculation of projected costs is essential to the estate planning process. Many people who do not have an estate plan purchase life insurance to cover costs that could be avoided at a fraction of the life insurance premium being expended.

Every person whose motivation in purchasing life insurance is to protect the estate should first plan that estate to reduce or avoid every cost possible. After projected costs have been reduced to the lowest dollar possible, life insurance should be purchased to cover the remaining costs. The estate planning process creates the car, gas tank, and gasoline gauge. Life insurance is the gasoline, in the right amount and in the right octane, that should meet the designer's specifications.

Often clients who have an estate of the size that will generate tax and other death expenses believe, incorrectly, that they have no need for life insurance. They envision that their property will be sold to pay the estate bills and that the balance of the property will be sufficient in value to accomplish their planning objectives. Too often clients believe that their estate assets can be sold at their fair market value to pay death costs when due. In our experience, this assumption is not practical and seldom proves true.

We have previously discussed the fact that federal estate taxes are due and payable nine months from the date of death, in cash. Nine months does not represent a great deal of time, particularly when the survivors have other matters on their minds. Death's aftermath is always frenetic, even with the best of estate plans. Buyers are usually aware of the time constraints placed on estate sellers. The more aware the buyer, the more likely the price offered will be reduced. Panic sales are seldom fair market value sales. They are usually distress sales.

Prudent estate owners should always plan to pay their estates' debts with cash. Estate property should be sold at the highest price, and that price should be negotiated without timing constraints. Life insurance should be considered a planning alternative to create instant estate cash. This entire discussion, and the problems it describes, is referred to by estate planners as the liquidity problem. The more nonliquid the estate, the greater the potential need for life insurance.

A panoply of insurance products are available in the marketplace, and more are coming on-stream every day. There are term policies and permanent policies and policies that cover everything in between as well. Like all other estate planning techniques, life insurance involves specialized knowledge. Most advisers are not experts in life insurance. Many life insurance salespeople are estate planning professionals; they are experts on the products within their industry. These insurance professionals are knowledgeable and can compare products in terms of cost, deductibility of those costs, benefits provided, and a host of other related issues that are critical to the total estate planning process.

Our advice is, "If you do not know jewels, know your jeweler." You should take the time to interview and select an insurance professional who is knowledgeable. You should select an insurance professional you like and one who will work comfortably with your other estate planning advisers. Once such an individual is found, you can test your preliminary feelings regarding the expertise of that individual through your other advisers. Attorneys, accountants, and financial advisers may not be insurance experts, but they recognize experts when they work with them. Your other estate planning advisers should share with you their opinions of your insurance adviser. This professional feedback should be both helpful and reassuring to you.

These insurance-related concepts are critical to the estate planning process:

Insurance is a third-party beneficiary contract. Leaving proceeds to third parties, whether directly or in trust, removes proceeds from the probate process.

Life insurance owned by the insured is subject to federal estate taxation on the owner-insured's death.

The owner of a policy does not have to be the insured. In fact, the owner should not be the insured if insurance proceeds are designed to avoid death taxes. We devote Chapter 28, The Irrevocable Life Insurance Trust, to this concept.

Most state death taxes do tax life insurance after certain dollar deductibles have been met. Some states do not tax life insurance proceeds at all.

Precisely written beneficiary designations are of critical importance.

Contingent beneficiary designations should always be made.

The estate of the insured should never be named as beneficiary; to do so is to subject the life insurance proceeds to the probate process.

Minors should never be named as primary or contingent beneficiaries, because they cannot receive the proceeds without court supervision until they are adults.

Insurance proceeds intended to benefit minors should be left to a trust created for their benefit.

Life insurance proceeds left to beneficiaries other than the estate of the insured owner are generally not subject to the claims of creditors. This is true with regard to creditors of the deceased, of the estate itself, and of the beneficiaries.

A life insurance program should always be coordinated with and become an integral part of the total estate plan.

Life insurance recommendations should always be discussed with and reviewed by other members of the estate planning team. The other advisers and the insurance professional should be encouraged to work closely with one another.

Life insurance can create an estate for loved ones. It can also protect an estate that has already been created. Policy proceeds can provide liquidity and the certainty of knowing that cash will be available to pay estate debts. Life insurance can be purchased in a host of ways to accomplish a host of objectives. It should always be considered in the estate planning process.

These analogies illustrate our feelings about the use of life insurance in the estate planning process:

The attorney's job, with the help of the accountant and the client's other financial advisers, is (1) to design an estate plan to enable the client to pass property to whom he or she wants in the way and at the time he or she wants, and (2) to avoid, in addition, every tax dollar, attorney's fee, and court cost possible.

The client, with the help of advisers, designs an automobile he or she wishes to drive. Color, size, and extras should be selected after discussion and thought.

The attorney cannot, and we stress *cannot,* provide the client with the fuel to power that car. The fuel is the client's responsibility.

The insurance professional sells fuel. It is the responsibility of the insurance professional to sell the fuel that will fill the vehicle's tank with the right fuel mixture at a price that is fair in the marketplace.

Attorneys have been accused (mainly by life insurance professionals) of saying: "You don't need life insurance; drop it. Insurance is too expensive, a waste of good money. I've written your will; your wishes have been executed; your planning is now complete."

Life insurance salespeople have been accused (mainly by attorneys) of saying: "Buy my product; I need the commission. Buy insurance, and you will discharge your planning responsibilities to your loved ones. Purchase insurance, and you won't have to worry about those death costs."

Both sets of statements, and others like them, are dead wrong. What good is a vehicle without fuel? What good can come from purchasing fuel without owning a vehicle that can be powered by it? What real good can come from either if it were not designed for the other?

We are now in a new era of the selling of financial products and services, including life insurance. This new era offers an opportunity to reconcile the old tension between the life insurance professional and the other estate planning advisors. While we have always advocated the team approach to planning, it has not always been effective. There has not been a real desire on the part of the team to do more than develop the initial plan. When that is completed, the team, more often than not, loses its cohesive nature. It is not uncommon for each professional to go on and do his or her own thing, usually without consulting the other team members. In just a few years, the carefully designed plan is no longer coordinated.

Thanks to changes in how planning is viewed, attorneys and accountants in many states can engage in the sale of life insurance products. We applaud this change, because it is better for clients. It allows a true collaboration among professionals, all of whom have a vested interest in the continuing performance of an estate plan.

There has been concern, primarily among American Bar Association members and the members of various state bar associations, that allowing attorneys to collect a commission on sales of life insurance will in some way create a conflict of interest or adversely affect an attorney's objectivity. While this may be an area of some concern, we think it is not as problematic as some would think.

According to some legal commentators, attorneys are likely to be held liable for the incompetence or malpractice of a life insurance agent who is recommended by the attorney or who sells life insurance to a client with the knowledge of the attorney. The attorney is not paid to take on this liability, and it is unlikely that the attorney's malpractice insurance will cover any damages incurred by the client. This situation puts the attorney at risk, making him or her less likely to become involved in a review of insurance or offer any advice on it.

If the attorney is compensated for his or her time, attention, and due diligence, the attorney will be much more willing to devote all the time and attention necessary to insure that a good job is done. But what about the potential conflict of interest when the attorney recommends the amount of life insurance, knowing that he or she will be paid more if the policy is larger? That is a risk. However, an attorney, or any other advisor who sells life insurance, should be able to demonstrate on an objective basis how much life insurance a person needs.

For some time there have been a number of objective methods to determine how much life insurance an individual or family needs. Protocols have been developed that forthrightly and correctly detail the information needed not only to determine the amount of the life insurance needed, but the type of life insurance that is most appropriate. There are also many very good ways to determine the financial security of the life insurance companies being considered, as well as the products.

In this new era of financial services, several organizations have dedicated themselves to the highest quality of planning on a collaborative basis. One such organization is called Quantum Alliance[3]. It is comprised of membership organizations for independent attorneys, accountants, and other financial advisors. Quantum Alliance[3] offers extensive training for members. It has developed the necessary protocols for all professionals as well as an environment of true collaborative professionalism. We are involved in the organization, and we believe strongly in its precepts.

Life insurance is a sensitive, serious, and complex subject. Clients and advisors need all the education and help they can get to make sure that a person's estate plan, including his or her life insurance portfolio, is appropriate for the client and his or her loved ones. Please make sure that you work with professionals who have the training and skills to coordinate your estate and life insurance planning.

27

Life Insurance: Who Should Own It?

"Good Engineering Requires the Right Fuel"

We have already discussed our belief that life insurance is generally purchased to satisfy one of two estate planning objectives: to create an estate or to protect an estate that has already been created. This chapter presents some ideas about how life insurance should be purchased to protect an estate that has already been built.

Most planning for U.S. citizen surviving spouses and other family members results in no tax liability on the death of the first spouse. This is true regardless of the size of the estate. The tax bite may be deferred to the second spouse's death.

Many existing life insurance policies insure the life of the wage-earner spouse; in our experience, this spouse is usually the husband. Sometimes life insurance is purchased to make sure that there is enough income if the wage-earner spouse dies. It is purchased long before there is an estate planning problem and ends up being used to pay for federal estate tax. In some cases, the insurance is actually purchased to pay federal estate taxes, with no thought given to the tax effects or cost of the insurance.

Actuarially, if the husband and wife are the same calendar age, the husband is older for insurance purposes and is therefore more expensive to insure. (Males die younger than females; that is a statistical fact.) If the husband does die first, the purpose for which the insurance was purchased may not materialize. There should be no federal estate tax on his death.

The bottom line with regard to life insurance for most estate tax planning is this: Do not insure a spouse for purposes of the first death; insure the second death, which is when the taxes will be incurred.

Insuring a second death presents another problem. How are you and your advisers supposed to know with certainty in what sequence death will occur? Obviously, there can be no precise answer to this question. What can be determined, however, is whether you or your spouse is less expensive to insure. The insurance company will tell you.

If your spouse is less expensive to insure than you are, why not insure your spouse's life rather than yours? If you, as the older spouse, fulfill the actuarial role and die first, there will be no federal estate tax and no need for life insurance proceeds to pay federal estate tax. On your spouse's subsequent death, there will be taxes, and there will be insurance proceeds.

If your spouse dies first, there will be no taxes but there will be insurance proceeds. Those proceeds could be invested in liquid assets, and on your death, funds would be available to pay taxes. In either case, regardless of the sequence of death, insuring the younger spouse (for insurance purposes) can save significant premium dollars.

By insuring the younger of the two spouses, premium dollars can be saved and, regardless of whose life is insured, the proceeds can be available to pay the taxes resulting from the death of the surviving spouse. This is important when significant insurance programs are in place or envisioned.

Many insurance companies provide a unique product called a joint and survivor policy or second-to-die policy. This type of policy insures two lives and pays out death proceeds only on the death of the second of the two insureds to die. As a method for insuring only the payment of death taxes, joint and survivor policies have merit. However, if life insurance proceeds are needed for any other purpose, insuring the younger spouse may be the better alternative.

The decision as to whether to insure the younger of the two spouses or to purchase a joint and survivor policy can generally be reduced to an economic decision based on the relative premium costs of each product. In our experience, different companies have different premium structures for each of their insurance products. This will necessitate a comparison between the two alternatives and their costs among companies.

The decision between these two products may not entirely hinge on economics. There may be many couples who will elect to insure the younger spouse rather than purchase the joint and survivor policy just in case the younger spouse does the unexpected and dies first. If the younger spouses do die first, the other spouses will have the insurance proceeds to use and invest.

Please remember that this discussion applies only to life insurance purchased solely to protect an estate already created.

Regardless of whether the younger spouse is insured or the joint and survivor policy route is taken, please read Chapter 28. In it, we discuss how life insurance proceeds can be protected from federal estate tax regardless of the insurance alternative selected.

One question that will certainly surface as a result of our discussion in this area is, "Can I afford to cash in existing policies that I've been paying on for years?" We do not recommend that existing policies be canceled until two steps are accomplished under the direction of your insurance professional:

1. Make a complete analysis of the relative costs between existing policies and new policies under the format we have discussed.

2. If the new method is truly less expensive, on an apples-to-apples basis, old policies should still not be canceled until the new policies are in force. Too many clients have made this mistake, only to find out that they were then uninsurable or very highly rated due to health problems.

We know that the insurance industry has gone through a rate revolution in the past few years, and from what we see, the revolution is continuing. As a result of low interest rates and a host of other economic factors, insurance rates have plummeted. We have been absolutely astounded at the rates many of the insurance professionals we have worked with have been quoting to our clients. The number of new policy formats recently introduced into the marketplace has equally astounded us.

The old rule that one should never cancel a policy that has been in existence for a period of years no longer seems to be a good rule of thumb. Seek out an insurance professional and redetermine whether your insurance portfolio is properly structured.

28

The Irrevocable Life Insurance Trust

"Having Your Cake and Eating It Too"

As we have said, life insurance proceeds provide the fuel that powers many an estate planning car, but most of the time the fuel mixture is taxed at the pump before it finds its way into the estate planning vehicle.

A disadvantage generally associated with the purchase of life insurance is that the life insurance proceeds usually increase the taxable estate of the policy owner. Upon the death of the insured owner, the life insurance proceeds are included in the insured owner's estate for federal estate tax purposes. Most people buy life insurance with the belief that insurance proceeds can be used by their beneficiaries free of federal estate tax. If the insured owns a life insurance policy on his or her own life, all the life insurance proceeds are included in his or her estate for federal estate tax purposes.

In order to avoid federal estate tax, many people have the life insurance on their lives owned by their spouses or others; then upon the death of the insured, the policy proceeds are paid to the owner's beneficiary free of federal estate tax.

There are problems with the cross-ownership technique:

The insured loses control of the life insurance policies.

Proceeds are usually taxed on the death of the policy owner if he or she is the beneficiary and dies after the insured.

Few people can plan for the contingency that the owner-beneficiary may die first.

If the proceeds are payable to other than the insured or the owner, there is a gift of the entire insurance proceeds to the beneficiary from the policy owner.

We discuss these problems at length in Chapter 29, Some Estate Planning Solutions.

The goal sought by insurance policy cross-ownership—to avoid federal estate tax on life insurance proceeds—is a noble one. But there is a better way to accomplish this goal. You can use an irrevocable life insurance trust (ILIT) to own life insurance policies that insure your life. By using an ILIT, the insurance proceeds will be free of federal estate tax on your death. In addition, if you plan for your spouse, the ILIT will keep the proceeds out of your spouse's estate as well.

The ILIT has been used as an estate planning technique since the federal estate tax laws were permanently implemented. These trusts were designed to keep life insurance proceeds free of federal estate tax. Because the government was losing tax revenue, the Internal Revenue Service attacked their use on many grounds, and as a result, the ILIT fell into disuse. Since World War II, however, their use has come back into vogue. Today they are frequently used and, quite frankly, are enjoying a heyday. It is important that you understand how an ILIT works. Once you understand how these trusts work, you will appreciate why they are so popular.

Generally, if a life insurance policy is given away, the value of the life insurance proceeds will not be included in the estate of the person who gave the policy away. Whoever gives a life insurance policy away must be careful not to retain incidents of ownership in the policy. This means that the person who gives the policy away must not retain control over the use of the life insurance policy in any way.

The ILIT is used to own an insurance policy, whether it is purchased by the ILIT or given to it. The ILIT, as its name implies, must be irrevocable. Once the trust is drafted and signed, it can never be changed, except by the courts and then only under very special circumstances. If an ILIT is not totally irrevocable or if the maker retains direct control over it, the insurance proceeds will not be free of federal estate tax.

Using an ILIT, three estate planning objectives can be achieved:

Insurance proceeds can be kept free of federal estate tax upon the deaths of both spouses.

Because of the terms provided in the trust document, the trust maker can control the insurance proceeds received by the ILIT to care for the maker's beneficiaries.

The life insurance proceeds received by an ILIT can be used to pay the death expenses, including taxes, of both the maker and the maker's spouse.

The beneficiaries of an ILIT are generally exactly the same as the beneficiaries of the maker's revocable living trust. In fact, the terms of the ILIT are almost identical to those of the maker's revocable living trust (main trust) and, believe it or not, the trustees under both the ILIT and the maker's revocable living trust are usually the same after the maker's death.

As we have discussed, assets receive a step-up in basis at death. To get cash (insurance proceeds) from the ILIT to the maker's main trust, a sale generally takes place. The ILIT buys nonliquid assets from the main trust, using cash provided by the life insurance proceeds. Because of step-up in basis rules, this sale can be accomplished income tax-free. Another technique often used to transfer the ILIT's cash to the main trust is a loan. Regardless of which approach is used, the net result is the same: The main trust has cash and can pay expenses. The ILIT has the nonliquid property either as collateral for the loan or as the owner after the sale. There are no distress sales or unreasonable borrowing requirements, and because the beneficiaries of the main trust are identical to those of the ILIT, there is no loss of asset value or control.

Too good to be true? Not if the ILIT is properly drafted and implemented by an estate planning professional. Irrevocable trust drafting is no place for rookies. One small mistake made in an ILIT, and all the tax benefits can be lost; remember, irrevocable is irrevocable. Good advice on the front end is essential so that flexibility can be incorporated into the ILIT, making irrevocability less ominous.

Your spouse can be the trustee of your ILIT as long as your ILIT is properly drafted. An ILIT that gives your spouse too much control over the terms of the ILIT may result in adverse tax consequences. Some professionals prefer to use an institutional trustee or another family member to alleviate potential adverse tax consequences.

An ILIT must be irrevocable, but its assets do not have to be. You can name a person other than the trustee, such as an adult child or other family member, as the holder of a special power to remove the life insurance policies owned by the ILIT, as well as any other assets owned by it, and distribute them to the beneficiaries of the trust. This power can be exercised at the holder's discretion, allowing for flexibility in your planning. If your planning objectives change, the assets can be removed from your ILIT. The ILIT will continue because it is irrevocable, but it might not have anything in it. In reality, a properly drafted ILIT might not be irrevocable at all.

How insurance policies find their way into an ILIT and how the premiums are paid on those policies are two issues of critical planning importance.

When an existing life insurance policy is transferred into an ILIT, a gift is made. Whether the gift is subject to federal gift tax is another matter. The value of the existing policy determines if it is subject to federal gift tax.

The value of the life insurance policy is sometimes hard to determine, and valuing a policy should be done with caution. The value of the life insurance policy is the replacement value of that policy. If you do not know the value of an existing life insurance policy, your insurance professionals can easily tell you.

You can transfer your existing policies into your ILIT, or you can have your ILIT purchase life insurance policies on your life. The latter is easier because you may not have to be concerned with policy values for federal gift tax purposes or about the three-year gift in contemplation of death rule, discussed later in this chapter.

Through gifts of cash from you or others, the ILIT receives funds so that it can pay premiums on life insurance policies it owns on your life, or it can pay those premiums from the income generated by other property you have already transferred into your ILIT. The federal gift tax consequences of these transfers must be examined.

The annual exclusion for gifts is $10,000 per recipient each year, although this amount is now subject to inflation adjustment, allowing it to rise if inflation increases. The annual exclusion can be used only when there is a gift of a present interest in property. A present interest is a gift of which the recipient can have the current use and benefit. A gift of a life insurance policy or the money to pay its premium is generally not a gift of a present interest when given to a trust. If there is no annual exclusion available for life insurance, the use of an ILIT may not be attractive, but this apparent problem has been solved. A man named Mr. Crummey established a special irrevocable trust for the benefit of his beneficiaries. Under his trust, his beneficiaries were to receive property from the trust sometime in the future. Mr. Crummey claimed the annual exclusion for the gifts he made to this trust, and the IRS took him to court. Mr. Crummey beat the IRS. Mr. Crummey won because his irrevocable trust had an added feature. This feature is called a demand right.

A demand right is the ability of a beneficiary, for a limited period of time, to ask for and receive from a trust the value of the current gifts made to the trust.

For example, on November 1, Dee Fox gives $5,000 to her ILIT. The trustee, pursuant to the terms of Dee's trust, notifies the beneficiaries that they have until December 1 to demand their share of the $5,000. If they choose not to make this demand, the demand right ends. This demand right can be given even if the beneficiary is a minor, because the minor's guardian may exercise the demand right for that minor.

Because of the demand right, a present interest is created in the property given to the ILIT, and the annual exclusion is available. Because of Mr. Crummey, your gifts to your ILIT can qualify for the federal gift tax annual exclusion.

There may be a practical problem with giving others a demand right. The beneficiaries may demand their share of the premium money; however, in our experience, this has not been a problem. The demand right is refused by the beneficiaries and the money is used to pay life insurance premiums. After all, the beneficiaries are your family members, and even though they are free to exercise their rights, they will likely understand that by not exercising them they are helping the family's overall tax situation.

Despite Mr. Crummey's groundbreaking efforts, when you give money or property to your ILIT, you can use only $5,000 of your annual exclusion for each beneficiary of your ILIT. Why? Because of a technical quirk in our federal estate and gift tax laws, use of more than $5,000 of the annual exclusion per beneficiary in an ILIT does create gift tax problems. There are ways to circumvent the $5,000 limitation. An understanding of these methods, however, is beyond the scope of this book. If you want to exceed the $5,000 limitation, consult your planning professionals.

If the terms of an ILIT require that the gift of the premium be used only to purchase life insurance on the maker's life, then any income or available deductions of the ILIT are included in the maker's income tax return. This rule is just one example of the income tax rules associated with the ILIT.

There are some income tax ramifications of trusts, many of which affect the ILIT. For example, if you name your spouse as a trustee or beneficiary of your ILIT, the income of the trust will be taxed to you. Usually, this does not present a problem, because an ILIT is generally not designed to create taxable income. However, this provision, as well as others, may have an effect on your planning. The income tax issues of an ILIT provide a good reason to check with an experienced professional before establishing an ILIT.

Having a friendly trustee is important. A second reading of Chapter 19, Trustees, is probably a good idea. Trustees and their successors must be provided for in the original ILIT trust document and cannot be changed.

There is one last pitfall in giving life insurance policies to an ILIT. If a life insurance policy is given to your ILIT within three years of the date of your death, the life insurance proceeds are brought back into your estate for federal estate tax purposes. This could also be true for insurance policies purchased directly by your ILIT. It is best for the trustee to apply for the life insurance policy as the owner, to reduce the risk that the insurance policies will be included in your estate if you die within three years after the date the insurance policy becomes effective.

Almost any type of insurance can be used in an ILIT. Term, whole life, universal life, variable life, group, or corporate insurance, properly structured, can all be used.

Creating an ILIT that will meet your objectives and will really work requires the hands of both an expert estate planning attorney and an expert insurance professional. To use less than the best is to invite disaster. If you use competent advisers, your ILIT will allow you to have your tax cake and eat it too.

An Irrevocable Life Insurance Trust:

Keeps life insurance proceeds free from federal estate tax upon the deaths of both spouses.

Allows the maker to control life insurance proceeds.

Allows the life insurance proceeds to pay the death expenses and taxes of both the maker and the maker's spouse.

29

Some Estate Planning Solutions

"Techniques and Gimmicks That Do Not Always Work"

There are many estate planning techniques that do not always work. There are also some estate planning gimmicks that never work. In this chapter, we discuss both the techniques and the gimmicks that are too frequently tried as solutions in the estate planning process. They are:

Techniques

Cross-ownership of life insurance

Joint tenancy

Uniform Transfers to Minors Act custodial accounts

General powers of attorney

Gimmicks

Hiding property in a safe-deposit box

Forms

Do-it-yourself estate planning

Constitutional trusts

Cross-Ownership
of Life Insurance

The proceeds of life insurance are subject to federal estate tax in the estate of the owner of the policy. They are not necessarily subject to federal estate tax in the estate of the insured. As a result, many insurance salespeople suggest that spouses purchase and own insurance policies on each other. For example, the husband is the owner of the insurance policy insuring the wife and vice versa. By doing this, each spouse is the beneficiary of the death proceeds from the policy he or she owns on the other spouse's life. On the death of a spouse, the insurance proceeds are paid to the other spouse free from federal estate tax.

Let us take a closer look at this technique. Under current law, the proceeds going to a U.S. citizen spouse would be tax-free anyway because of the unlimited marital deduction. On the second death, the entire amount of the remaining insurance proceeds will be included in the estate of that spouse and will be subject to federal estate tax.

The tax consequences of cross-ownership are even worse if the insurance proceeds are payable to someone other than the spouse who owns the policy. If this occurs, there is a gift under federal law of the entire insurance proceeds to the beneficiary from the spouse who owns the policy.

Cross-ownership is not a good technique for avoiding federal estate tax. In reality it does not accomplish a thing for spouses. There are better techniques available to avoid death taxation on insurance proceeds, techniques that can keep the proceeds free of federal estate tax on both deaths.

Cross-ownership also results in loss of control over the policy and the proceeds. The owner of the policy, not the insured, controls the policy. What if a divorce occurs? The insured may be left without insurance. On the death of the insured, the owner-beneficiary will receive the proceeds without any requirement as to how, why, or for whom the proceeds should be used.

Cross-ownership between nonspouses is equally dangerous. Here, though, the benefit is potentially greater: There will be no federal estate tax on the death of the insured where there might otherwise be if the insured were the owner. But remember, the insured loses all control in the policy and its proceeds.

The better technique to avoid federal estate tax is establishing an irrevocable life insurance trust, which can keep control of the policy and its proceeds in the insured. This technique was discussed in Chapter 28.

Joint Tenancy with Right of Survivorship

Because of its importance and frequent use as an estate planning technique, we have discussed joint ownership in several other chapters. A summary of its weaknesses is apropos here, however.

Putting property in joint ownership with a nonspouse creates a gift for federal and some state tax purposes. This is true when one party paid for the property or already owned it.

Joint ownership results in loss of control of the joint property because the other owner can require that it be split up or sold. On death, there is no control; it is a mini estate plan. The entire property could be subject to the other owner's creditors. The property cannot be planned. There is a loss of step-up in basis that is particularly detrimental in spousal planning.

Joint tenancy is an estate planning technique that should be avoided, because other techniques can accomplish estate planning goals far better.

Uniform Transfers to Minors Act Custodial Accounts

Uniform transfers to minors custodial accounts can be created in all states. These custodial accounts come in two forms. Which kind you can use depends on the state's law that is in effect where the account is set up.

The original form of special custodial accounts for minors was the Uniform Gifts to Minors Act. This legislation was essentially passed to allow an adult to give stock to minors; some states' acts also apply them to savings accounts and annuity contracts. The gifts to minors law allows an account to be created for the benefit of a minor child in the name of an adult and, in some states, in the name of a bank or trust company. The adult or institution in whose name the account is created is called a custodian.

Gifts to minors laws allow certain property to be given to minor children without necessitating the creation of a trust. When a child reaches the age of twenty-one, the account is closed and the property transferred to the child.

Most states have adopted a newer version of the Uniform Gifts to Minors Act, called the Uniform Transfers to Minors Act. The newer version is aimed at eliminating some of the shortcomings of the Uniform Gifts to Minors Act. Essentially, the new law allows all types of property to be held in the custodial account, rather than only the limited types allowed under the older act; and the new version broadens how custodial accounts can be established and used. For property that cannot be held in an account, such as real estate or personal property, the new law allows title to the property to be placed in the name of a custodian on behalf of a minor. In most other respects, both versions of the law are the same, with almost the same problems and pitfalls.

The problems resulting from these accounts and other custodial transfers can be weighty:

If the dividends or other income generated by the stocks are used to support the child and the person who created the account is legally obligated to support the child, the income will be taxed to the person who created the account.

If the person making the gift is the custodian of the account, the entire value of the account will be taxed in that person's estate on death.

The custodian cannot invest in property other than stock in some states, but may put the income in a savings account for the child's benefit. There is little investment flexibility in these accounts.

The custodian is liable to the child for the negligent handling of these accounts and must, on the child's request, make a complete accounting with respect to the transactions in the account.

The child must receive the account property, including the income earned from the account, on the child's twenty-first birthday. What the child does with the account proceeds then is the child's business.

The creation of these accounts is a gift under both federal and state gift tax laws. If the value of the gift to a minor exceeds the annual exclusion amount ($10,000 plus any adjustments for inflation) in any given year, gift tax may have to be paid.

We believe that, more often than not, this technique does not accomplish the objectives of the account creator. Too often these accounts are abused, cannot be controlled sufficiently by their makers, and result in adverse tax consequences.

A better way to accomplish your objectives in this area is to establish a minor's trust. Estate-planning professionals call this a 2503(c) trust. The use of this trust provides much greater flexibility as to the investment of your funds, because the trust investments are not limited to stock and the trust property is not included in your estate on death. Gifts to a minor's trust, like gifts under the Uniform Transfers to Minors Act, qualify for the annual exclusion under federal gift tax law. In addition, the 2503(c) trust allows the maker more control over the property in the trust and over the income it earns. Always be wary of making gifts under the Uniform Transfers to Minors Act and, when appropriate, use the 2503(c) trust as a potentially better alternative.

General Powers of Attorney

Many older people concerned about their ability to conduct their affairs grant a general power of attorney to loved ones. By giving their loved ones a general power of attorney, these mature adults hope to avoid the confusion that could occur should they become ill or mentally incompetent. They want their children or other loved ones to be in charge of their affairs, not attorneys or courts of law. Their objectives are sincere and patently reasonable.

However, a general power of attorney generally does not accomplish the objectives of its maker. Under the laws of most states, a general power of attorney is invalid upon the death or adjudicated incapacity of its maker. Thus, when the event the maker feared occurs, the solution that was envisioned will not work.

The granting of a general power of attorney is exceedingly dangerous. The person who has a general power of attorney can control all the property of the maker. This means the holder can spend or dispose of the property for the holder's own benefit.

The concerns that motivate individuals to use these general powers of attorney are real, however, and should be addressed. If you are concerned about your affairs, create a revocable living trust, spelling out how you wish to be taken care of in case of your incapacity. Name a trustee you can trust, whether child, friend, or adviser. If these alternatives are not available or acceptable to you, name an institutional trustee.

By using a revocable living trust, you can reduce the likelihood that others will appropriate your property for unauthorized purposes. This alternative is discussed at length in Chapter 17, The Revocable Living Trust.

General powers of attorney should not be confused with limited or durable special powers of attorney. A discussion of these powers can be found in Chapter 18, Funding a Revocable Living Trust.

Hiding Property
in a Safe-Deposit Box

We have found that many of our clients believe that if assets are placed in safe-deposit boxes, family members can go to the bank after their deaths, take the assets out, and nobody will be the wiser.

This kind of thinking could not be further from the truth. Our public officials are not so naive. The first public act, generally through each state's death tax division, is to lock or freeze a safe-deposit box upon the death of the owner. The box stays frozen until the proper public official can inventory every asset in the box.

On being so informed, many clients do not relent but become even more creative: "I'll put my assets in someone else's box so that the state won't know about it." Not a bad idea, except for the fact that a gift has been made without a receipt, total control over the contents has been lost, and a potentially fraudulent transaction has been entered into. Not reporting assets for federal estate tax purposes is like not reporting income; it is a crime. Need we say more?

Forms

In 1965, Norman F. Dacey authored *How to Avoid Probate*. The book was a national best-seller. In it, as we have indicated elsewhere, Mr. Dacey made a vicious attack on attorneys and the probate process. His thesis was that probate should be avoided.

Most of the Dacey book represented his views and suggestions—complete with tear-out forms—on how probate should be avoided and how estate plans should be drafted. Mr. Dacey was not an attorney; his forms were to be filled in and used by the readers of his book to effectuate their estate planning goals. Mr. Dacey did not encourage his readers to seek the advice and counsel of attorneys, accountants, insurance professionals, or other estate planning advisers in using his forms.

We partially agree with Mr. Dacey: Probate should be avoided. We do not believe, however, that his "forms" approach represents a sound estate planning process. We do not believe that the reading of one book (including this one) qualifies anyone to properly plan an estate without the additional help and knowledge of experts in the field. We believe that filling out forms is a gimmick that should be avoided.

Do-It-Yourself Estate Planning

An extension of the Dacey forms is the growing industry of buying estate plans through the mail, through software, through the Internet, or by having advisers other than lawyers prepare estate plans. These are gimmicks that should be avoided at all cost.

Wills, trusts, and all other aspects of estate planning almost invariably involve legal and tax rules. The rules apply in certain ways based on an individual's particular personal and financial situation. For an individual to plan his or her estate without legal counsel is akin to a person performing brain surgery without the aid of a physician.

Mail order, software, or Internet planning and planning provided by those who are not lawyers may sound attractive, but engaging in it is a big mistake. Lawyers are the only professionals who can, by law, draft legal documents and render legal advice. They are trained in the information that is critical to perform certain legal tasks.

Some of the people who sell forms or who provide mail order or Internet planning make the claim that their documents have been drafted and reviewed by lawyers. This is a weak and misleading statement. For a lawyer to draft a form for a particular fact situation without having any specific information about the client's family, financial situation, and particular wants and needs is unethical in every state in the United States. These boilerplate plans that have not been tailored to the needs of a particular client do not result, for the most part, in responsible planning.

The definition of estate planning is giving what you have to whom you want, the way you want, and when you want, and, if possible, saving every fee and tax possible. Mail order or other long-distance planning and estate plans sold by nonlawyers do not even begin to meet that definition.

Attempting to circumvent lawyers in estate planning may cost more money in the short run—many software or mail order trusts are more expensive than those drafted by lawyers. It may cost more in the long run too. When do-it-yourself plans, mail order plans, software plans, or plans drafted by nonlawyers are put to the test because of disability or death, it may well be that undoing one of these plans is much more expensive than doing the right plan. Do yourself and your loved ones a favor: Use a lawyer as well as other professionals and form an estate planning team that will clearly meet your planning needs.

Constitutional Trusts

Many of the techniques we refer to in this chapter have some basis in fact and in law. They are honest attempts at planning.

The constitutional trust does not fall into this category. The constitutional trust, or as it is sometimes referred to, the pure equity trust, is an out-and-out fraud. It is a hoax being promulgated by hucksters masquerading as professionals.

The hucksters claim that by using a constitutional trust, estate tax can be avoided and no gift tax liability will be incurred. They even claim that income tax will be avoided through the use of their technique. Can you believe it? A triple play! They are selling these trusts and the planning kits that go with them at prices ranging from \$4,000 to \$25,000 or more. Generally, they present or sell their packages to professionals, with some emphasis, it seems, on the medical profession.

This scheme does not work, nor does it accomplish any of the benefits claimed. The Internal Revenue Service has watched these trusts for some time and has been coming down very hard on the often innocent participants who were taken in by this hoax. *Time* magazine exposed these devices as hoaxes. These trusts are shams and nothing more than page after page of nonsense.

If you have been taken in by this type of hoax, we strongly suggest you seek competent counsel immediately, or if you prefer, your local district or prosecuting attorney.

Beware of any income, gift, or estate tax scheme that seems too good to be true, because they are. There are many legitimate methods for saving substantial amounts of taxes. If you are willing to pay for the expertise, you will find out how to reduce or eliminate taxes in a safe manner that will hold up to scrutiny. When faced with a proposal from business hucksters that guarantees you will not pay taxes, get a professional opinion.

30

Freezing
Techniques

"Putting Your Estate in Cold Storage"

Congress has reduced the number of estates that will be subject to federal estate taxation. Many estates, however, will continue to qualify for federal estate tax, and it is probable that inflation and real growth will push estates that currently are not taxable into the realm of taxability. This chapter deals with traditional techniques that stop or at least control the growth of your estate by passing that growth to other family members. We explain how these traditional techniques have been radically altered by Congressional attempts to prevent their abuse. The techniques are known as freezing techniques.

By using a freezing technique, you can accomplish the following with respect to your assets:

Transfer future appreciation from your estate to your children and grandchildren while you are alive, with little or no federal gift tax implications.

Keep control of your assets during your life.

Continue to receive income from your assets.

Traditional Freezing Techniques

Prior to 1988, freezing techniques could be used for almost any asset, such as stock of closely held corporations, partnership interests, sole propri-

197

etorships, and real estate. Beginning in 1987, Congress began to enact tough legislation to address what was considered the abusive use of a tax-avoidance measure. Since 1987 Congress has made two major revisions to the tax laws, enacting in quick succession two completely different methods to discourage the use of freezing techniques.

The Revenue Act of 1987 introduced a new section, 2036(c), to the Internal Revenue Code. That section substantially eliminated many of the freezing techniques used prior to 1988 by bringing the value of certain transferred interests back into the federal taxable estate of the person who made the transfer. Section 2036(c) was very complex. It covered a broad spectrum of transactions, not just traditional freezing techniques, and was very difficult to administer.

In the Revenue Reconciliation Act of 1990, Congress completely repealed section 2036(c), but did not abandon trying to limit the use of freezing techniques. The 1990 Act replaced section 2036(c) with an entirely new set of rules. The new rules focus more on the valuation of transfers for gift tax purposes, rather than on interests retained under section 2036(c) that were taxed at the donor's death. The new provisions have a substantial effect on the use of traditional freezing techniques.

In order to understand the freezing techniques that are still available, it is important to understand the traditional freezing techniques. After an explanation of freezing techniques as they were used prior to 1988, we explain the new valuation rules introduced by the Revenue Reconciliation Act of 1990, which continue to be in effect.

One of the most popular freezing techniques was called a recapitalization. A recapitalization restructures stock ownership in a corporation. Exchanging growth stock for nongrowth stock restructures a corporation.

There are two types of corporate stock—common stock and preferred stock. Common stock is the growth stock. As a corporation prospers and grows in value, so does the common stock of the corporation. If the value of the corporation goes down, so does the value of the common stock. Owning common stock is risky.

Preferred stock is nongrowth stock. Its value is fixed when it is issued. As a corporation prospers and grows in value, the preferred stock does not grow in value, and if the value of the corporation goes down, the preferred stock does not necessarily go down. Preferred stockholders get the first right to receive dividends paid by the corporation. If the corporation is sold or liquidated, preferred stockholders have the right to get paid for their stock before common stockholders. When a corporation issues preferred stock, it has a predetermined dividend. For example, 15 percent preferred stock with a face value of $100 means that if a corporation pays a dividend, the preferred stockholders will receive $15 of dividend income for each $100 of preferred stock they own.

Preferred stock can be issued so that the corporation is required to pay the agreed-upon dividend, or it can be issued so that the payment of the dividend is left to the corporation's discretion. If the preferred stock is cumulative preferred stock, the corporation must pay the agreed-upon dividend every year. If the corporation cannot afford to make a dividend payment to cumulative preferred stockholders, then it must make up the missed dividends in future years.

If the preferred stock is noncumulative preferred stock, the corporation may or may not pay dividends each year. If dividends are not paid, they do not have to be made up in later years.

If a corporation is sold or dissolved, the preferred stockholders receive all the proceeds, after all creditors are paid, until the face value of their preferred shares, plus any dividends owed, is paid. Preferred stockholders get paid before common stockholders.

A corporate recapitalization occurs when a common stockholder exchanges common stock for shares of preferred stock. While there are many variations on how these tax-free trades are made, here is a description of one of the more common types that was used prior to 1988:

An independent appraiser valued the existing common stock.

The corporation issued preferred stock to the common stockholder in exchange for all or part of the common stock owned by that stockholder.

The corporation issued new common stock to the preferred stockholder's children or grandchildren or other designated individuals; or the original stockholder gave the common stock to his or her children or grandchildren or to other designated individuals.

The recipients of the common stock paid for their common stock if the corporation issued it. Because the corporation was only worth the value of the preferred stock, the price of the common stock would be very low.

The end result of this stock trade (recapitalization) was that the children or grandchildren had all the growth (common) stock. The original stockholder had no-growth (preferred) stock and had removed the future growth of the corporation from the stockholder's estate.

The most difficult and risky aspect of a corporate recapitalization is valuing the preferred stock. Because preferred stock in a closely held corporation is often structured in such a manner as to make its value problematical, it is not uncommon to have it valued significantly below the value of the corporation as a whole. When this occurs, the common stock is worth more, which may result in federal gift tax implications when the common stock is given to children or grandchildren. The IRS issued some guidelines in 1983 as to how preferred stock is to be valued in a corporate recapitalization. These guidelines should be adhered to in a recapitalization to avoid later problems.

Here is an example of how a recapitalization worked prior to 1988:

> John Walls, a man in his late sixties, and his wife Betsy, who is the same age, have spent all their lives accumulating an estate. They own a small print shop that designs and produces a line of greeting and Christmas cards. Their business was incorporated years ago. All the corporation's common stock is in John's name.
>
> John and Betsy have three children. Their son, Dave, works for the corporation. Their two daughters, Sally and Betty, have never worked in the business. Sally is a successful businessperson, Betty a homemaker.
>
> John and Betsy depend on their corporation for their livelihood.
>
> Both John and Betsy want their son, Dave, to operate and own the business upon their deaths. They also want to be fair to their daughters. If John dies, Betsy needs to receive cash from the business. If the estate continues to grow at its present rate, the federal estate taxes that will ultimately have to be paid by the children may force the sale of the family business.
>
> John and Betsy's advisers recommend a recapitalization to them. A report is issued by a professional appraiser stating that the common stock of the family's business is worth $750,000. After conferring with their appraiser and tax advisers, they agree that the preferred stock can be valued at $710,000. This will leave $40,000 worth of common stock to divide among Dave, Sally, and Betty.
>
> John trades $710,000 worth of his common stock for $710,000 worth of 15 percent noncumulative preferred stock. The preferred stock has the right to vote on all corporate matters. John, however, still owns $40,000 worth of common stock, which he can divide up among Dave, Betty, and Sally in any manner he and Betsy decide. John and Betsy can give up to $20,000 a year to each of their children free of federal gift tax. If they want to give Dave more than $20,000 worth of stock, either they can use up part of the exemption equivalent, or they can make a $20,000 gift in the current year and the remainder the next year. No matter how the gifts are made, any future growth in the value of the corporation will be passed on to John and Betsy's children, free from federal gift, estate, or income tax.

In our example, John transferred the future appreciation of the corporation to the children in the percentages that he and Betsy desired, free of federal income tax and gift tax. John and Betsy also retained control of the corporation because the preferred stock had voting rights. John and Betsy continued to work in the family corporation and continued to take their salaries. They have also assured themselves that if the business does well, they can receive dividend payments upon retirement. On John's death, he can leave the preferred stock to Betsy so that she may continue to enjoy all the ownership benefits. On Betsy's death, Dave will own and control the family corporation, fulfilling John and Betsy's desires.

Figure 30-1 illustrates our example.

The example of John and Betsy is illustrative of how a recapitalization used to work. A recapitalization could be structured to accommodate almost any family situation that involved a family-owned corporation. This was not a technique that was commonly used because only trained tax advisers understood it and knew how to implement it.

There is a second freezing technique known as a partnership freeze. It is used to freeze assets other than corporate stock. This technique accomplishes all the objectives that are accomplished by a recapitalization. It is more advantageous than a recapitalization. Because no corporation is involved, many of the valuation problems encountered in a recapitalization are avoided. In addition, there is no double tax on income when using a partnership.

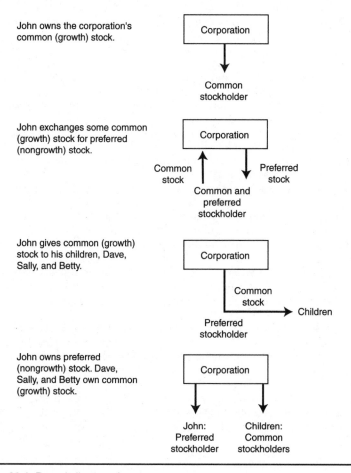

Figure 30-1. Recapitalization of a corporation.

The definition of a partnership is any endeavor entered into by two or more people with a view to making a profit. Profit can be made through operating a business or investing in assets for a later sale. Either way, the business or assets can be placed in a partnership. A partnership may either be a general partnership or a limited partnership. In a general partnership, all partners have an element of control and therefore have unlimited liability. A limited partnership has both general and limited partners. The general partners control a limited partnership and have the same liability they would in a general partnership. The limited partners do not have control and are liable only to the extent of their partnership investment.

Either a general partnership interest or a limited partnership interest can be frozen for estate planning purposes. Just like no-growth preferred stock, partnership ownership can be established in such a manner that its value does not increase. Any nonfrozen partnership ownership then becomes growth ownership. To illustrate this concept, we will continue the example of John and Betsy.

> John and Betsy own a building in a joint tenancy. Like the corporation, it is increasing in value. John and Betsy want the building's appreciation out of their estates but want to keep the income they receive from the building.
>
> John and Betsy have the building appraised. It is worth $650,000. John and Betsy then form a limited partnership and transfer the building into the partnership in exchange for a 50 percent general partnership interest for each of them.
>
> John and Betsy each owned 50 percent of the building before the partnership was formed, and nothing has changed except that there is a new name on the deed—the name of the partnership.
>
> The formal partnership agreement states that upon the sale of the building or the liquidation of the partnership, the general partners, John and Betsy, will receive the value of the building as it was appraised when put into the partnership. The value at that time was $650,000. Thus the most John and Betsy could receive in the future is $325,000 each. The value of the building is frozen in the same manner as a corporate recapitalization.
>
> After the partnership is formed, Dave, Betty, and Sally will buy limited partnership interests of the partnership. The price for these limited partnership interests will not be high, however, because as in the recapitalization of the corporation, John and Betsy will decide the amount each can purchase. If John and Betsy decide to sell $10,000 worth of limited partnership interests, $4,000 worth each may go to Betty and Sally and $2,000 to Dave. Betty and Sally would each have 40 percent of the future growth of the building, and Dave would have 20 percent.

John and Betsy retain the income from the building. The partnership can provide an income to them before any of that income is paid to the children.

In the example of a partnership freeze, John and Betsy transferred the future appreciation on the building to their children in the percentages that John and Betsy decided, free of federal income tax and gift tax. John and Betsy also retained control of the building because they became general partners. As general partners, they control the partnership. John and Betsy continue to receive the income from the building. On either John's or Betsy's death, the survivor will continue to receive income from the building. On the deaths of both John and Betsy, Betty, Sally, and Dave will own the partnership and therefore will own the building. The partnership freeze, like the recapitalization, has accomplished all of John and Betsy's planning objectives.

The second example involving John and Betsy illustrates one of the many ways that a partnership freeze was used prior to 1988. Like the recapitalization of a corporation, a partnership freeze was understood and properly used only by trained tax advisers. Figure 30-2 illustrates how this concept worked.

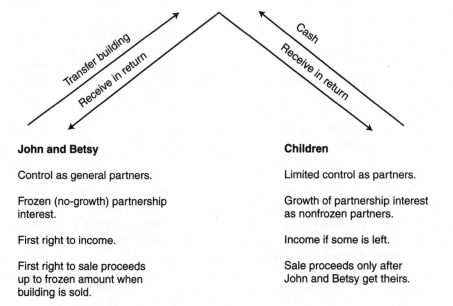

John and Betsy

Control as general partners.

Frozen (no-growth) partnership interest.

First right to income.

First right to sale proceeds up to frozen amount when building is sold.

Children

Limited control as partners.

Growth of partnership interest as nonfrozen partners.

Income if some is left.

Sale proceeds only after John and Betsy get theirs.

Figure 30-2. Frozen limited partnership.

Changes in Freezing Techniques Made by the Revenue Reconciliation Act of 1990

In the Revenue Reconciliation Act of 1990 (which we will shorten to "1990 Act"), Congress repealed code section 2036(c) retroactively to the date of its enactment and replaced it with a new set of rules. Every transaction that has the potential to freeze an estate must be analyzed in light of these new rules.

Traditional freezing techniques were based on the assumption that the value of future appreciation is very low and that the value of the retained interest is very high. Under our earlier example of a traditional recapitalization, when John transferred common stock to his children, his advisers valued it at a much lower value than the preferred stock that John retained. By doing this, the cost of transferring the future appreciation of the business to John's children was very low.

The new rules take a different approach. Instead of allowing the taxpayer to value the property, the new law sets out how property is to be valued. In addition, instead of imposing federal estate tax at the death of the person who makes the transfer, the new rules immediately subject the transfer to federal gift tax.

The new rules, in most situations, require John to value the preferred stock at a low or no value. Under John's plan to recapitalize the corporation, federal gift tax may well be generated when he gives the common stock away to his children, because it will be valued at a substantially higher amount than it would have been prior to the new rules.

The same is true in a traditional partnership freeze. Again, under the new rules, the general partnership interest is valued lower and the limited partnership interests are valued at a higher amount. This allows Uncle Sam to subject the property to federal gift tax immediately. It also makes a recapitalization much less attractive from a planning point of view.

Under the new rules, some of the valuation issues are addressed under certain distribution rules for corporations and partnerships. Now, if an individual transfers an interest in a corporation or partnership and retains a right to distributions from a corporation with respect to its stock or a right to distributions from a partnership with respect to a partner's interest in the partnership, that distribution right is given a zero value. The transferred interest—the part that will appreciate—is thus deemed to have all the value.

These distribution rules also apply to persons who control an entity immediately prior to the transfer. Control is defined as holding at least 50 percent, by vote or by value, of the stock of a corporation or at least 50 percent of the capital or profit interests in a partnership, or having any interest as a general partner in a limited partnership. As with section 2036(c), the ownership of certain family members is lumped together for purposes of the 50 percent requirement.

For transfers of other types of interests, the valuation rules apply regardless of whether the person making the transfer or a group of family members has control. Some of these types of interests include rights upon liquidation and conversion, and puts and calls.

The new rules recognize that a retained interest is not always worthless. If a corporation, for example, is paying periodic dividends to holders of cumulative preferred stock at a fixed rate, and that stock is the retained interest, then the zero-value concept does not apply. These payments are called qualified payment rights under the new law. By properly structuring a recapitalization to include qualified payment rights, the value of the gift may be decreased to such an extent that the recapitalization may be attractive. There are other exceptions to the zero-value rule for other types of interests.

As usual, the new law comes with its own complexities. For example, the 1990 Act introduced special valuation rules for different types of transactions. One set of rules applies to transfers of certain types of interests in corporations or partnerships. Another set of special valuation rules applies to transfers of interests in trust. Still another set of rules provides that the value of property is determined without regard to certain rights, options, or restrictions; this set of rules applies to buy–sell agreements. Another set of rules deals with the valuation of rights that terminate or lapse.

For transfers in trust, the valuation rules disregard the value of any retained interest that is not a qualified interest. A qualified interest is the right to receive fixed amounts, payable not less than annually; or the right to receive amounts that are a fixed percentage of the fair market value of the property, not less than annually; and any remainder interest that is not contingent on some event occurring in the future. Thus, if an interest retained by a person making a gift to a trust is not a qualified interest, the retained interest is treated as having no value and does not decrease the value of the gift. This concept is much like the qualified payment right for recapitalizations.

There are other exceptions to the valuation rules for transfers in trust. The valuation rules do not apply if there is no completed gift. This includes the situation in which a maker funds a revocable living trust. There is no gift made when transferring one's property to one's revocable living trust; it is an incomplete gift. Another exception applies to the holding of a personal residence in a trust.

Similarly, in the context of buy–sell agreements, the value of property being transferred is determined without regard to any option, agreement, or other right to acquire or use the property, at a price less than the fair market value of the property, or without regard to any restriction on the right to sell or use the property. This means that a price established in a buy–sell agreement to purchase the stock of a shareholder will not be binding for estate, gift, or generation-skipping transfer tax purposes unless the buy–sell agreement is a bona fide business arrangement and is not a device to transfer property to members of a person's family for less than full market value. Also, its terms must be comparable to similar agreements entered into by persons in arms-length transactions.

The valuation rule for lapsing rights provides that if a person who makes a transfer fails to exercise any retained voting or liquidation rights in a corporation or partnership, then that failure to exercise lapses and is treated as a transfer by the individual by gift, or it may be included in the person's estate for federal estate tax purposes.

The new rules introduced by the 1990 Act are extremely complex, and we have only scratched the surface of many of the provisions contained in the law. The implications of the new valuation rules are not clear and will likely not be for some time, because of its broad scope and its lack of history in terms of court cases and IRS rules explaining its effects. The general provisions of our federal tax laws have changed several times in the last several years, making it much more difficult to freeze estates and pass on any future appreciation in a business or other enterprise.

One of the most effective methods for avoiding the new rules and shifting appreciation to family members is to plan ahead. Creating more than one class of stock in a new corporation may allow you to steer clear of the estate-freezing rules.

For example, Tammi decided to begin a new basket-decorating and gift business. Her children, Shayna, David, and Brian, will be running the business with her, and Tammi hopes they will take over the business one day.

Prior to the new rules, if Tammi incorporated her new business, she would own all the common stock. Now it may be appropriate to have preferred stock issued to Tammi and common stock issued to Shayna, David, and Brian before the business begins, especially if Tammi has a large estate. This would keep the growth in the value of the corporation out of Tammi's estate and there should be no gift tax consequences, assuming Tammi and the children each contribute their own funds to the business.

Putting your estate in cold storage has traditionally been a most effective estate planning tool. In certain situations it is still possible to freeze the value of property. The advice of your estate planning experts in the planning and implementation of family freeze techniques is of critical importance if you wish to put your estate in cold storage.

31

Discounting
the Value
of Your Estate

"Reduce Value—and Taxes—by Restructuring Your Assets"

In Chapter 30, we discussed freezing techniques and the fact that they have been virtually eliminated in terms of estate planning. In this chapter, we address a new generation of planning techniques that allow you to give your assets away for pennies on the dollar. Sound too good to be true? Not at all. However, the price you pay for discounting is some complexity and Internal Revenue Service frustration. These techniques work so well that the Internal Revenue Service has attempted to squelch their use by encouraging audits and issuing private letter rulings that are less concerned with the state of the law than they are with stopping the use of the techniques.

The techniques discussed here are family limited partnerships and special trusts known as grantor retained income trusts.

Family Limited Partnerships

Family limited partnerships are not new. In fact, an Internal Revenue Code provision specifically allows their use. This provision has been in the Code for at least fifty years.

A family limited partnership (FLP) is structured in the same manner we explained in Chapter 30: A husband and wife (or a single parent) set up a limited partnership and own the general partnership interest and all of the limited partnership interests. Usually, the husband and wife own a 1 or 2 percent general partnership interest and a 99 or 98 percent limited partnership interest. Recall from Chapter 30 that a general partner has full control of a limited partnership even if the general partner owns a very small percentage of the overall partnership.

When the FLP is formed, the husband and wife transfer assets into the partnership. The assets can be cash, stocks, bonds, or other investments. They can be real estate or a business. They can include stock in a closely held corporation (other than an S corporation), and other partnerships or limited liability companies.

Assets such as personal residences, vacation homes, or other personal assets should not be transferred into an FLP. The FLP must be a trade or business of some kind, even if that business is investments. It is important that the FLP agreement itself state the business purposes of the FLP. The Internal Revenue Service has tried to attack more than one FLP because they had no business purpose.

The FLP agreement must be carefully drafted. It must follow state law and cannot create any restrictions on the actions of the limited partners that are in excess of state law. If extra restrictions are added, the FLP may fall under special rules that prevent making effective gifts of the limited partnership interests.

Even without extra restrictions, limited partners have limited rights in an FLP. By law, limited partners may not participate in the management of the FLP. They cannot force the general partner to pay them income that is generated by the FLP. In fact, limited partners can be prohibited from transferring their limited partnership interests to third parties without the consent of the other partners.

Because a limited partnership interest is subject to restrictions, its value is less than its proportionate share of the underlying assets. This reduction in value is a called a discount. It works this way:

Sean and Jane have three children. Sean and Jane would like to make a substantial gift to their children of stocks, bonds, and investment real estate. However, Sean and Jane would like to continue to decide how their assets are invested. In addition, Sean and Jane would like to make sure that their children do not give or sell their shares of the assets to others, at least not without their consent.

The value of the assets that Sean and Jane wish to give away is a little over $2,000,000. Of course, Sean and Jane would like to reduce the value of the gift to their children, if they can.

Let's assume that Sean and Jane, with the advice of their attorney and other professional estate planning advisors, decide to create an FLP. Initially, Sean and Jane are the general partners and are also limited partners. This dual role is acceptable under all state laws, even though limited partners are not supposed to have management control.

Sean and Jane fund the FLP with a little over $2,000,000 worth of assets by transferring them to the name of the FLP. In exchange, Sean and Jane, general partners, receive a 1 percent general partnership interest; and Sean and Jane, limited partners, receive a 99 percent limited partnership interest.

Sean and Jane want to give all of the limited partnership interests equally to their children. However, the Internal Revenue Code requires that when an asset is given away, it must be valued at its fair market value for gift tax purposes. Fair market value is defined as the amount that a willing buyer will pay a willing seller, each being under no compulsion to buy or sell and each having full knowledge of all relevant facts about the asset.

If a person were to buy a limited partnership interest, he or she would not pay full value for the interest if it were subject to restrictions. In fact, a buyer would not pay full value for the limited partnership interest if it would be hard to resell the asset.

To assess the fair market value of a limited partnership interest, it is imperative that an appraiser be used. An appraiser in this case has two jobs: Value the assets put into the FLP, and value the general and limited partnership interests. There is a difference. The assets that are put into the FLP have their own fair market value. However, the limited partnership interest's fair market value must be adjusted for lack of marketability and lack of control. Lack of marketability means that it will be hard to find a buyer for the limited partnership because of its restrictions on ownership. As an incentive for a buyer to purchase the limited partnership interest, it must be discounted. Lack of control is self-explanatory; a person will not pay full value for an asset that offers no control.

The fair market value of a limited partnership interest generally ranges from 25 percent to 50 percent less than the value of the underlying assets. In some cases, the discount is greater if the assets inside the FLP are also restricted in some way. For example, if an FLP owns stock in a closely held business or another limited partnership, it may be that the value of the FLP's limited partnership interests will be discounted up to 60 percent or more.

Let's assume that Sean and Jane's FLP is subject to a total of 30 percent in discounts. That means that they can make a gift of all the limited partnership interests to their children at a gift tax value of $1,400,000, while still controlling the assets within the FLP and how the income and principal are distributed to the limited partners.

It is possible to get similar discounts for gifts of stock in closely held corporations and ownership interests in limited liability companies. However, limited partnerships are preferred for a number of reasons. The primary reason is that the law for discounts of limited partnerships is well-settled and familiar. Limited liability companies are new entities in the law and do not have a history to rely on. Also, the state laws allowing limited liability companies are generally more liberal than laws governing limited partnerships. Because of control and voting issues, you are more likely to get a greater discount in a limited partnership than in a limited liability company.

Corporations must overcome many issues. A C corporation, which is a regular corporation with its own income tax structure, lacks the ability to pass through income to shareholders with only a single tax. A limited partnership is a pass-through entity; the partners include in income their pro rata share of partnership income. In a C corporation, the corporation has its own income tax liability. Any amounts paid to shareholders are subject to a second tax. When making gifts to children or grandchildren, most people would prefer that income be passed through without a second tax.

S corporations are pass-through entities. Their shareholders share income on a pro rata basis just as partners do. Voting can be restricted in an S corporation by the use of voting and nonvoting stock. However, there are many restrictions on S corporations that sometimes make them difficult to deal with.

The state laws governing corporations are not as restrictive as the laws governing limited partnerships. In addition, certain provisions of the Internal Revenue Code make it difficult to use restrictive provisions in a corporate shareholders' agreement to increase the amount of the discounts used in valuing the stock.

All in all, FLPs tend to be the most effective structures for discounting gifts. State and federal law, as well as legal precedent, favor the use of FLPs for making discounted gifts.

If you are interested in forming an FLP, seek out expert advice. Because of the Internal Revenue Code minefield surrounding FLPs, only advisors who have a thorough understanding of what can and cannot be done with an FLP should be hired to design and create of one of these complicated entities. Also, make sure that you use a top-notch business appraiser. The old saying that an ounce of prevention is worth a pound of cure applies here.

Grantor Retained Income Trusts

Grantor retained income trusts (GRITs), like family limited partnerships, are not new. At one time, a technique known as a statutory GRIT was used by many estate planners as a very effective way to transfer assets to children with little or no gift tax. The use of statutory GRITs has been curtailed, but other grantor retained interest trusts can be used effectively to make gifts to family members.

To understand how grantor retained interest trusts work, let's examine the old statutory GRIT. A GRIT was a trust that generally lasted for a term of years. A maker created an irrevocable trust, placed certain assets in it, and retained the income from those assets for the term of the trust. At the trust's end, the assets passed to the trust's beneficiaries.

The value of the gift to the GRIT's beneficiaries was the assets' fair market value at the time of their transfer into the GRIT, less the value of the maker's right to income over the term of the trust. The Internal Revenue Code provided a mechanism to compute the value of the income interest.

GRITs proved to be quite effective because the method of determining the value of the maker's retained income interest did not allow for the actual income generated by the assets. So, for example, a maker could place assets that were assumed to pay out a certain amount of income, but actually did not. The net result was that a gift was made, over time, to beneficiaries. The value of the gift could be greatly understated.

Statutory GRITs are still allowed in limited circumstances. The Internal Revenue Code prohibits the use of GRITs if members of the maker's immediate family are beneficiaries. However, a maker can create a GRIT that names people other than immediate family members. Immediate family members include the maker's spouse, ancestors, lineal descendents of the maker or the maker's spouse, any brother or sister of the maker, and their spouses.

The use of GRITs even for non-family members is not as effective as in the past. There is a requirement that income-producing assets be used in the GRIT; if non-income-producing assets are used, then the Internal Revenue Service will attempt to increase the gift element of the trust to reflect that the income interest held by the maker is not worth very much.

GRITs can be used in one more area. It is possible to put certain tangible property in a GRIT, such as artwork, undeveloped property, or antiques. However, the Internal Revenue regulations make use of these devices very difficult, if not impossible. You may want to discuss tangibles GRITs with your advisors to determine whether they may be applicable to your situation.

The most common type of grantor retained interest trust that is used today is called a Grantor Retained Annuity Trust (GRAT). A variation of this trust is a grantor retained unitrust (GRUT).

A GRAT works very much like a GRIT except that the grantor retains an annuity interest rather than an income interest. An annuity interest is a periodic payment that is based on the value of the assets initially put into the trust. For example, if $100,000 is transferred to an 8 percent GRAT, then the maker of the GRAT will receive $8,000 per year for the term of the trust. If the assets do not created enough income to pay the $8,000 per year, then trust principal (part of the $100,000) must be paid to make up the difference.

In a GRUT, the income interest that the maker retains is called a unitrust interest. A unitrust interest differs from an annuity interest in that the unitrust interest is a payment based on the fair market value of the trust's assets as valued each year. If $100,000 worth of assets are placed in an 8 percent GRUT, the payment the first year is $8,000. However, if in the second year of the GRUT the assets have grown to a value of $110,000, then the second year payment is $8,800 (8% of $110,000). If in the third year, the value has dropped to $80,000, then the payment would be $6,400 (8% of $80,000).

For a number of reasons, GRATs are much more commonly used than GRUTs. The primary reasons are that GRATs tend to result in a lower gift to the beneficiaries and their assets do not have to be valued each year to determine the amount of the payout.

The value of the gift to the beneficiaries of a GRAT or a GRUT is determined based on the following:

The value of the assets initially transferred into the trust.

The length of time the trust pays its income interest to the maker.

The payout rate to the maker.

The maker's life expectancy.

An interest rate provided each month by the Internal Revenue Service.

The timing of the payments (monthly, quarterly, annually, etc.).

The interest rate provided by the Internal Revenue Service is an assumed rate of return of the trust based on current interest rates. For example, if the current rate published by the Internal Revenue Service is 6 percent, then it is assumed, for purposes of computing the value of the gift to the beneficiaries, that the trust will make a total rate of return of 6 percent for its full term.

In essence, the longer the trust pays its income interest to the maker and the higher the payout amount is, the lower the value of the gift.

A simple example will illustrate how a GRAT works to discount the value of a gift:

Margo Maker wants to make a substantial gift to her three children. Margo is 56 and has $1,000,000 in stocks and bonds. She would like to retain an income interest of $85,000 a year for ten years, at which time she would like her stocks and bonds to pass to her three children. The current interest rate for GRATs, as published by the Internal Revenue Service, is 6.2 percent.

Assuming that the stocks and bonds actually grow at the rate of 10 percent over the ten-year term of her GRAT, the amount of Margo's gift is about $396,000, and the amount her children will receive will be around $1,188,000. Margo's gift will be sheltered by her applicable exclusion amount. Gifts to a GRAT do not qualify for the annual exclusion.

GRATs should only be funded with assets that will grow faster than the current interest rate required by the Internal Revenue Code. If they do not, then the efficiency of using a GRAT is greatly reduced.

There are two drawbacks to using GRATs. The first is that if the maker dies during the GRAT's term, the full value of the GRAT's assets will be included in the maker's estate. There is no adverse gift tax effect; the transaction is treated as if the gift never occurred. This contingency must be planned for. If not planned correctly, especially if the maker is married, excess estate taxes can be generated.

The second drawback to a GRAT involves its use for generation-skipping. Because of special language in the Internal Revenue Code, the valuation of the assets in a GRAT occurs when the payout term ends, not when the gift is made.

When the payout term does end, the GRAT's assets do not have to pass directly to children. Just as in any other trust, it is possible to retain the assets in trust. If the maker has concerns about making outright gifts, then appropriate provisions can be added to the GRAT.

In this chapter we have surveyed two very sophisticated planning techniques. A complete analysis of a family's financial and estate planning objectives must take place before these concepts should be considered. Even then, the family's advisors should run the numbers to ensure that these techniques make sense. If they do make sense, the discounting available will allow the transfer of a great deal of wealth at substantially discounted values.

32
Protecting Your Assets

"Safety from Unexpected Liability"

One of the common reactions to the concept of asset protection is that an individual, family, or business is trying to avoid paying well-deserved creditors. That is not the purpose of asset protection.

We live in a litigious society. It is common for unhappy people to attempt to solve their problems by resorting to a lawsuit. Creative attorneys and receptive courts have had the effect of broadening the reach of litigation. As a result, huge judgments are awarded in cases that one would not expect to even go to court.

The purpose of asset protection is to title assets in such a manner as to discourage lawsuits that are unreasonable in their scope, as well as avoid the horrendous monetary demands of plaintiffs. Short of discouraging the lawsuit itself, asset protection encourages plaintiffs to settle their claims on a more reasonable basis because of the difficulties they encounter in collecting from the defendant.

There are numerous asset protection techniques. This chapter deals with the best-known methods.

Insurance

A great deal of the liability risks most of us face can be insured against. One of the first steps in asset protection is to meet with your liability insurance carrier to assess your assets and your lifestyle to determine your need for basic liability coverage and amplified umbrella insurance. Find out what the coverage costs and what it covers. You are then better able to determine whether asset protection is necessary and whether the cost of insurance is such that other forms of asset protection are warranted.

Holding Property in Tenancy by the Entirety

An inexpensive and relatively effective method of asset protection for married couples is to hold title to marital property as tenants by the entirety. In Chapter 2, we discussed this form of title holding.

In the states that allow tenants by the entirety ownership, neither a creditor of only the husband nor a creditor of only the wife can get a judgment against tenancy by the entirety property. For example, let's say that John is an executive with a large company and his wife, Terri, is a physician. John's exposure to litigation may be small, but Terri's could be very high. If all of John and Terri's property were held in tenancy by the entirety, a patient could sue Terri for millions and win a judgment for an amount far greater than her malpractice coverage. Even though there is a judgment, the patient could not take John and Terri's assets if they were held in tenancy by the entirety.

However, if John and Terri were to divorce and split the property, Terri's separate assets would then be subject to the judgment. Also, if John were to die while the judgment was outstanding, then all the assets would pass to Terri by law. At that point, they would be subject to the claims of her creditors.

The more likely outcome is that when the patient's lawyers find out that Terri is judgment-proof because of the way her property is titled, they will want to settle the case. It is also likely that the settlement will be within Terri's malpractice insurance limits. Settling within these limits is a clear victory for Terri and John; it allows them to preserve their assets while paying for the consequences of Dr. Terri's actions.

Tenancy by the entirety planning is not compatible with basic estate planning, however. If a married couple has all of its assets titled in both names, then all of the other disadvantages of jointly held property apply. Thus this type of planning should be used only if a couple's advisors can provide for other estate planning objectives. This is most often difficult, if not impossible, to do; we most often recommend that other asset protection devices be used.

Community Property and Asset Protection

Community property offers no asset protection. In community property states, a creditor of one spouse has the ability to seize community property. The only property that is protected from creditors is the separate property of the spouse who does not have a judgment against him or her.

In order to reduce the risk of having a creditor of one spouse take all community property, it is possible to sever a couple's community property. By severing the property, each spouse owns half, usually as a tenant in common, which protects half of those assets from the creditors of one spouse. An alternative is to title all or a majority of the assets in the name of the spouse who appears to have the least amount of exposure to creditors.

There are some disadvantages for each of these techniques. By severing community property, the couple loses the full step-up in cost basis on all of the property when the first spouse dies. While asset protection may be more important than the full step-up in basis, loss of this significant income tax benefit can be quite costly.

Transferring the bulk of a married couple's assets to the spouse who has less exposure is no more than a gamble. If the spouse who owns all of the property is in a car accident that results in a huge judgment, then all the property may be lost. Unfortunately, it is not always the expected liability that creates exposure. In fact, it is the unexpected that often results in loss of assets.

Other alternatives such as limited partnerships or offshore trust planning should be considered for those couples living in community property states. The other choices do not, in the main, make a great deal of planning sense.

Investing in Exempt Assets

One simple method of asset protection is to invest in assets that are free from the claims of creditors by either state or federal law. While state law provides for more exempt assets than does federal law, each can be taken advantage of for purposes of asset protection.

The primary exempt asset under federal law is a qualified retirement plan such as a profit sharing plan, a money purchase pension plan, or a defined benefit pension plan. Assets in these plans, by law, cannot be taken by creditors of the plan participant. However, plans that are not considered to be qualified, such as Individual Retirement Accounts (IRAs), are not protected under federal law. A majority of the states do protect IRAs and other nonqualified retirement plans from creditors. Because this protection is not always available, it is important that you ask your estate planning professional what the law is in your state.

State law varies as to what assets are exempt from creditors. Most states provide a homestead exemption. The objective of a homestead exemption is to protect a person's primary residence from being taken by creditors. A majority of states provide for a certain dollar amount to be exempt from creditors. This means that the house can be seized, but the homeowner can retain some of the sales proceeds. A few states, such as Texas and Florida, have an unlimited homestead exemption; the entire value of the homestead, no matter how much it is worth, is protected.

Life insurance proceeds paid to named beneficiaries are generally protected from the claims of creditors of the insured. Sometimes the proceeds are also protected from creditors of the beneficiary. In addition, a number of states protect the cash value of life insurance, when the policy is owned by the insured. The value of an annuity and the proceeds from an annuity may also be protected from creditors of the annuitant.

Finally, most states have some minor exemptions for personal property. However, none of these exemptions are very large and they should not be relied upon as any sort of comprehensive asset protection planning.

Using a Corporation to Protect Assets

One of the primary reasons that businesses incorporate is for the asset protection of their shareholders. If a corporation is sued or goes bankrupt, the shareholders generally can lose only the value of their stock. Theoretically, they are not personally liable. We say "theoretically" because if a shareholder takes some action that is deemed to be fraudulent or in violation of the corporate charter, the shareholder could be liable for some or all of the corporate debts. In the case of closely held corporations (those with very few shareholders, who are also involved in the corporation's operations), it is very possible that in any lawsuit against the corporation, the shareholders will be sued also.

Corporations are often used for limited asset protection. When they are used, it is to isolate particular assets. For example, let's say that Harvey owns a fireworks company. If the entire operation blows up, Harvey would not like to lose his other assets. Harvey would be wise to incorporate his business. Now, Harvey could still be sued, but if he has kept his business entity up by paying annual fees, filing annual reports, making sure the public is aware that it is dealing with an entity, not Harvey, and meeting all other state requirements, odds are that Harvey has protected his other assets.

A corporation can protect an owner's other assets, but only if the business entity is clearly separate and apart from its owners. This does not mean the owners cannot work in the business, but it does mean that the owners must observe all formalities of the business. If Harvey does work in the business and he is the person who negligently packed the fireworks that exploded, then he still can be sued for his personal negligence. A corporation does not protect an owner, an officer, or an employee from his or her own acts. That is why a corporation may not be the best asset protection in the world for an individual who wants to protect more than his or her investment in a business.

One of the problems of using a corporate structure without other asset protection planning is the application of Murphy's Law: "What can go wrong, will go wrong." If Harvey gets into an automobile accident and is sued for millions of dollars over and above his insurance coverage, then he may lose his corporate stock as well as the remainder of his assets. In asset protection, it is not always the obvious liability that comes back to haunt you. It is just as likely that some unexpected action will cause the need for asset protection.

Limited Partnerships

A limited partnership is a business structure that has two types of owners. The general partner is in charge of the management of the partnership, and has unlimited liability. The other owners are called limited partners. Much like shareholders in a corporation, they do not have any liability other than the value of their limited partnership interests. Limited partners are not allowed to participate in the management of the partnership; if they do, then they lose their liability protection.

Well-structured limited partnership agreements provide that the general partners and the limited partners cannot sell, give, or in any manner dispose of their interests in the limited partnership without the consent of all the other partners. This provision works well in the asset protection arena. If a creditor has a judgment against a partner, that creditor cannot be a legitimate owner. Therefore, the creditor has no standing to "step in the shoes" of the partner who owes the creditor. This provision makes partnership interests unattractive for creditors.

The best a creditor can hope for is to go to court and obtain a legal instrument called a charging order. A charging order allows the creditor to seize any distributions from the partnership that would otherwise go to the partner who owes the judgment to the creditor.

If the limited partnership is comprised of family members or related parties, as in asset protection limited partnerships, then it is unlikely a distribution will be forthcoming. Thus the creditor may have to wait a long time to collect the amount of the judgement. This encourages the creditor to settle rather than wait.

A charging order does cause a very serious potential problem for the creditor. The Internal Revenue Service takes the position that a creditor holding a charging order is responsible for the partner's share of taxable income. Let's say that a limited partnership has $100,000 of taxable income, but the general partner decides not to distribute any cash. The partners are still responsible for their share of the partnership's taxes. If Limited Partner A owns 25 percent of the partnership, but A's creditor has a charging order, the creditor must include 25 percent of the partnership's taxable income on the creditor's income tax return, even if the creditor has not been paid a dime! This feature discourages some creditors from seeking a charging order; again, it is a method to help settle the debt with the creditor.

One of the weaknesses of a limited partnership is that the general partner is liable for all partnership debts and liabilities. Often, a general partnership is held in a business entity, such as a corporation or a limited liability company, to reduce the exposure of the individual who would otherwise be the general partner.

Another potential weakness of a limited partnership is that a court may find that the partnership is a sham and should be ignored for purposes of a judgment. Courts do this if the partnership is not properly formed, not properly funded, or not properly operated, or is clearly set up solely for purposes of defrauding creditors. For these reasons, it is imperative that an individual or family consult with an attorney who is an expert in asset protection planning before setting up a limited partnership. These are complex business organizations that need the attention of a professional.

Limited Liability Companies

A limited liability company is a hybrid between a corporation and a limited partnership. Like a corporation, all of a limited liability company's owners are protected from the debts and liabilities of the company. Like a partnership, a limited liability company does not have its own tax liability; income and losses are passed through to the owners, based on their percentage of ownership.

Limited liability companies are popular for several reasons. The primary reason for their popularity is that the owners of a limited liability company can participate in management. Contrast this participation to that of a limited partnership; in order to maintain limited liability, the limited partners cannot participate in management.

Another reason for the popularity of limited liability companies is that they are taxed like an S corporation or a partnership. Limited liability companies do not have a separate tax liability, so all income, deductions, and credits are passed through to the owners based on their ownership percentages. Unlike an S corporation, which is subject to a number of rules respecting who can and cannot be owners, practically any person or entity can own a limited liability company.

Just as in corporations, however, limited liability companies offer only limited asset protection. They protect the owners from losing more than their investment, assuming all the required limited liability formalities are met, but do not necessarily prevent a creditor from taking the ownership interest itself. The remedy of a charging order for a limited liability company is not necessarily available, so absent state legislation to the contrary, limited liability companies are not used for overall asset protection.

Using Domestic Trusts
for Asset Protection

It has long been a basic tenet of law that a person cannot set up a trust, transfer assets to the trust, name himself or herself as the beneficiary, and then prevent creditors from taking the trust assets. This principle of law applies whether the trust is irrevocable or revocable.

However, at least one state, Alaska, has passed a trust statute that offers trust makers the possibility of asset protection in a trust that they created. In an Alaska trust that is drafted correctly and has an Alaskan trustee, the maker of a trust can be a discretionary beneficiary of the trust. By Alaskan law, creditors of the maker cannot take trust assets even though the maker is a beneficiary. The legal theory behind this law is that because the trust has an independent trustee who can unilaterally make the decision to make income or principal distributions to the maker, the maker has no legal rights to the trust. If the maker has no legal rights, then neither can his or her creditors.

As yet, the courts have not ruled on whether or not someone who lives outside of Alaska can create one of these trusts in Alaska and still avoid creditors who are not in Alaska. There are some constitutional issues that must be addressed, so these trusts, at least for asset protection purposes, are not ironclad for non-Alaskans. But, as the cases evolve, the courts and other states may eventually allow this type of asset protection trust.

An irrevocable trust that names someone other than the maker as the beneficiary can be used for asset protection. If the trust contains a spendthrift provision, in most states those trust assets are protected from the creditors of the beneficiary. A spendthrift provision states that neither the trustee nor the beneficiary can use trust assets to pay creditors, and that the beneficiary is prohibited from using trust assets as collateral.

Not all states recognize spendthrift provisions, but they should nevertheless be included in all trusts, even revocable trusts. Here is why: Suppose you create a revocable living trust that provides, among other things, that upon your death some of your assets will pass to an irrevocable subtrust for the benefit of your children. You allow the trustee to make the decision as to whether or when income and principal will be paid out to your children. You also allow the trustee to pay out trust income and principal on behalf of a child. That means that instead of giving the money directly to the child for rent, for example, the trustee pays the rent directly. The trust also includes a spendthrift provision.

After your death, one of your children has creditor problems. Creditors will seize any money he or she receives directly. However, if the trustee makes payments on behalf of your child, then the creditors cannot seize either the money paid or the trust assets.

Now, let's further assume that when you made the trust, you lived in a state that did not recognize a spendthrift provision, but your child lives in a state that does allow spendthrift provisions. It is possible, in a properly drafted trust, to change the location (situs) of the trust to the state in which the beneficiary lives. This will likely protect the assets.

As you can see, spendthrift planning is important in trusts for the beneficiaries. That is one reason why you should work with a highly skilled estate planning attorney and other advisors so that these issues can be addressed properly.

Offshore Asset Protection Trusts

The most sophisticated method for asset protection is the offshore asset protection trust (OAPT). These trusts have become quite popular over the last decade and have proven to be effective in asset protection, despite critical articles to the contrary.

In a nutshell, an OAPT is an irrevocable trust that is set up in a country outside of the United States. A number of countries can be used, but some of the most popular are the Isle of Man, the Cook Islands, and the Cayman Islands. Even though the trust is irrevocable, it provides provisions that in essence allow the maker to have the benefit of the assets. There are built-in mechanisms that allow the maker to retrieve the assets if he or she needs them.

Unlike a domestic irrevocable trust, OAPTs require that creditors bring their lawsuits in the foreign country rather than the United States. The countries that are used for the situs of an OAPT do not recognize United States judgments. So, for example, if a creditor has a court order to seize the assets of a United States person who has his or her property in an OAPT, the creditor cannot go to a court in the foreign jurisdiction and ask the courts there to enforce it. The courts in the foreign jurisdiction will require a full trial there in order to determine the validity of the claim.

Even if the claim is valid, the foreign jurisdictions do not allow creditors of the trust maker to take trust assets unless the creditor can prove that the assets were fraudulently conveyed to the trust. Typically, these countries make proving fraudulent conveyances very difficult. In addition, they have relatively short statutes of limitations for bring a fraudulent conveyance action; it is highly likely that the statute of limitations will expire prior to the time that the creditor comes to the foreign country.

Because of the way OAPTs are drafted, the maker of the trust does not lose a great deal of control over his or her assets. Most practitioners who draft these trusts start with a domestic family limited partnership that owns all, or substantially all, of the maker's assets. The maker then transfers his or her assets to the partnership in exchange for the general and limited partnership interests. The limited partnership interests are transferred to the OAPT. The maker controls the assets in the partnership because he or she is the general partner.

The limited partnership allows the maker to invest assets freely, with few restrictions. However, at the first sign of litigation, the maker can liquidate the assets in the partnership and transfer the proceeds into the OAPT. The liquidation and transfer get the assets out of the reach of United States courts.

OAPTs are not as effective for real estate as they are for other types of property such as stocks, bonds, and investment accounts. The latter assets are movable; real estate is not. Because real estate is not movable, a United States court can seize it even if the property is technically owned by an OAPT.

One common fear of people thinking about creating an OAPT is that they will get in trouble with a court and a judge may send them to jail if they do not take assets out of their trust. A unique feature of an offshore trust that is created in a proper jurisdiction is that the foreign jurisdiction's laws will prohibit the trustee from paying the assets to a maker who is under duress. So, if a court orders the maker to force the foreign trustee to give the assets back, the maker can agree to do so. But the trustee cannot comply under the laws of the foreign jurisdiction. The trustee can only pay over assets if the maker requests that the trustee do so and if the maker is not being forced to make the request.

Do not ever attempt to set up an OAPT by yourself or with someone who does not have absolutely impeccable credentials in offshore asset protection planning. These are complex trusts that require precision in their drafting and implementation. Generally speaking, OAPTs fail because they are not drafted correctly or they are incorrectly funded. Handled with expertise, they are very effective in motivating creditors to settle on a reasonable basis.

Fraudulent Conveyances

All states in the United States and most foreign jurisdictions make it un-lawful to make a conveyance that is designed to hinder, delay, or defraud an existing creditor or a creditor who is known and could have a basis for a valid claim. That type of transfer is a fraudulent conveyance, and the re-cipient of the conveyance must return the asset.

Fraudulent conveyance statutes vary from jurisdiction to jurisdiction. Prior to entering into any asset protection planning, consult with an attor-ney who will give you guidance about these statutes, as well as others that may apply. Please understand that asset protection should be accomplished prior to encountering a problem, not afterward. If you have a creditor problem now, or you think that you may, asset protection planning may not be for you. An attorney or other advisor who helps you make such a con-veyance can get in a lot of trouble, as you can.

It is in the area of fraudulent conveyances that OAPTs are commonly—and correctly—criticized as being immoral, potentially ineffective, and crooked. However, if they are created innocently before a cause of action arises, none of these labels can attach.

Asset protection planning, even at its base level, is no area for rookies or do-it-yourselfers. Use a team of professionals if you want asset protection to be a part of your estate planning.

33

Loans to Family Members

"It's Hard to Be Your Family's Banker"

Loans to family members have the potential to be a good method of freezing the value of an estate and shifting income to family members in lower tax brackets. Unfortunately, the Supreme Court and Congress have done a great deal to discourage the use of loans to family members.

In the past, two types of intrafamily loans have been used for estate and income tax planning purposes. They are below-market loans and interest-free loans.

Below-market loans are loans made by one family member to another for less than the going interest rate. For example, a child could go to a bank and borrow money at 12 percent interest, but a parent could lend the child the money for 6 percent. If this could be done, the child would only pay 6 percent interest, and would receive an income tax deduction for the interest. The parent would only pay income tax on the 6 percent received.

Interest-free loans are based on the same principle, except no interest is charged. There is no payment of interest by the child and no income to the parent.

For many years, the IRS felt that if a parent made a below-market or interest-free loan to a child, a gift had been made. The amount of the gift, according to the IRS, was the difference between the prevailing market rate of interest and the interest, if any, charged by the parent. In our example, the IRS considered the gift to be 6 percent of the amount loaned if a below-market loan was made, or 12 percent if an interest-free loan was made.

Whether or not a gift was made was generally inconsequential to most Americans. Because every American can give away $10,000 each year to as many people as the giver desires, and a husband and wife can team up to give away $20,000, most loans were not big enough to generate a gift tax. For a $100,000 loan, when the going interest rate was 12 percent, the gift on a below-market loan at 6 percent would be $6,000 per year, the difference between $12,000 if full market interest rates were charged and the $6,000 actually charged. On an interest-free loan, the difference would be $12,000 per year.

A $6,000 gift is below the $10,000 annual exclusion, making it gift-tax-free. A $12,000 gift could be made gift-tax-free by having both parents make the gift. Thus, the gift tax, even if the IRS contention was correct, would only come into play on very large interest-free or below-market loans.

For those Americans who made large interest-free or below-market loans, demand loans were used to avoid the gift tax. A demand loan is a loan that that can be called or demanded by the lender at any time. This type of loan does not have a fixed due date. Because interest-free or below-market demand loans had no actual due date, the theory was that the amount of a gift could not be computed.

When the IRS contested this theory in the courts, it invariably lost. The courts agreed that the amount of the gift could not be computed and, in addition, held that a gift had not really been made. The courts did hold, however, that if a below-market or interest-free loan was made and a demand note was not utilized, a gift did occur. For example, a note for five years at no interest had a gift element. The market interest rate on the note for a five-year term, which was easily computed, was the amount of the gift. The only difference between this transaction and a demand note was that the demand note was not fixed as to time of payment.

The Supreme Court, in an historic 1984 decision, held that interest-free or below-interest loans, whether on a demand basis or for a fixed term, were subject to the gift tax. Worse, the Supreme Court overturned court cases that untold numbers of tax advisers and their clients had relied upon for many years. This decision allows the IRS to assess gift taxes for loans made prior to the Supreme Court's decision, even though a vast majority of lower courts had come to an opposite conclusion for years.

Congress got into the act, too. In the Tax Reform Act of 1984, all interest-free and below-market interest loans were addressed. Massive changes were made in the tax code that severely curtailed interest-free and below-market loans as viable planning devices.

Any interest-free or below-market loan is considered as a whole economic package, encompassing not only gift tax but also income tax.

The amount of interest that is not charged, that is, the difference between the amount charged and the market rate of interest, is considered a gift from the lender to the borrower. The gift is computed on an annual basis, or for the term of the note if less than a year. For term loans of a year or longer in duration, the interest is compounded semiannually. The Treasury Department determines the market rate of interest, and the amounts are announced periodically.

Interest deductions for personal interest are no longer allowed. Personal interest is interest that is not related to a trade or business; is not investment interest; is not interest considered in computing income or loss from a passive activity; is not interest on a loan used to acquire a qualified primary or secondary residence; or is not interest on certain estate tax payments. Now, interest-free or below-market loans are even more unattractive, given that it will be more difficult to take a deduction for the interest without securing the loans with the residence of the individual who receives the loan.

The difference between the interest rate charged and the government-imposed rate will be considered income to the lender and an income tax deduction to the borrower, assuming the borrower can itemize his or her deductions. The effect is to recharacterize the family loan as a business transaction. The assumption is that the lender really did charge interest, the borrower really did pay interest, and a gift was made.

For example, if the prevailing federal rate is 10 percent and an interest-free loan of $100,000 is made from a grandparent to a grandchild for a term of six months, the transaction will be viewed as a gift loan. The grandparent will have income of $5,000, representing the income that the grandparent would have earned on the money in six months at the federal rate. The grandchild may have a tax deduction of $5,000, if the loan is secured by the grandchild's home or second home, or is otherwise not personal interest, and the grandchild can itemize deductions. There also is a gift of $5,000 from the grandparent to the grandchild.

There are two additional rules that may aid taxpayers who are considering a below-market or interest-free loan to a family member. The first is that for all loans of less than $100,000, the amount considered as income to the lender and a deduction by the borrower cannot exceed the investment income of the borrower. If the borrower does not invest the loan proceeds in an income-producing investment or does not have other investment income, generally the income tax provisions will not apply. This leaves the opportunity for below-market interest or interest-free loans for college, buying a house, or other non-income-producing uses. The loan cannot be one that is aimed at tax avoidance, however, and it must be secured by the borrower's primary or secondary residence for the interest to be deductible.

The second rule deals with loans of less than $10,000 per year. As long as the proceeds from these interest-free or below-market loans are not used to buy or carry income-producing property, the loans do not fall under the otherwise complex rules.

Below-market and interest-free family loans are not viable planning tools in most situations. The complex gift tax and income tax rules make them economically unattractive and difficult to use. Avoid them, unless you are advised to the contrary by a tax expert.

Below-Market Rate or Interest-Free Loans to Family Members:

Create income to the lender.

May allow a deduction to the borrower if secured by a residence or not otherwise considered personal interest.

Are gifts to the extent that market interest is not charged.

Are only free from complex rules if less than $10,000.

34

Sales to Family Members

"Caveat Emptor"

It is possible to freeze the value of certain assets in an estate by selling them to family members on an installment basis. Just like a loan, an installment sale appears to be easy on its face. Also like a loan, this technique, in order to work, has to be implemented properly.

As a result of inflation, most assets are continually going up in value. As we have discussed, inflation forces taxpayers and their estates into higher tax brackets.

Giving an appreciating asset away may not be feasible because either the annual exclusion may not be sufficient to prevent federal gift tax or the applicable exclusion amount may not be available. Also, many of us are reluctant to give away assets because we want to make sure we have our assets to provide for our security and comfort as we grow older. Under these circumstances, an installment sale to a family member can be an attractive planning alternative.

A sale to a family member is the same as any other sale. A decision is made by the seller as to what asset or assets are to be sold, for what price, and under what terms. The sale is then consummated.

A sale to a family member removes an appreciating asset from the estate of the seller. The asset is replaced by a promissory note. A promissory note has a calculated time value. Whatever this calculated value is determined to be at the death of the note owner is the amount that is included in the estate for federal estate tax purposes. Thus the value of the promissory note is less than the value of the asset it replaced in the estate of the seller.

By selling an asset on the installment basis, you may convert a non-income-producing asset to an asset that can provide you with income. Many older taxpayers who are asset-rich but cash-poor can use this technique to generate needed income and remove the appreciating value of an asset from their estates.

An installment sale to a family member should be entered into only after careful thought, because of the tax and economic results that can occur.

The profit from an installment sale is subject to income tax. However, the favorable maximum capital gains rate may make a sale income-tax attractive.

The type of property chosen for sale is an important consideration for sales between family members. Sales between family members of property subject to depreciation do not qualify for installment sales. The same is true for installment sales of publicly traded securities.

On most installment sales, the interest is not deductible. Interest deductions for loans secured by a primary or secondary residence are deductible subject to certain limitations, but structuring an installment sale to meet this requirement is difficult. The deductibility of interest is clearly a tax and economic factor that must be considered before an installment sale is entered into.

Recently, another sales technique that eliminates the adverse income tax results of typical sales to family members has been used to increase the effectiveness of sales between family members. This technique is called an intentionally defective grantor trust. Professionals refer to this technique as an IDGT. For convenience, we will too.

An IDGT is an irrevocable trust that is drafted in such a way that it is a grantor trust for income tax purposes. A grantor trust is a trust over which the maker has sufficient control to be considered the owner for income tax purposes, but not for estate tax purposes. This is a critical distinction.

If a trust is a grantor trust, any income or expenses of the trust are attributed to the maker; he or she must put them on his or her income tax return. However, if the maker has more control than simply as the income owner, the whole trust could be included in the maker's estate. Special language must be added to a grantor trust to achieve the income and estate tax balance. When this language is intentionally included in an irrevocable trust, the trust is an IDGT.

Here is how a typical IDGT works:

Alex and Jane, a married couple, own a successful business. It is held in a limited liability company and was just appraised for $1,750,000. Alex and Jane want to sell this business to their two children, who work in the business. As a first step, Alex and Jane create an IDGT and make a gift of $175,000 to it. Their two children are the trustees and beneficiaries of the IDGT.

The IDGT offers to buy the business from Alex and Jane for $1,750,000. The terms of the sale are 10 percent down, with payments of only interest for nine years. A balloon payment is due at the end of nine years. All this is put in a formal promissory note.

Now, here is the effectiveness of the IDGT. When the sale is made, Alex and Jane are the sellers and the buyers. You see, they are the tax owners of the IDGT. It has long been established under our tax laws that if you buy something from yourself, you do not owe any income tax. So, when Alex and Jane sell the business, the interest and principal payments come to them tax-free. Over time, they divest themselves of their business, get an income (the interest), and get their principal back. The children own the company, can run it, and will get all of the future appreciation. They will also get an income tax deduction for the interest paid.

To make an IDGT work, it must have economic substance, at least according to the Internal Revenue Service. That is why 10 percent of the value of the asset to be purchased should be put in the trust as a gift to the beneficiaries. In addition, the sale must be for fair market value, so an appraisal is necessary. The interest rate used must be the rate published by the Treasury Department in the month the sale takes place. Finally, the children must be able to amass enough principal to pay Alex and Jane in nine years. Of course, Alex and Jane can decide to forgive the note. This gift would be sheltered by their applicable exclusion amounts, resulting in a transfer of the business free of gift tax.

An IDGT can be effective in freezing an estate. These trusts are not always appropriate, but given the right circumstances, they can help in effective planning, especially if the business is appreciating at a rate significantly greater than the current interest rate required on the promissory note.

Make sure that your advisors run the numbers if you are thinking about using this technique. Expect some Internal Revenue Service scrutiny. This is another technique that works, but upsets the Service because it transfers property very effectively at a reduced tax cost.

When you sell an asset to a family member, you must be sure that the family member has the economic ability to make the payments to you. This is a problem that is often overlooked. If, after a sale is made, your loved one is financially unable to meet the payments, what are you going to do? Are you going to foreclose on the note? Probably not. You will probably be inclined to forgive the note. If you do, you will not have the income you need or the asset you sold. Worse yet, you will have made a gift and may have to pay federal gift tax to boot.

If an asset is sold to a family member at a price below its fair market value, the difference between the fair market value of the asset and the actual price paid for it is a gift. Fair market value, remember, is the amount a willing buyer would pay to a willing seller when neither is subject to any compulsion to buy or sell and both are aware of the facts relevant to the sale.

The best way to determine an asset's fair value is to obtain a professional appraisal. If this is not accomplished, be ready to defend the purchase price used. If there is an IRS audit as to the sale and a professional did not value the asset, the price will be scrutinized by the IRS. Under our tax law, the burden of proof as to the asset's value is always on the taxpayer. This means the IRS can disagree with your sales price and make you prove that it was the fair market price.

The interest rate that you use in your installment note can have tax consequences. If a note has an interest rate lower than prevailing market rates, the difference between the value of the property and the time value of the note can be construed as a gift for federal gift tax purposes. In addition, the rules for below-interest loans discussed in Chapter 33 may apply to the transaction.

The Treasury Department issues interest rates that are to be used for sales between family members. The rates are adjusted every month. The rates vary based on the time period involved; they are issued for short-term periods, mid-term periods, and long-term periods. Long-term periods are longer than nine years; mid-term periods are from three to nine years; and short-term periods are less than three years.

You can combine a gift and a sale if you choose. If you sell an asset to a family member, you may forgive any installment payment as it becomes due. For example, if you sell property to your two children for $50,000 at 15 percent interest over ten years in equal payments of principal plus any interest due, the first payment would be $12,500. Of that amount, $5,000 is principal ($50,000 divided by 10 years) and $7,500 is interest ($50,000 multiplied by 15 percent). Because you have two children, you have two $10,000 annual exclusions available, a total of $20,000. Thus the whole $12,500 payment (or any part of it) can be waived. Because the amount waived is less than the combined annual exclusions, there is no federal gift tax.

Before you waive an installment payment, be aware of the income tax ramifications. The $12,500 is still income to you, and any income tax you would have paid had the installment actually been paid to you will still be due. Your children will still have the advantage of deducting the interest as if it were paid.

The advantages of the gift–sale technique are twofold: The children may not have to come up with cash to make the installment payment, and the $12,500 you would have received (less income taxes, of course) is not added to your estate.

The courts have held, however, that if there was no intent that the note be paid because the sale was really a plan to avoid paying federal gift tax, the sale can be defeated and the entire sales price treated as one big current gift.

Family members who buy property under this technique receive a step-up in basis for income tax purposes. For example:

> Sandy and Rich buy a piece of property from their parents for $100,000. Their parents paid $10,000 for the property. If Sandy and Rich sell it for $110,000, only $10,000 ($110,000 less $100,000) is subject to federal income tax.

The family installment sale technique has been used so creatively that, in the eyes of Congress, it has been abused. The most common abuse involves a two-sale method. In this method, Dad and Mom own a second home worth $100,000. They bought it for $20,000. They now wish to sell it. If they sell it for cash, $80,000 (the difference between the selling price of $100,000 and their cost of $20,000) will be income taxable to them. As a result, if the potential buyer wants to pay cash, Dad and Mom will realize all the gain in the year of the sale. So Dad and Mom sell the house to the kids for $100,000 for ten years at a fair interest rate. The kids sell it immediately to the real buyer for cash. The result of the transaction appears to be beneficial for everyone. The kids bought the house for $100,000 and sold it for $100,000. They have no taxable gain. Mom and Dad pay taxes over ten years as opposed to one year. The kids put the money in the bank and draw interest. They use this same interest and some of the principal each year to pay Mom and Dad. What a great method to save taxes.

In 1980, Congress closed this tax-avoidance door. Today, if the kids were to sell the house within two years of buying from Mom and Dad, Mom and Dad cannot pay their taxes over ten years; they will pay their total tax in the year the kids sell the house. The solution, of course, is for the kids to wait two years and then sell the house.

Another loophole that Congress closed was forgiving an installment note on the death of the note owner. At one time, a parent could, at death, leave an installment note owed by a child to that child. The result was that the installment note was forgiven with no income tax consequence.

This technique is no longer effective. Income tax will be due if this technique is used. In our experience, many estate plans use this outdated device. If your planning includes this device, you should amend your plan.

Installment sales are complicated. By way of review, look at the following lists.

Installment Sales Help Sellers Because:

They can get appreciating assets out of sellers' estates.

Non-income-producing assets can be favorably converted into income-producing assets.

Installment Sales Help Buyers Because:

Buyers get appreciating assets at a fair price on favorable terms.

Buyers receive a step-up in basis when they buy the asset.

Family installment sales may accomplish some of your estate planning objectives. They have been abused in the past and may not be as attractive as they once were, but they still represent a viable planning tool. Let your professional estate planning advisers guide you in their use.

35

Private Annuities

"The Ultimate Gamble"

The private annuity has long been a favored estate planning technique. It is discussed by many but, in our experience, understood by few.

A private annuity has three elements. An individual called an annuitant (seller) transfers property to a family member called an obligor (buyer). The buyer promises to pay the seller certain payments. These payments are paid to the seller for the duration of the seller's life. Sounds like a sale? It is, but this sale has several unique twists that we will examine.

An installment sale, as we discussed earlier, can eliminate an appreciating asset from your estate; however, the asset removed from your estate is replaced by a promissory note. Because of the asset replacement, the installment sale converts appreciating assets to a nonappreciating asset. The value of the nonappreciating installment note, however, still remains in your estate. The installment note creates income to the seller and may create interest deductions for the buyer. The installments are paid for a definite period of time, no matter what happens to either the buyer or the seller.

A private annuity is designed so that the value of your appreciating asset and the value of the promissory obligation are both totally eliminated from your estate.

An annuity is a promise by the buyer to pay the seller fixed payments for the life of the seller. When the seller dies, the buyer owns the asset and does not have to make any more payments. If the buyer dies before the seller, the buyer's heirs must continue the payments.

Annuities are governed by the Internal Revenue Code. Its regulations provide a method to value a private annuity and spell out what the payments for the annuity must be. This method must always be used.

The value of the annuity and the payments resulting from its value are based on two factors. The first factor is how long the seller is expected to live. The number of years that any seller is expected to live is included in the regulations of the Internal Revenue Code in the form of actuarial (life expectancy) tables. The second factor is the interest rate that must be charged. The interest rate is equal to 120 percent of the federal mid-term rate in effect for the month in which the annuity is being valued. Your estate planning adviser can help you find this rate.

If you place a value on the property you sell through an annuity and that value is not fair market value, you also make a gift subject to the federal gift tax. Does this sound familiar?

Using a private annuity is a little bit like gambling. If the seller dies before he or she is statistically supposed to, the buyer wins, because the payments end. In addition, the seller's estate wins, because the annuity is not includable in the seller's estate. On the other hand, if the seller lives longer than predicted, the buyer continues to make the payments for as long as the seller lives. Remember, an annuity is an agreement by the buyer to pay fixed payments to the seller for the seller's life, no matter how long or short the seller's life is.

There is no requirement that the seller be in good health. If the seller has a terminal illness, however, a private annuity cannot be used. An individual who is in poor health but does not have a terminal illness is an excellent candidate for a private annuity.

Care must be taken when an older person contemplates using a private annuity. As age increases, life expectancy decreases. That means that the number of annuity payments decreases and the value of the payments increases. If there are fewer payments to pay for an asset, it necessarily follows that each payment will be higher. These payments may be so high that the buyer cannot afford to make them, particularly if the seller fools everyone and turns into Methuselah.

There may be disadvantageous income tax consequences with a private annuity. The federal income tax treatment of the payments made to a seller is similar to that afforded installment sales. A portion of each payment is a return of the seller's original adjusted cost basis, which is tax-free. Another portion of each payment is the capital gain element, which is the difference between the fair market value of the asset transferred under the annuity and the asset's original cost to the seller, as adjusted for depreciation and other factors. The remainder of each payment is the interest factor.

A private annuity is an estate planning technique that allows a seller to remove an asset completely from the seller's estate, still maintain an income stream from that asset, and assure the buyer that all payments cease on the seller's death.

Annuities, properly drafted and implemented, still represent the ultimate gamble: Will the seller live longer—or shorter—than he or she is supposed to?

36

Personal Residence Trusts

"Give the House, but Not Your Home

Congress allows a tax-efficient way to give your residence or a vacation home to your children. A personal residence trust allows you to reduce the value of your residence or vacation home for gift tax purposes, remove the value of the home from your estate, and enjoy the use of the home for as long as you want. Sound too good to be true? It is all true, but there are a number of rules to be followed and pitfalls to be avoided.

Personal residence trusts are short-term irrevocable trusts in which the trust maker, called the grantor, has the right to retain the use of the residence for a period of years. At the end of the period of years, the home becomes the property of the beneficiaries of the trust. Even then, the grantor can continue to use the home, but must, at that point, pay rent in order to continue to live in the home.

To better understand how a personal residence trust works, an example is in order. Let's say that Edwina Edwards, age 58, owns a home that is worth $750,000. It is in a great neighborhood and will continue to increase in value. In fact, it appears that it will appreciate at the rate of about 7 percent per year. Edwina would like to get the value of the house, and its future appreciation, out of her estate so that it will not be taxed, but she wants to live in the house for as long as she wants, but for at least ten years. It will be worth about $1,475,000 at that point.

Edwina can set up a personal residence trust that, at the end of ten years, will allow ownership of the house to pass to her children. Let's further assume that the prevailing interest rates are 6 percent (we need to make this assumption in order to compute the value of the gift). The amount of the gift to Edwina's children is about $352,000, all of which can be sheltered by her applicable exemption amount. If Edwina dies after ten years, the full value of the home will be out of her estate. That means the $1,475,000 will not be subject to federal estate tax.

Types of Personal Residence Trusts

There are two types of personal residence trusts: a qualified personal residence trust, referred to as a QPRT, and a personal residence trust, called a PRT. The difference between the two is that a PRT cannot hold any assets other than a residence and the residence cannot be sold during the term of the trust. A QPRT is allowed to hold some cash and the trustee can sell the residence during the trust's term. Most practitioners prefer to use a QPRT because it is more flexible. For those clients who want to insure that their residence is not sold, a PRT may be the better choice.

Definition of a Personal Residence

In order to be eligible for a personal residence trust, the home that is transferred must be the maker's primary residence or a vacation home. A person may transfer up to two homes in personal residence trusts, one primary residence and a vacation home. A maker does not have to own the whole residence to use a personal residence trust. For example, if a husband and wife own a residence as joint tenants with right of survivorship, each of them may transfer his or her respective interest in the residence to one trust or they may create separate trusts for their interests in the property.

There is flexibility in the definition of a personal residence. For example, a home that is rented out for part of the year can qualify as a personal residence trust, but it cannot be a bed and breakfast or a hotel. A personal residence can consist of outbuildings as long as they are part of the residence; there have even been instances in which rental units that are part of a residence have qualified for personal residence trust status. However, a personal residence does not usually consist of a home and a great deal of acreage. Farms or ranches cannot be put into personal residence trusts, but the farm or ranch house, and a reasonable amount of acreage around it, can be put into a personal residence trust.

Income Tax Rules for Personal Residence Trusts

A personal residence trust, whether a PRT or a QPRT, is a grantor trust. A grantor trust is treated as being owned by the maker of the trust for income tax purposes. This means that all of the tax benefits and deductions that are attributable to a home during the term of the personal residence trust are passed through to the maker. For example, if a QPRT sells the residence, any gain is sheltered, up to $250,000 ($500,000 for married couples). For all income tax purposes, the trust is ignored as a separate taxable entity and the maker (grantor) is considered the direct owner.

Gift Tax Rules for Personal Residence Trusts

The amount of the gift that a personal residence trust generates depends on several factors. These include the age of the maker, the value of the residence, the term of the trust, and prevailing interest rates. All of these are taken into account in special tables that are part of the Internal Revenue Code and regulations.

The older the maker, the lower the value of the gift. The reason for this is that there is a higher probability that the maker will die during the term of the trust. The death of the maker causes the value of the residence to be included in his or her estate. The probability that the residence will revert to the estate is important in valuation.

Of course, the value of the residence makes a big difference in the value of the gift. The higher the initial value of the residence, the higher the gift. This value can be reduced, however. A long-term trust can reduce the value of the gift. Also, if a husband and a wife each create their own personal residence trusts and transfer their undivided one-half interests in the residence to their respective trusts, then the value of each ownership interest can be discounted. Generally, when a person who owns property with another transfers his or her interest, that interest is not valued at one-half of the total value of the property. The interest is worth less than one-half of the total. The value is discounted to reflect the fact that a third party would pay less for a one-half interest in property, because that third party would not have full control of the property.

Let's assume Don and Cathy own a vacation home in joint tenancy. The home has been appraised at $250,000. Don and Cathy create separate personal residence trusts and transfer their ownership interests into their respective trusts. The appraiser, when valuing the separate interests (the trusts would own the residence as tenants in common), would likely discount the value by around 25 percent, although that figure could be higher or lower. In our example, the value of the partial interest of the residence is be reduced by 25 percent. The value of the partial interest, prior to final valuation of the total gift, is $93,750 rather than $125,000. Obviously, this is an excellent tax result.

The longer the term of the trust, the lower the gift. You want to retain ownership for a long period of time. Of course, if you die during the term, the value of the gift will be affected. A term of twenty years creates a much smaller gift than a term of five years.

It is easy to be confused by what the "term" of the trust really is. A personal residence trust can last far past the term of the retained interest. For example, you may have your attorney draft a personal residence trust that states:

> I will retain the right to live in my home for ten years without paying rent and with all of the benefits of owning a home, including the tax benefits. At the end of ten years, I will relinquish my right to live in the home without paying rent, and I will no longer have the benefits of owning a home. However, I want my home to remain in trust for the remainder of my life, and I wish to have the right to rent my home from the trust at its fair rental value, as determined by appraisal.
>
> Upon my death, the home shall be transferred to my living children in equal shares as tenants in common.

The term of the trust, for purposes of determining the value of the gift to the personal residence, is ten years. The trust may last for a longer period of time, but this is not relevant to the valuation of the gift.

The final factor that is taken into account when valuing the gift to a personal residence trust is an interest factor. The Internal Revenue Code requires that an assumed rate of growth be factored into the valuation of a gift to a personal interest trust. The interest rate is 120 percent of the federal mid-term rate that is in effect at the time of the transfer. The Treasury Department publishes this rate on a monthly basis. The higher the rate, the lower the gift. A personal residence trust is more tax-efficient when interest rates are high, the maker is young, and the term of the trust is long.

Estate Tax Rules for Personal Residence Trusts

After the term of a personal residence trust expires, the value of the residence is not included in the maker's estate. But if the maker dies while the trust term is in effect, the value of the residence at its the date of death is included in the maker's estate. It is for this reason that personal residence trusts are not used for people who may die during the trust's term.

One of the fundamental considerations in creating a personal residence trust is that its term should not exceed the life expectancy of its maker. While a person who is 50 years old could consider a personal residence trust that lasts 20 years, an 80-year-old will require a term that is substantially shorter. Moreover, if a person is ill or there is a family history of early death, a long-term personal residence trust may not be a good choice.

It is important that a personal residence trust be drafted to take into account the early death of the maker. If a maker dies and the trust instrument does not allow the residence to flow back into the maker's estate, it may be that federal estate tax will be generated, but the asset is in a separate trust. Bifurcating the two may make it difficult to pay the taxes.

Also, if spouses create separate personal residence trusts and one of them dies, it usually makes sense to have the value of the residence trust qualify for the unlimited marital deduction. To do so, special language must appear in the trust.

Personal Residence Trusts and Generation-Skipping

Personal residence trusts are not used to skip generations. Under the generation-skipping provisions of the Internal Revenue Code, any trust that can be pulled back into the maker's estate precludes using the $1,000,000 generation-skipping exemption amount (adjusted for inflation) at the time the gift is made. The time when the generation-skipping tax exposure is known is when the term of the trust expires. If the value of the residence were $750,000 at the time the trust was made, one would expect that if the grandchildren were the beneficiaries, part of the maker's generation-skipping exemption could be applied. Not so. Let's say that the value of the residence is $2,000,000 when the trust term ends. At that point, the residence passes to grandchildren. If this is the case, and the generation-skipping exemption is then $1,100,000, the difference between the exemption and the value of the residence is subject to generation-skipping tax. That tax will be in addition to any federal gift tax that was paid when the trust was established.

In most cases, the risk and cost of the generation-skipping transfer tax are too high for a personal residence trust to be used for generation-skipping transfers. That is why personal residence trusts are used to make transfers to children, but not to other generations.

Subsequent Sale of a Residence

In a QPRT, the trustee has the ability to sell the residence. The Internal Revenue Code and regulations set out complex rules governing those sales. The rules also apply if the home is destroyed or is taken in a condemnation proceeding.

Generally, the trustee has two years to use the sales proceeds or insurance proceeds to acquire a new residence or to repair a damaged one. If, at the end of the two-year period, neither of these events have taken place or all of the proceeds have not been used, then the trust has to state what is to happen. There are basically two alternatives. The first is that the extra money is returned to the maker. This is not a particularly good result, because the maker ends up with the very assets he or she gave away, back in the maker's estate. In addition, the maker may have used valuable unified credit, which is irretrievably gone, wasted on a transaction that should have never been entered into.

The second alternative to using the proceeds is to create a grantor retained annuity trust (GRAT). Under the GRAT rules, the maker receives an annuity for the remaining term of the QPRT. Generally, a GRAT is not as gift-tax-efficient as a QPRT; the maker receives income back, which will be part of his or her estate.

It is not a good idea to create a QPRT with the thought that the residence will be sold. If it is sold, then a new residence of equal value should be purchased. If this is not done, then the alternatives are not attractive from an estate planning perspective.

Personal residence trusts can be very useful in transferring a valuable home to children. They are sophisticated and subject to a number of very exacting rules and regulations. Before embarking on personal residence trust planning, it is extremely important to understand all the ramifications of creating a trust, and to set up a trust that is state-of-the-art and backed by professional advisors.

37
Retirement Planning
"Long Life Deserves Good Planning"

Since the 1970s, there has been an explosion in retirement planning. Congress has passed numerous laws allowing all kinds of innovative retirement plans. Business in general has added and expanded retirement planning opportunities for employees. And, of course, there is a great deal of interest in retirement planning as America ages and the baby boomer generation begins to enter its silver years.

Retirement plans have an enormous impact on estate planning. How they are planned for and structured during one's lifetime and at one's death can have significant income and estate tax consequences. To understand these consequences, it is important to have a general understanding of the common types of retirement plans.

Types of Retirement Plans

There are a number of ways to classify retirement plans: employer-sponsored plans and individual plans; qualified plans and nonqualified plans; deferred compensation plans, stock bonus plans, stock option plans, death-benefit-only plans, and hybrid plans.

We have found that the easiest way to understand the many types of plans is to begin with plans that are qualified under the Internal Revenue Code. Generally speaking, qualified plans are those plans that are sanctioned by the Internal Revenue Code and that provide income tax incentives to employers and employees. These types of plans are instituted by employers for the benefit of employees.

The most common qualified plans are profit sharing plans (including 401(k) plans), money purchase pension plans, and defined benefit plans. Each of these plans allows the employer to take an income tax deduction for the amounts paid into the plan. An employee does not have to take his or her share of the contribution into income until the employee has the right to the share and actually takes it out of the plan and has access to it.

Within the categories of qualified plans, there are specific types of plans. For example, employee stock ownership plans (ESOPs) are allowed to hold the stock of the sponsoring company. There are separate and distinct rules for these types of plans, even though they are qualified plans. Other examples of qualified plans are savings incentive match plans for employees (SIMPLE plans) and simplified employee pension (SEP) plans.

Qualified plans are required to cover most of the employees in a business. There are very complicated rules about who must be allowed to participate in these plans. These rules also make sure that employees are vested in the plans over a relatively short period of time. The rules may require that the plan be subject to strict funding rules and that the plan be insured by an agency of the federal government.

Individual retirement accounts (IRAs) are not qualified plans. They are individual plans and, as such, are not generally used by employers as part of compensation plans. In fact, IRAs are covered under separate provisions of the Internal Revenue Code, and are not part of ERISA, the law that governs qualified plans.

Some companies sponsor IRA plans, but IRAs are not designed as compensation plans for business; they are savings plans. Contributions to these types of plans are made directly by the participant, not by the employer. There are rules as to who can contribute to these plans and how much of the contribution is tax deductible. The tax deductible amount that can be contributed to an IRA is far less than the maximum contributions allowed in qualified plans.

Some retirement plans are not qualified. For the most part, a nonqualified plan is one for which a company cannot take an immediate income tax deduction. On the employee's side, a nonqualified plan is usually one in which the company promises to make certain payments in the future.

A typical nonqualified plan is a deferred compensation plan. Under one of these plans, the company promises to pay compensation to the employee at some time in the future, usually at retirement. There is no assurance that the money will be paid, other than the company's promise. The payments are not deductible to the company until paid. Likewise, the employee does not take the payments into income until they are received.

Nonqualified plans do not have to cover all employees in a company and are almost always reserved to a few employees. Sometimes these plans are funded by life insurance or by a pool of money that is set aside for the future payments. The funds that are set aside, including life insurance contracts, must be subject to the claims of the company's creditors. That is why when the funds are set aside for the employees, they do not have to be included as income. If a company offered a nonqualified plan that actually set aside money in a way that the company's creditors could not access it, then the employees would have to take the amounts into income immediately.

Because nonqualified plans are mere promises to pay rather than separately funded plans, employees are concerned about the money being available when they retire. Methods have been invented to separate the funds while not making them so separate as to avoid the creditors of the company.

A Rabbi trust is such an attempt. A company that sets up a separate irrevocable trust to fund a nonqualified deferred compensation plan is said to have set up a Rabbi trust. Although the trust does hold separate funds for payment of the nonqualified benefits on behalf of the company, those funds must remain subject to the claims of the creditors of the company. The trust is merely a holding vehicle so that the company itself cannot spend the funds.

The Rabbi trust got its name because the concept of using a trust to set aside funds was first used by a synagogue for the benefit of its rabbi. The Internal Revenue Service attacked the device as being a funded plan, making the rabbi liable for income taxes on the amounts set aside. The courts held that the trust was subject to the claims of creditors and therefore the rabbi did not have to take the amounts in the trust into income.

Another method that is used to segregate funds is life insurance. Typically, the company purchases a cash value life insurance policy on the life of the employee. The company is the owner and beneficiary of the policy. When the employee retires, the company borrows funds from the policy to pay the deferred compensation that is owed to the employee.

If the employee dies during the period when he or she is being paid, then the death proceeds are used to pay off the remainder of the payments. If the employee dies before retirement, all or part of the death proceeds are paid to the family, trust, or estate of the employee. In all cases, when the funds are paid as part of compensation, they are deductible to the company and income to the recipient.

A variation of a nonqualified deferred compensation plan is a death-benefit-only plan (DBO). With a DBO, the company promises to pay a death benefit to a beneficiary who is named by the employee. Generally, the amount to be paid is funded by a life insurance policy on the life of the employee. When the death benefit is paid, the company takes an income tax deduction and the recipient pays income tax on the proceeds received.

Estate Tax Results
of Retirement Plans

With a few exceptions that we will discuss, both qualified and nonqualified retirement plans can have substantial negative estate planning consequences. Anytime retirement funds are paid after the death of the plan participant, at least two taxes apply: the federal estate tax and the federal income tax.

The full value of qualified retirement plans, including IRAs, is considered to be part of the participant's estate. The only exception to this rule is for pension plans that terminate on the death of the participant. For many reasons, it is impractical for a person to give a qualified plan to another, so there are very few methods for avoiding federal estate taxation of qualified plans and IRAs.

Nonqualified retirement plans are also included in the estate of the employee unless at some time the employee gave the rights to the plan to another person or a trust. Because nonqualified plans are not controlled by the same laws as qualified plans, it is possible to remove the proceeds from the estate of the employee with good, forward-thinking planning. However, this planning is not easy and should only be accomplished by an expert in nonqualified plans.

Now let's explore what it means to have the value of the plan included in the participant's estate. First, if the participant's spouse is the beneficiary of the plan, the value of the plan will be subject to the unlimited marital deduction. No estate tax will be due, regardless of the size of the plan, when the participant dies so long as the spouse is the beneficiary. When the spouse dies, the full remaining value of the plan will be included in his or her estate.

When the proceeds are included in an estate, they do not get a step-up in basis. Also, even if the proceeds are paid over a period of time, the tax is due nine months after the death of the owner or his or her spouse. This may create a situation in which tax is due, but there are no funds to pay the estate tax. Obviously, this is a result that should be avoided or planned for in advance.

Income Tax Results
of Retirement Plans

The technical term given to income that is earned by a decedent before his or her death, but paid after death, is income in respect of a decedent (IRD). Special income tax rules are associated with IRD, none of them very positive.

Not only is IRD included in the estate of the decedent, but the proceeds are also subject to income tax when received by the beneficiary. Yes, you read that right. IRD is taxed at least twice, once under the estate tax and once under the income tax. If you live in a state that has a death tax and an income tax, these taxes may also be assessed.

There is a small tax break that reduces the impact of the taxes: The beneficiary gets an income tax deduction for the estate tax attributable to each payment. At the end of each year, the recipient computes the estate tax that was associated with the IRD payments made during the year and itemizes the amount as a deduction. If the beneficiary does not itemize or cannot qualify for itemization, then the benefit is lost. Please understand that a tax deduction is only a partial offset to the estate taxes actually paid; it softens the blow, but it doesn't eliminate the impact. And federal income taxes are a maximum of 39.6 percent; estate taxes are as high as 55 percent. The rate differential creates a mismatch that the beneficiary has to pay.

Depending on the beneficiary's income tax rate and the amount of estate taxes paid, the overall tax rate on IRD may reach as high as 95 percent.

An exception to the income tax results of IRAs is the Roth IRA. The proceeds from a Roth IRA are not subject to income tax, but they are subject to estate tax. For purposes of estate planning and income tax planning, a Roth IRA is generally superior to a standard IRA.

Retirement Planning Alternatives

Because of the nature of IRD, there are few retirement plan alternatives that will substantially reduce its income and estate tax consequences. However, there are alternatives that may work for you.

For those who have large IRAs or qualified plans that will be subject to income and estate tax, the first step is to understand that eventually any funds left in these plans will be subject to taxes. Once that stark fact is assimilated, then a decision has to be made as to what impact that will have on an estate.

A number of people come to the conclusion that it is better to give the proceeds to charity than to see a vast majority of the fund go to taxes. These people, if married, name their spouse (or revocable living trust) as the primary beneficiary of their plan because of the unlimited marital deduction. After the death of the spouse, their planning names a favorite charity or charities as fund beneficiaries.

By naming a charity as the beneficiary, the money passes directly to charity without diminution from taxes. Because much of it could pass to the government otherwise, this allows people to at least control how the proceeds will be used.

A second solution is to create an irrevocable life insurance trust (ILIT) and fund it with enough life insurance to pay the taxes on the retirement plan. The ILIT proceeds are not subject to federal estate tax, so they can be fully used to pay all estate and income taxes on the retirement plan proceeds. ILITs are also used when the proceeds of a plan are paid to charity; the life insurance proceeds are used to replace the retirement plan proceeds.

The retirement plan itself can be the source of the premium payments for the ILIT, even though after-tax dollars are used. Because a majority of the funds in a retirement plan could be lost to income and estate tax anyway, plan participants should not avoid taking money out of the plan and buying life insurance to protect or replace the retirement plan proceeds. While buying life insurance as protection for heirs is not always the most efficient use of funds, in the majority of cases it can nevertheless be well advised.

ILITs are also used to fund the taxes on nonqualified retirement plans. Because the proceeds from these plans are also IRD and subject to estate and income tax, an ILIT is a source of tax-free cash to pay the taxes generated by the nonqualified deferred compensation amounts.

Finally, some financial planners have taken the view that it is better not to touch retirement plan proceeds for as long as possible. When forced to take the proceeds, they say to take the minimum amount out. The rationale behind this concept is that by growing the retirement funds on a tax-deferred basis (and delaying the payment of taxes for as long as possible), even after taxes, more assets will pass to heirs. Not all planners agree with this point of view, but it should be explored.

Perhaps deferral will create a better tax result; but be careful of the assumptions that are being made. Many of the favorable computations look good only if the participant lives for a long period of time and receives a fairly decent rate of return. If the deferral route is taken, it is wise to hedge the result by creating an ILIT with at least some life insurance, in case the growth projections are not as accurate as hoped.

Because of the complexity of the rules surrounding retirement planning, the better course for everyone is to read and study as much as possible. Consulting with advisors who rationally and patiently share the available alternatives is also important.

In our view, retirement planning is not sound planning at all unless you have a clear goal in mind. Many times, tax savings are not of the greatest concern to families. Factors such as health, family makeup, and availability of assets outside of the retirement plan all influence the type of planning that is appropriate.

38

Special Use Valuation

"Keeping the Farm in the Family"

Farmers and ranchers face unique federal estate tax problems. Over the years, farm and ranch income has been declining dramatically as a percentage of land value. Thus farmers and ranchers are continually forced into higher federal estate tax brackets and are unable to generate the income to pay those taxes. This inability to pay can, and often does, force their families to sell all or part of the family farm or ranch.

A family farm or ranch purchased forty years ago may have cost as little as $10 per acre. During that forty years, a city and its suburbs might have expanded to within a mile of that farm or ranch. Developers might pay $5,000 or more per acre in order to build houses on the farmland or ranchland. The farm or ranch may produce only enough income to feed and provide the basics for the agricultural family. If the land is valued in terms of its ability to produce agricultural income, it will not have a very high value. The difference in values depending on whether the property is valued at its agricultural use or its residential use can be staggering. If the federal government used the residential value for federal estate tax purposes, it would force almost every farm and ranch family off their land.

Recognizing this massive problem, Congress, as part of the Tax Reform Act of 1976, passed a relief provision for the special valuation of family farm and ranch property, and for real estate used in other types of family businesses as well. This relief provision is called special use valuation. Congress has tinkered with special use valuation over the years, and it has gotten easier to use. It has been helpful to many farmers and ranchers.

Special use valuation allows farmland and ranchland to be valued at its agricultural value instead of its value as residential property for federal estate tax purposes. This valuation method decreases the value of the farmer's or rancher's estate for federal estate tax purposes and gives the farm or ranch family a better opportunity to continue farm and ranch operations.

The value of farmland and ranchland in an agricultural estate can be reduced through special use valuation by as much as $750,000. The $750,000 amount, beginning in 1999, is subject to adjustment for inflation. The inflation adjustment is not necessarily made every year. Inflation must increase enough so that at least $10,000 is added to the previous year's inflation-adjusted amount. Check with your tax advisors to determine what the current amount is.

To qualify for special use valuation, the value of the farmer's or rancher's assets, including the land and personal property used in the farm or ranch, *less* the debt secured by that land and personal property, must be at least 50 percent of the total value of the estate. In addition, the value of the land itself must be equal to at least 25 percent of the estate. In qualifying under these percentage rules, the agricultural land is valued at its residential value. The agricultural land must have been used as farmland or ranchland for five of the eight years prior to the owner's death, and actively managed by the owner or other family members. This means that the owner or family member must materially participate in the decision making rather than being out in the field. Material participation generally means that they must regularly advise those persons managing the farm and participate in most decisions. Active management can include having the current owner rent the property to a family member. The owner must be a U.S. citizen or resident at the time of death.

The land also must pass upon the death of the owner to an heir who is a close family member. The qualified heir then must operate the farm or ranch for a period of time after the death of the original owner. All these rules must be met to qualify for special use valuation.

Owning agricultural property in joint tenancy or in a community property state may affect the application of the percentage test. If one-half of the estate is considered to be owned by the surviving spouse, a significant portion of the agricultural property will be ignored for purposes of the percentage test.

A family member can actively manage the farm or ranch on behalf of the owner, special use valuation can be retained, and the owner can qualify for Social Security benefits.

Special use valuation does not end with the closing of the original owner's estate. If the heirs dispose of all or part of the property subject to special use valuation within ten years of the original owner's death, the tax savings that originally resulted from special use valuation must be paid back to the government.

The Internal Revenue Service monitors the ten-year requirement by placing a tax lien on the property that was subject to special use valuation. Because it has a lien on the property, the IRS will know if the property is sold. The seller cannot sell the property until the lien is removed. The IRS gets paid.

A federal tax lien on property makes it difficult for its current owners to mortgage the property. As a result, the family members actively engaged in farming or ranching may find it difficult to borrow money to keep the farm or ranch going.

With the advent of the unlimited marital deduction, the farm and ranch owner will not owe any estate tax if sufficient property passes to the surviving spouse as long as the surviving spouse is a U.S. citizen, or special planning has been done for a noncitizen. Special use valuation is of no value to the owner under this circumstance because of the marital deduction. However, the special use valuation is available for the surviving spouse's estate, provided the surviving spouse actively manages the farm or ranch. This means that the surviving spouse must make some management decisions but does not have to be involved in the day-to-day operating decisions.

Special use valuation is a potential life saver for farm or ranch families. Like many provisions of the Internal Revenue Code, it has its traps. Applied wisely, however, special use valuation can keep our farms and ranches where they belong—in the family.

Requirements for Special Use Valuation

The value of the farm or ranch assets (*less* debts on them) must be at least 50 percent of the deceased owner's estate.

The value of the farmland or ranchland (*less* debts on it) must be at least 25 percent of the deceased owner's estate.

The property must have been actually managed by the deceased owner for five of the eight years prior to death and must have been used for farming or ranching during the same period.

A qualified heir must actually manage the property after the owner's death.

The land must be used as a farm or ranch for ten years after the owner's death.

The land is subject to a federal tax lien.

The land value can be reduced through special use valuation by as much as $750,000, which is subject to increase for inflation.

Special use valuation also applies to other types of family businesses.

Special use valuation may be particularly valuable to the surviving spouse.

39

Qualified Family-Owned Business Interests Exclusion

"Leaving More of Your Business to Your Family"

Sometimes, Congress has the best of intentions when it passes legislation; often, the law does not measure up to the intent. Great intentions with bad execution pretty much sums up the qualified family-owned business interests deduction. As a matter of fact, the law as first passed was so confusing and hard to apply, it was substantially changed a year later. The new law, however, remains terribly confusing and challenging.

The idea behind the qualified family-owned business interests deduction is to give an estate tax break to owners of a qualified family-owned business interest (QFOBI) so that it may pass to heirs who are active in that business.

This noble concept is obscured by a convoluted legislative scheme that appears to be more concerned about preventing abuse rather than allowing qualifying families to properly use it. With this warning, we will attempt to reduce the complexities of this convoluted tax law to their essence. As in all other complex tax matters, your professional advisors should be consulted to apply these intricate rules to your particular situation.

For those who qualify, there is a maximum estate QFOBI deduction of $675,000. However, for estates electing this deduction, the ability to use the applicable exclusion amount (unified credit) is generally limited to $625,000, and this is true regardless of future increases in the applicable exclusion amount. The result of combining these two independent tax laws is that a maximum of $1,300,000 of business value can be excluded from tax, even though the applicable exclusion amount will reach $1,000,000 in the year 2006.

Estates that cannot use the full $675,000 QFOBI deduction are not unduly penalized. For these estates, the $625,000 applicable exclusion amount is increased by the difference between $675,000 and the amount of the QFOBI deduction allowable. The formula for computing the applicable exclusion amount is $625,000 + ($675,000 − the value of the family-owned business). An easy way of remembering this formula is that the sum of the applicable exclusion amount and the value of the family-owned business must be $1,300,000 or less. Here is an example of how the interplay between the QFOBI deduction and the applicable exclusion amount works:

> Charlene owns a small sheep operation that produces fine wool. She dies in 2004, when the applicable exclusion amount is $850,000. The value of her ranch is greater than $675,000. Her estate is entitled to a QFOBI deduction of $675,000, and the applicable exclusion amount for her estate is $625,000.
>
> Had Charlene's ranch been worth $450,000, the applicable exclusion amount for her estate would be the full $850,000, and her estate could take the full deduction of $450,000. If the ranch's value were $560,000, the applicable exclusion amount would be $790,000. If Charlene died in a year in which the applicable exclusion amount was more than $850,000, say 2006 when it is $1,000,000, then the applicable exclusion amount would be $850,000.

Remember, the formula for computing the applicable exclusion amount is $625,000 + ($675,000 − the value of the family-owned business). The higher the value of the business, which can never exceed $675,000, the lower the applicable exclusion amount. The applicable exclusion amount will never be less than $625,000 or more than $1,000,000, and the amount of the QFOBI deduction will never exceed $675,000.

Qualifying for the QFOBI Deduction

There are five requirements to take advantage of the QFOBI deduction:

1. The deceased owner must have been a citizen or resident of the United States at death.

2. An election must be made on the federal estate tax return.

3. A written agreement consenting to the deduction must be signed by all who received an interest in the QFOBI property and must be attached to the federal estate tax return.

4. The sum of the adjusted value of all of the owner's QFOBIs plus includable gifts must be greater than 50 percent of the adjusted gross estate.

5. The deceased owner (or his or her family) must have owned and materially participated in the business's operation for five or more of the eight years preceding the owner's death.

Adjustments to Value

Adjustments have to be made to the value of the deceased owner's estate in order to determine if the estate will qualify for a QFOBI deduction under the greater than 50 percent rule. The adjusted value of the qualified family-owned business interests is the amount of those interests that would otherwise be included in the estate, reduced by claims against and debt of the estate that exceed:

qualified residence debt;

medical or educational debt for the deceased owner (or his or her spouse or children); and

any other debt not exceeding $10,000.

For example, assuming that Charlene's QFOBI interest is valued at $675,000, if the total claims against her estate and other debt totaled $200,000, including a $50,000 residential mortgage, the QFOBI deduction would be $525,000. This amount is computed by reducing the $675,000 value by the $200,000 debt, which equals $475,000, and adding back the $50,000 of debt on her residence. If Charlene had medical or educational debt, this too would be added back.

It is not uncommon for business owners to make lifetime gifts to family members to reduce the value of their estates. To prevent gifts to family members of family-owned businesses from being used to reduce the owner's estate to qualify for the QFOBI deduction, gifts made to family members after 1976 (provided the recipient of the gift still owns the property at the owner's death) are added to the adjusted value of the owner's QFOBI property for purposes of the 50 percent test. These gifts are also added back to the adjusted gross estate.

In contrast, if the owner makes gifts of other property in order to qualify for the QFOBI deduction, most property, other than family-owned business interests given by the owner to his or her spouse within ten years of death, and gifts made to others within three years of death, are added back to the adjusted gross estate. Annual exclusion gifts to family members are **not** added back to adjusted gross estate.

Qualifying Business Interests

A business interest must be an interest in a trade or business carried on by the deceased owner or one or more of his or her family members. Family members are the same as those listed under the special use valuation rules. The business may be a proprietorship, a partnership (or a limited liability company), or a corporation. If the business is a partnership or corporation, the owner and his or her family must own at least 50 percent of the entity. Alternatively, if two families own at least 70 percent of an entity, or three families own at least 90 percent of an entity, the deceased owner and his or her family must own at least 30 percent.

Businesses with principal places of business outside the United States, businesses whose stock is traded on established securities markets, and businesses in which more than 35 percent of the adjusted gross income is personal holding income cannot qualify as QFOBIs. In addition, if a business holds cash and marketable securities in excess of the business's needs for working capital, then these assets reduce the value. Likewise, assets not used in the active conduct of a trade or business, and which produce personal holding income, do not constitute QFOBI assets.

Recapture

The estate tax savings resulting from the QFOBI are subject to recapture for ten years. This recapture is not as harsh as special use valuation recapture, however. In addition, the recapture amount is reduced 20 percent per year after six years.

Some Planning Tips

If you are interested in qualifying for the QFOBI deduction, consider making annual exclusion gifts of non QFOBI assets to help ensure that your estate will meet the 50 percent threshold.

Consider revising the marital deduction formula clauses in your estate planning documents to reflect this new deduction. Generally, QFOBI property should pass to the decedent's family members in a specific bequest or to a nonmarital trust with only family members as beneficiaries. Passing the QFOBI property to the marital trust will waste the QFOBI deduction.

If you own a farm or ranch on which you live, it is important to allocate some of your debt, if you have any, to the farm or ranch house. The amount allocated will qualify for residence debt, which may help your deduction.

Finally, it is important that you work with knowledgeable advisors. As you can see, the rules to qualify for the QFOBI deduction are extremely complex, and we have only scratched the surface in terms of the complexities. Good advisors will be familiar with the QFOBI rules. They can assist you in such matters as documenting the working capital needs of your business and helping your business to rid itself of passive assets that will reduce the QFOBI deduction.

Planning for the QFOBI deduction should not occur in isolation. Rather, estate planning practitioners should utilize the deduction as part of an overall estate and business succession plan for their clients. For closely held business owners, and particularly farm owners, the QFOBI deduction offers significant planning opportunities if properly coordinated with the overall estate plan.

If family members do not want to continue the business for at least six years after the client's death, or if clients have entered into buy –sell agreements for the business with someone who is not a qualified heir, the QFOBI deduction is largely irrelevant. Under these circumstances, practitioners should utilize other methods to minimize clients' estate taxes.

40

Using Assets
of a Corporation
to Pay Death Costs
"Trading Dollars for Stock"

Many of our clients own all or part of the stock of a successful corporation that has cash or assets that can readily be converted to cash. Their estates consist primarily of their corporate stock. This stock may be hard to sell or difficult to borrow against at their deaths. The money needed by their beneficiaries to pay death taxes and expenses is, unfortunately, in the wrong place; it is in the corporation, not the estate.

The federal government has long recognized the difficulty of using corporate assets to pay personal death taxes and, as a result, passed section 303 of the Internal Revenue Code. Section 303 allows corporations to provide their assets to pay the federal and state death taxes, funeral expenses, and other death expenses of deceased stockholders. Professional estate planners refer to this technique as a section 303 redemption.

A section 303 redemption is merely the purchase by a corporation of enough of a deceased stockholder's stock of that corporation to pay all or part of the deceased shareholder's state and federal death taxes, funeral expenses, and administrative expenses. Administrative expenses include expenses involved in the operation and maintenance of an estate.

For example, a deceased businessperson owned one million shares in XYZ Corporation worth $1 million, or $1.00 per share. The state and federal death taxes and the funeral and administrative expenses of the estate total $325,000. Assuming the stock meets all of the technical requirements of section 303, the estate may sell $325,000 worth of stock (325,000 shares) back to XYZ Corporation. The cash received by the estate in exchange for the stock *must* be used to pay the deceased stockholder's death expenses. As a result, cash or other liquid assets in the corporation have been successfully exchanged for the nonliquid stock.

Section 303 is also a benefit to a corporate owner because of the income tax savings it can generate. Generally, a stockholder who sells only part of his or her stock in a corporation back to that same corporation will be subject to federal income tax on the sale proceeds as if those sale proceeds were a dividend. A dividend is a terrible way to be taxed—a dividend creates two federal income taxes.

Double taxation occurs with a dividend because the money that a corporation uses to buy its own stock is usually money that has already been subject to corporate federal income tax. For example, assume that a corporation is in the 34 percent tax bracket. A dollar of profit is made and the corporation pays $0.34 on that $1. This is the first tax. The $0.66 left is then used by the corporation to purchase its stock from the selling stockholder. The selling stockholder receives the $0.66 for his or her stock and, if the stockholder has held the stock for more than one year, the $0.66 will likely be taxed at 20 percent. The result is that the selling stockholder has about $0.53 of the dollar that was originally profit in his or her corporation. Because of the double tax, this represents a combined income tax rate of 47 percent.

On the death of a stockholder, the stock's cost basis is increased, or stepped up, to its value as of the day of the stockholder's death. We have discussed step-up in basis rules in other chapters. If the stock is sold back to the corporation, there should be little if any income tax. An example will help you understand:

> The deceased stockholder originally paid $100,000 (cost basis) for 325,000 shares of stock that the estate sold back to the corporation. If the stockholder sold that same stock to a third party before death, the gain would have been $225,000 ($325,000 less $100,000). If the stock was worth $325,000 on death, however, the step-up in basis rule gives the stock a new cost basis of $325,000. As a result, if the stock were sold back to the corporation for $325,000 under section 303, there would be no gain or federal income tax at all.

Now that we have explained the advantages of section 303 for the estates of corporate owners, let's discuss some of the requirements that must be met in order to use it. (Please refer to Figure 40-1.)

The value of the stock that was owned by the deceased stockholder has to be 35 percent of the value of the adjusted gross estate to qualify for section 303. Basically, the adjusted gross estate is the value of the estate *less* expenses and debts of that estate.

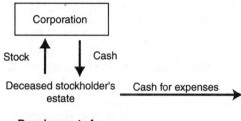

**Requirements for
Section 303 Redemption**

The value of all the stock in the deceased
stockholder's estate must be at least
35% of the adjusted gross estate.

The cash received from the corporation
must all be used for federal and state
death taxes, funeral expenses, and other
death expenses.

Figure 40-1. Requirements for section 303 redemption.

There are other requirements that must be met in order to qualify under section 303. Some of these requirements deal with the time periods under which the stock must be sold. These are complicated and should be discussed with your professional advisers.

There can be disadvantages related to the use of a section 303 redemption. If the corporation does not have liquid assets, section 303 may not be beneficial. The corporation is allowed to distribute property other than money in a section 303 redemption, but if the property distributed cannot be sold by the estate within the time provided in section 303, then the distribution will be taxed as a dividend, a catastrophic result.

Another potential disadvantage of a section 303 redemption is that the deceased stockholder's family may lose control of the family corporation. For example, if the deceased stockholder owned 51 percent of the corporation before death and enough stock is sold back to the corporation under section 303, the family may be left with far less than 50 percent ownership; this can occur when there are stockholders other than family members. When a section 303 redemption is used without proper advice, outsiders can end up controlling a family corporation.

A section 303 redemption usually takes cash out of a corporation. If that corporation needs its cash to survive after the death of its principal shareholder, a section 303 redemption may kill the goose that could lay more golden eggs.

The last disadvantage of section 303 is that it can create a tax trap for the unwary. This section of the Internal Revenue Code is fairly simple when compared with other code sections; however, the technical requirements of section 303 are intricate and, if not thoroughly understood, can result in a tax-planning disaster. The following example should prove our point:

> Bob, a stockholder of Bolt Corporation, reads a book on estate planning and is interested in the chapter on section 303 redemptions. Bob discovers that 35 percent of the value of his estate must be corporate stock to qualify. He calculates the value of his Bolt stock and finds its value is less than 35 percent of the value of his estate. As a result, our self-taught stockholder figures out that if he gives some property (other than Bolt stock) to his spouse, his estate will qualify. He gives property to his spouse and then dies two years later.
>
> Because of one of the intricacies of section 303, the amount of the gift Bob made to his spouse is *added back* to his estate. The result is loss of section 303 treatment.
>
> If Bolt Corporation, following the section 303 planning, buys its stock back, all the proceeds received by the estate are taxed *as a dividend.*

Section 303 provides an easy way to convert nonliquid stock into liquid dollars on the death of a stockholder. Used wisely, it can be of great benefit to the beneficiaries of a corporate businessowner's estate; but it is a technical section of the Internal Revenue Code, and it should never be used without expert professional advice in both its conception and its application.

41

Giving It to Charity

"Good Works Deserve Good Benefits"

Methods of charitable giving have been the subject of significant numbers of technical texts. In a society attuned to charity, it is only logical that a myriad of methods is available to all of us to make charitable giving attractive. This chapter is aimed at the person who wants to obtain a rudimentary knowledge of the vast income tax, gift tax, and estate tax opportunities afforded by making gifts to charity.

Charitable giving falls into a few general categories. These categories include outright gifts, gifts of a part of or an interest in property, and gifts in trust. All these methods can be used during one's lifetime or at one's death; each has separate federal income tax, gift tax, and estate tax implications.

Outright gifts of property are probably the most commonly used form of giving. People making an outright gift can make their gifts in money, personal property, or real property.

To receive all the tax benefits that can result from a charitable gift, the gift must be made to an Internal Revenue Code qualified charity. To qualify, the charity must be a public, semipublic, or private foundation that has received special approval from the IRS. When you make a gift, either during lifetime or after your death, it is important that you check with the charitable organization to make sure that it has IRS approval. IRS approval is generally given if the charity is a governmental agency; a religious, charitable, scientific, literary, or educational organization; or a war veterans' or domestic fraternal organization.

A lifetime charitable gift has two distinct tax advantages. The first is that an income tax deduction is generated. The second is that assets, along with their future appreciation, are removed from the value of an estate.

Normally, the income tax deduction that can be taken by the giver is limited to 50 percent of adjusted gross income (AGI). AGI is not taxable income; it is all income *less* certain deductions. The income tax deduction is limited, however, to 30 percent of AGI when the gift is made to semipublic or private charities. These include certain veterans' and fraternal organizations and certain private foundations. When checking to see whether an organization is IRS-approved, you should also check its status as a public, semipublic, or private charity.

There is another income tax deduction limitation that can apply when giving property to charity. It applies generally to property which, if sold would be taxed at the capital gain rate. It applies generally to property which, if sold, would be taxed at the capital gain rate. The deduction that applies to this type of property is limited to either 50 or 30 percent of AGI when it is given to a public charity and 20 percent of AGI when it is given to a semipublic or private charity.

When giving capital gain property to a public charity, you can elect to have the gift qualify for either the 50 or 30 percent deduction limits. Qualifying for the 30 percent limitation is the simplest. The full fair market value of the property can be deducted from AGI, as long as the deduction does not exceed 30 percent of AGI. If it does, the excess can be used in the next five years.

If you wish to use the 50 percent limitation, then the total amount of the deduction is not allowed. The deduction is limited to the basis or cost of the property. This amount is then subject to the 50 percent limitation. Any excess cannot be carried forward.

These rules can be illustrated as follows:

> If your AGI is $100,000 and you give $60,000 in cash to a public charity, then only $50,000 can be deducted in the current year. The remaining $10,000 can be used in the future for up to five years. But if the $60,000 is given to a semipublic or private charity, only $30,000 can be deducted in the current year (30 percent of $100,000). The remainder can be carried forward to the next five years.
>
> Let us assume that your gift is of stock that you bought for $45,000 and that it is currently valued at $55,000. A sale of the stock would create a $10,000 taxable gain.
>
> A gift of the stock to a public charity using the 30 percent rule would result in a $30,000 deduction from your AGI in that current year. The remaining $25,000 could be deducted in a future year, as long as it is deducted within the next five years.
>
> If you choose the 50 percent limitation, then your cost basis, $45,000, is deducted in the current year.

A gift of this stock to a semipublic or private charity will result in a deduction that will be limited to 20 percent of your AGI, or $20,000. The remaining $35,000 can be carried over for the next five years.

There are further limitations on the amount that you can deduct when making a gift of appreciated property to a public charity. One example is that, if you give a work of art to a hospital, your deduction is limited. Because the hospital cannot generally use artwork to further its exempt purpose, you can only deduct the original cost of the work of art.

These income tax rules, believe it or not, are not exhaustive. A lot of other income tax rules can come into play, depending on the nature of the property and the type of charity to which you are giving it. For example, under TRA 1986 and the Revenue Reconciliation Act of 1990, giving away real property and some types of personal property owned for less than one year generates another tax called the alternative minimum tax, which may result in making the gift less attractive. You can see how important it is for you to consult a tax adviser before making a charitable gift other than a gift of cash.

While charitable giving almost always has income tax ramifications, direct charitable giving, providing it follows the rules, never results in gift taxes. A charitable gift made within three years of your death generally cannot be brought back into your estate for federal estate tax purposes. An exception to this rule is a gift of life insurance as well as other minor types of gifts.

An outright gift upon death has no income tax advantages or disadvantages. But for federal estate tax purposes, the value of a gift made to a qualified charity does result in a deduction equal to the fair market value of the gift.

Unlike the income tax deduction rules for charitable gifts, there is *no* percentage limitation for gifts made at death.

If a charitably minded individual is in ill health and may not live, a lifetime charitable gift should be considered instead of a charitable gift on death. A lifetime gift has the potential advantage of reducing income taxes as well as reducing the giver's estate for federal estate tax purposes, as shown in Figure 41-1.

Many people want to give property to charity at their deaths but want to retain the property for their use during their lifetimes. They would also like, if possible, to receive a current income tax deduction. The Internal Revenue Code allows both of these benefits through the gift of a remainder interest to charity.

A gift of a remainder interest that is not in trust is restricted to a farm or a personal residence. This type of gift allows the giver to retain a life estate in the property. Thus the giver can use the property, receive income from

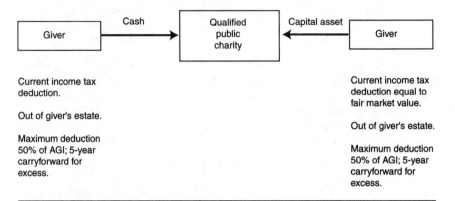

Figure 41-1. Outright gift of cash or capital asset while giver is alive.

the property, and live on the property during life. At the death of the giver, the property automatically passes to the charity.

The value of the remainder interest can be determined under Internal Revenue Code guidelines. Valuation is based on the life expectancy of the giver of the property; if a husband and wife are joint givers, their joint life expectancy can also be calculated. The value of the remainder interest is a deductible expense in the year the remainder interest is given. In addition to this income tax advantage, the asset passes to charity at death and is therefore removed from the estate of the giver. Remember, the gift of a remainder interest that is not in trust is restricted to a farm or personal residence. (See Figure 41-2.)

Gifts to charity from a trust can take many forms. In our experience, the most commonly used charitable trusts are the remainder trust and the lead

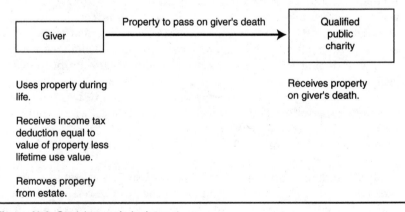

Figure 41-2. Outright remainder interest.

trust. These vehicles are extremely complex in terms of the rules that govern them. Our discussion is directed toward an understanding of their basic principles.

Charitable Remainder Trust

A charitable remainder trust is a trust to which the maker of the trust transfers income-producing property irrevocably and then retains an income interest in the trust property for the maker or the maker's family. (See Figure 41-3.)

When the income interest retained by the giver or the giver's family is a fixed amount of the value of the property at the time it is transferred to the trust, the trust is called a charitable remainder annuity trust. When the income interest that is retained by the giver or the giver's family can vary depending on changes in the annual value of the trust fund, the trust is called a charitable remainder unitrust. Regardless of which trust is used, the income must be at least 5 percent of the value of the property in the trust.

A charitable remainder annuity trust is not popular during inflationary times because of its inflexibility. It tends to benefit the charity more than the giver or the giver's family because inflation increases the value of the trust, but the income distributions are fixed as a percentage of the value of the trust property when the property was originally placed in the trust. Thus more of the trust property is left to charity.

A charitable remainder unitrust, however, tends to favor the giver and the giver's family because the income distributions increase as the trust assets increase.

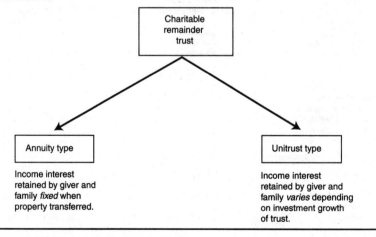

Figure 41-3. Types of charitable remainder trusts.

In both these remainder trusts, the beneficiaries of the trusts have a lifetime interest in a percentage value of the assets. At death, the remaining trust assets pass automatically to the named charity or charities. (See Figure 41-4.)

All charitable remainder trusts are similar to remainder interests in property. The income belongs to the beneficiaries, and whatever is left belongs to charity. There is an income tax deduction available to the giver at the time the property is put into the trust in the amount of the present value of the remainder interest. This amount can be calculated by using Internal Revenue Code guidelines, as we discussed earlier.

Charitable Lead Trust

A charitable lead trust is the reverse of a charitable remainder trust. Instead of providing income to the beneficiaries and giving the property to chari-

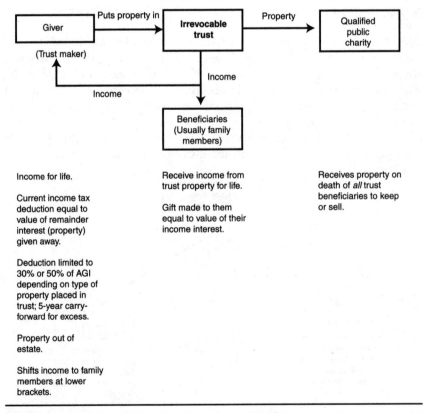

Figure 41-4. Charitable remainder trust (annuity or unitrust).

ty, a lead trust gives income to charity for a period of time and passes property to the giver's beneficiaries, free of federal estate tax. (See Figure 41-5.)

A lead trust involves valuing the remainder interest of the property to be placed in trust. As we mentioned, it is possible to value the remainder interest of property. The value of the remainder interest in this case, however, results in a taxable gift to the beneficiaries. It is a gift of a future interest and therefore is not eligible for the annual exclusion. If the lead trust is structured properly by a professional estate planner, however, the gift tax, in many instances, can be virtually eliminated.

The value of the income interest in a charitable lead trust must also be valued. The value of the income interest may be income tax deductible to the giver in the year the property is placed in the lead trust. The income tax deduction that the giver can take is limited to 30 percent of AGI. This is true regardless of whether the charity is public, semipublic, or private. The big limitation is, however, that the giver only gets an income tax de-

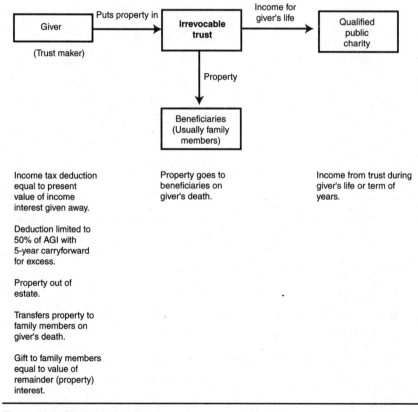

Figure 41-5. Charitable lead trust.

Table 41-1
Gifts to Public Charities

Gift Method	Description	Benefits to Maker or Family	Limitation	Income Tax Consequences	Gift Tax Consequences	Estate Tax Consequences	Charity Receives
1. Cash	Outright while giver alive	Tax	50% of AGI; 5-year carryforward for excess	Current deduction	None	Out of	Cash
2. Cash	On death from estate	Tax	None	None	None	Deduction	Cash
3. Capital assets	Outright while giver alive	Tax	30% or 50% of AGI; 5-year carryforward for 30% limit	Current deduction	None	Out of	Capital assets to keep or sell
4. Capital assets	On death from estate	Tax	None	None	None	Deduction equal to fair market value	Capital assets to keep or sell

Table 41-1 (continued)
Gifts to Public Charities

Gift Method	Description	Benefits to Maker or Family	Limitation	Income Tax Consequences	Gift Tax Consequences	Estate Tax Consequences	Charity Receives
5. Outright remainder interest	Giver keeps income and use of property for life	Tax and use of property for life	Personal residence or farm *only*	Deduction equal to value of remainder interest	None	Out of	Property on death of giver
6. Remainder trust	Giver puts property in trust	Tax and family retains income for their lives	50% or 30% of AGI depending on type of property put in trust; 5-year carryforward for excess	Current deduction equal to value of remainder interest	Gift to family members equal to value of their income interest	Out of	Exclusive control of property on deaths of all trust beneficiaries, to keep or sell
7. Lead trust	Giver puts property in trust	Tax and property goes to family beneficiaries when trust terminates	30% of AGI; 5-year carryforward for excess	Deduction limited to first year, if taken at all	Gift to family members equal to value of remainder interest they will receive	Out of	Income from trust for giver's life or term of years

duction in the year the property is given to the trust. Worse yet, in future years, the income is taxed to the giver.

Because of this income tax disadvantage, many people elect not to take the income tax deduction. If they so elect, and the trust is drafted correctly, none of the lead trust income will be taxed to them.

A lead trust can be beneficial for several reasons:

The maker removes property from the estate, free of federal estate tax, while passing it to chosen beneficiaries.

The charity has full use of all the income from the property.

As shown in Table 41-1, charitable giving is a broad area, encompassing not only federal estate and gift tax planning but also federal income tax planning. The array of charitable giving techniques is limited only by one's imagination and, as always, certain provisions of the Internal Revenue Code. If you are genuinely interested in charitable giving, seek expert assistance.

42

An Estate Planning Summary

"Passing the Bucks"

We know of no average or representative estate planning situation that could be used as an example or illustration to summarize all the estate planning principles and techniques we have discussed. In our experience, people have individual estates requiring individual planning techniques.

There are, however, certain basics or universals common to the estate planning process. We summarize them here:

Inventory the assets that you own.

Know where all of your title papers are located, and understand how you have taken title.

If title is in your name alone, you own the property in fee simple and can give it away, sell it, or leave it to whom you please. If you own it in tenancy in common, you only own part of it and can only give, sell, or leave your part. If you own property in joint tenancy, you own all of it with someone else. You may give your interest away or even sell it, but you cannot dispose of it on death.

The laws of the state of your domicile will provide an estate plan for you if you do not provide your own.

If you choose to accomplish your planning by using a will, you should remember that wills are only effective on death and require a public probate process. In addition, your will may not control the passage of all your property. If you move to another state, you should have your will reviewed—each state's laws are different, and your will may have to be rewritten.

Your will does not help you if you become so disabled that you can no longer handle your financial affairs. Absent disability planning, you may have to face a living probate.

Probate, whether for disability or death, involves unnecessary red tape and expense; it puts the real control in the judge's chambers. Probate can and should be avoided.

Federal estate taxes are imposed on your right to transfer almost all your property interests on death. Estate tax is levied on the fair market value of your property and is generally paid within nine months of death; it is paid before your beneficiaries receive their inheritance.

The federal estate tax rules generally only apply to estates greater than $1,000,000 beginning in 2006. Prior to that time, the amount that is sheltered from estate tax is phased in. The maximum tax bracket is 55 percent (60% for asset values between $10,000,000 and $17,184,000). Spouses in all states can give or leave an unlimited amount of property to their U.S. citizen spouses tax-free. The only requirement associated with the unlimited marital deduction is that surviving spouses receive all of the income from the property during their lifetimes.

Federal estate tax can be deferred in estates that lack liquidity or in those in which 35 percent of the value consists of closely held business interests. If a family business is incorporated and certain technical tax requirements are met, the surviving family may trade corporate dollars to the estate in return for stock with no adverse tax consequences. Congress has also provided special relief for businesses and farm and ranch families who wish to retain ownership of their farms or ranches following the deaths of the farm or ranch owners.

The federal estate and gift tax systems have been unified for some time. The $1,000,000 applicable exclusion amount and the unlimited marital deduction apply to gifts made during life as well as on death.

The law allows you to make annual exclusion gifts to anyone of up to $10,000 (adjusted for inflation) without the requirement of filing a federal gift tax return. If your spouse chooses to split the gift with you, the amount doubles. You should exercise care to avoid inadvertent gifts. How you give may be as important as the amount and nature of your gifts.

If you make a gift to your noncitizen spouse, the annual exclusion is $100,000 because the unlimited marital deduction only applies to U.S. citizen spouses. This amount is also adjusted for inflation, as is the $10,000 annual exclusion. Most states have their own death and gift taxes. Always consider your state's laws when planning.

Your property interests receive a step-up in basis at your death. This fact should be taken into consideration when structuring your plan.

Trusts are truly the estate planner's golf clubs because they can accomplish just about any of your objectives. Any number of separate trusts can be created in a single trust document. A death trust is called a testamentary trust and can only be created in your will. A living trust is always created during your lifetime. A living trust that allows you the right to change your mind and thereby change the trust is called a revocable living trust; one that cannot be changed is called an irrevocable living trust. A revocable living trust does not involve a gift; an irrevocable trust does.

An irrevocable living trust commonly used to give property to minors is the 2503(c) trust.

A revocable living trust can provide for the control, coordination, and distribution of your property while you are alive as well as on your death. It can also provide for your care and needs as well as those of your beneficiaries. Revocable living trusts are not public and are good in all states. They are extremely difficult for disgruntled heirs to attack.

Your revocable living trust can be unfunded, partially funded, or totally funded during your lifetime. It can also be funded subsequent to your death. Your trust can be funded directly, through the use of a nominee partnership, or, in some states, through other techniques such as unrecorded deeds, POD designations, and postmortem assignments. A properly funded revocable living trust avoids the probate process.

Your trust planning will only be as good as the performance of your trustees. Trustees are totally responsible for expert performance and judgment while following the written instructions provided in your trust document. Trustees have awesome power, accountability, and liability, all wrapped together in their roles as superagents.

Both individual and institutional trustees have their strengths and weaknesses. You should select the types of trustees that best serve your planning purposes. Trustees are compensated. Institutional trustees publish fee schedules that are pretty much the same. Individual trustees usually negotiate their fees within parameters set by local state statutes or court rules.

Giving property to a minor can be difficult. Under the laws of most states, in order to make a gift to a minor, you must set up a Uniform Gifts to Minors Act or Uniform Transfers to Minors Act account, establish a Totten trust, or fund a living trust created for the minor's benefit.

Property left directly to a minor will be waylaid in a court-imposed custodianship until the minor reaches legal age. Leaving property directly to a minor involves a great deal of red tape; it depersonalizes the planning process and can create confusion and insecurity for your loved ones while generating substantial expense and delay.

When planning for children, you should provide for a succession of guardians and discuss your situation with the guardians you choose; it is always a good idea to share your planning objectives with them.

How you divide and distribute your property among your loved ones is your business. However, some general rules of thumb are: Do not divide your property among your children until the youngest of your children is an adult. Once your property is divided, you can provide for different distribution dates for each child to allow for specific thoughts you may have with regard to each. It is important for you to recognize that you *can* control how you wish your property to pass to your children and grandchildren. If you wish to bypass your children in favor of your grandchildren, you must take into account the generation-skipping federal estate tax rules.

When planning for your spouse, you must consider your own state's law and the rights it gives your spouse to your property regardless of your planning attempts to the contrary. You may, however, avail yourself of two planning techniques: premarriage and after-marriage contracts. Given a choice between the two, always opt for the former; they are valid and binding if fair and fairly made and have always been favored under the laws of most states.

The number of planning possibilities available when planning for a spouse is staggering. There is no hypothetical best or optimum planning approach that can be used when planning for a spouse today. Great care must be taken to analyze all the spousal planning possibilities before you select that best personal tax choice.

Your life insurance program should be coordinated with, and become an integral part of, your total estate plan. Life insurance that you own on your life will be federal estate taxable on your death and may be taxed by your state as well. It is important for you to properly record both primary and contingent beneficiary designations with your agent. Never make your estate or minors the direct beneficiaries of your insurance proceeds.

Reexamine your life insurance portfolio. Insuring the life of the younger spouse makes excellent sense in light of the federal estate tax rules.

Life insurance can be purchased and structured to totally avoid federal estate tax. In general, this is best accomplished through the use of an irrevocable life insurance trust. ILITs can be structured by estate planning specialists to accommodate almost any type of insurance you may own.

Some estate planning techniques are often not appropriate and do not always work. These include cross-ownership of life insurance policies, joint tenancy, Uniform Transfers to Minors Act accounts, and general powers of attorney. There are also some estate planning gimmicks that never seem to work. These include form books, hiding property in a safe-deposit box, and attempting total tax avoidance through the use of a so-called constitutional or pure equity trust.

Protecting your assets from creditors is always an estate planning consideration. There are a number of ways that you can protect your assets, including insurance, investing in exempt assets, and creating entities such as limited partnerships and offshore asset protection trusts.

Often, retirement benefits represent the largest assets in an estate. Knowing how to treat retirement benefits as part of your estate planning is critical in creating an effective estate plan.

While Congress has curtailed many of the traditional estate freezing techniques, many opportunities remain. Family limited partnerships and grantor retained income trusts can be very effective in freezing an estate. In addition, these devices can be used to substantially discount the value of gifts, allowing a much greater amount to be given away.

Installment sales are complicated and have been substantially curtailed. Under some circumstances, especially when used with an intentionally defective grantor trust, they can help you as a seller because they can allow you to get appreciating assets out of your estate and, at the same time, create tax-free cash flow. If you are a buyer, an installment sale will allow you to purchase an appreciating asset under favorable terms. If you like the installment sales law but desire potentially higher benefits, you may wish to consider a private annuity. A private annuity can be designed so that the value of your appreciating assets and the value of the promissory obligation are *both* totally removed from your estate; the danger is in the gamble between your real and anticipated life expectancy.

A personal residence trust is an excellent method for reducing the value of your estate by giving your primary residence or a vacation home to your children. The value of the home is discounted, you may treat it as your own for the duration of the trust, and after the trust ends, you may rent your home back from your children. Substantial tax benefits can be derived from such an arrangement.

If you desire to make contributions of cash or assets other than cash to qualified charities, either currently or on death, you may receive tax benefits for your good works. The rules surrounding the income tax, estate tax, and gift tax deductibility of your munificence are extremely complex. Always seek out expert assistance in planning for your charitable objectives.

Estate planning is no place for loners. Professional advisers should be selected for the knowledge they possess within their particular disciplines. All your advisers should participate in your estate planning process and should work well not only with you, but also with each other.

It may be worthwhile for you to seek the advice and counsel of a collaborative group of professionals who work together on a regular basis. These professionals should be from the law, accounting, insurance, and financial planning professions. This type of collaborative group will be able to help you far more than the traditional team of unrelated advisors.

If you properly approach the estate planning process, you can be assured that you will be successful in "passing your bucks."

Appendix A

Getting Organized

PERSONAL INFORMATION

FAMILY INFORMATION

Name _____Nickname _____

Home address _____City _____State _____Zip _____

Home telephone _____Birthdate _____Social Security number _____

Employer _____Position _____

Business address _____City _____State _____Zip _____

Business telephone _____

Spouse's name _____Nickname _____

Birthdate _____Social Security number _____

Employer _____Position _____

Business address _____City _____State _____Zip _____

Business telephone _____

Your Children (use full names)   BIRTHDATE

_____ _____

_____ _____

_____ _____

_____ _____

Spouse's Children (if different from above)   BIRTHDATE

_____ _____

_____ _____

_____ _____

_____ _____

Advisers   TELEPHONE

Accountant _____ _____

Attorney_____ _____

Primary personal bank_____ _____

Stockbroker_____ _____

Referred to our firm by _____ _____

CASH

Name of Institution	TYPE*	A/C NUMBER	OWNER†	AMOUNT

*Checking Account (CA), Savings Account (SA), Certificate of Deposit (CD).
†Husband (H), Wife (W), Joint (JT), Tenants in Common (TC), Community Property (CP).

NOTE: If account is in your name for benefit of a minor, please specify and give minor's name.

NOTES RECEIVABLE

Name of Debtor	DATE OF NOTE	DATE NOTE DUE	OWED TO*	CURRENT BALANCE OWED

*Husband (H), Wife (W), Joint (JT), Tenants in Common (TC), Community Property (CP).

BONDS

Description (*U.S. Savings Bonds, corporate, municipal, etc.*)	OWNER†	FACE VALUE

†Husband (H), Wife (W), Joint (JT), Tenants in Common (TC), Community Property (CP).
If bond is owned either JT or TC with someone other than spouse, please furnish name and relationship.
Note: Please put ✓ next to bearer bonds.

REAL ESTATE

For which you have either a deeded or land contract interest *(Land or buildings that you own in partnership with someone else should be listed in the Partnership Interests section.):*

General description and/or address	OWNER*	FAIR MARKET VALUE	MORTGAGE
_____	_____	_____	_____
_____			
_____	_____	_____	_____
_____			
_____	_____	_____	_____
_____			
_____	_____	_____	_____
_____			
_____	_____	_____	_____

*Husband (H), Wife (W), Joint (JT), Tenants in Common (TC), Community Property (CP).
If property is owned either JT or TC with someone other than spouse, please furnish name and relationship.
NOTE: If two or more names are on deed or contract without stating type of ownership, please use "?".

CORPORATE BUSINESS INTERESTS

Privately owned *(not publicly traded)*

Company	NUMBER OF SHARES	BUY/SELL AGREEMENT*	PERCENTAGE OWNERSHIP	OWNER†	VALUE
_____	_____	_____	_____	_____	_____
_____	_____	_____	_____	_____	_____
_____	_____	_____	_____	_____	_____
_____	_____	_____	_____	_____	_____
_____	_____	_____	_____	_____	_____
_____	_____	_____	_____	_____	_____
_____	_____	_____	_____	_____	_____
_____	_____	_____	_____	_____	_____
_____	_____	_____	_____	_____	_____

*Please check (✓) if a buy/sell agreement exists.

†Husband (H), Wife (W), Joint (JT), Tenants in Common (TC), Community Property (CP).
If stock is owned either JT or TC with someone other than spouse, please furnish name and relationship.

STOCKS

Please list all stock ownership in publicly owned corporations *(stock traded on an exchange or over the counter)*. Stock owned in a family or nonpublic company should be listed in the Corporate Business Interests section.

Name of Institution	OWNER*	NUMBER OF SHARES	FAIR MARKET VALUE
_____	_____	_____	_____
_____	_____	_____	_____
_____	_____	_____	_____
_____	_____	_____	_____
_____	_____	_____	_____
_____	_____	_____	_____
_____	_____	_____	_____
_____	_____	_____	_____
_____	_____	_____	_____
Total	_____	_____	_____

*Husband (H), Wife (W), Joint (JT), Tenants in Common (TC), Community Property (CP).
If stock is owned either JT or TC with someone other than spouse, please furnish name and relationship.

If any of your shares are held in a street name account with your broker, please furnish:
Brokerage firm _____
Broker _____
Exact name and number of account _____

PARTNERSHIP INTERESTS

Partnership Name	PERCENTAGE OF PARTNERSHIP INTEREST		OWNER*	VALUE
	GENERAL PARTNER	LIMITED PARTNER		
_____	_____	_____	_____	____
_____	_____	_____	_____	____
_____	_____	_____	_____	____
_____	_____	_____	_____	____
_____	_____	_____	_____	____
_____	_____	_____	_____	____
_____	_____	_____	_____	____

*Husband (H), Wife (W), Joint (JT), Tenants in Common (TC), Community Property (CP).

SOLE PROPRIETORSHIP BUSINESS INTERESTS

Name of Business   DESCRIPTION OF BUSINESS   OWNER*   VALUE

_____   _____   _____   _____
_____   _____   _____   _____
_____   _____   _____   _____
_____   _____   _____   _____
_____   _____   _____   _____

*Husband (H), Wife (W), Joint (JT), Tenants in Common (TC), Community Property (CP).

FARM AND RANCH INTERESTS

Description *(livestock, machinery, leases, etc.)*   OWNER*   VALUE

_____   _____   _____
_____   _____   _____
_____   _____   _____
_____   _____   _____
_____   _____   _____
_____   _____   _____
_____   _____   _____

*Husband (H), Wife (W), Joint (JT), Tenants in Common (TC), Community Property (CP).

OIL AND GAS INTERESTS

Description *(lease, overriding royalty, fee mineral estate,*
working interest, pooling agreement, etc.)   OWNER*   FACE VALUE

_____   _____   _____
_____   _____   _____
_____   _____   _____
_____   _____   _____
_____   _____   _____
_____   _____   _____

*Husband (H), Wife (W), Joint (JT), Tenants in Common (TC), Community Property (CP).

ANTICIPATED INHERITANCE, GIFT, OR LAWSUIT JUDGMENT

Description _____
_____
_____
_____
_____
_____
_____

Total estimated value _____

RETIREMENT PLANS

Type of Plan*	COMPANY	BENEFICIARY ON YOUR DEATH	PERCENT VESTED	VALUE
_____	_____	_____	____	____
_____	_____	_____	____	____
_____	_____	_____	____	____
_____	_____	_____	____	____
_____	_____	_____	____	____
_____	_____	_____	____	____

*Pension (P), Profit Sharing (PS), H.R.10, IRA.

PERSONAL EFFECTS AND OTHER ASSETS

(Furniture, automobiles, jewelry, collectibles, and other personal assets of more than nominal value.)

_____
_____
_____
_____
_____
_____
_____
_____
_____

Total estimated fair market value _____

LIFE INSURANCE POLICIES

Policy Number and Company _____

Type* _____ Insured _____
Owner _____
Primary beneficiary _____ Secondary _____
Who pays premium?† _____ Cash value _____
Amount of loans on policy _____ Face amount _____

*Term, whole life, split dollar, group life, annuity.
†Husband (H), Wife (W), Corporation (C).

Policy Number and Company _____

Type* _____ Insured _____
Owner _____
Primary beneficiary _____ Secondary _____
Who pays premium?† _____ Cash value _____
Amount of loans on policy _____ Face amount _____

*Term, whole life, split dollar, group life, annuity.
†Husband (H), Wife (W), Corporation (C).

Policy Number and Company _____

Type* _____ Insured _____
Owner _____
Primary beneficiary _____ Secondary _____
Who pays premium?† _____ Cash value _____
Amount of loans on policy _____ Face amount _____

*Term, whole life, split dollar, group life, annuity.
†Husband (H), Wife (W), Corporation (C).

Policy Number and Company _____

Type* _____ Insured _____
Owner _____
Primary beneficiary _____ Secondary _____
Who pays premium?† _____ Cash value _____
Amount of loans on policy _____ Face amount _____

*Term, whole life, split dollar, group life, annuity.
†Husband (H), Wife (W), Corporation (C).

_____

Policy Number and Company _____

Type* _____ Insured _____
Owner _____
Primary beneficiary _____ Secondary _____
Who pays premium?† _____ Cash value _____
Amount of loans on policy _____ Face amount _____

*Term, whole life, split dollar, group life, annuity.
†Husband (H), Wife (W), Corporation (C).

_____

Policy Number and Company _____

Type* _____ Insured _____
Owner _____
Primary beneficiary _____ Secondary _____
Who pays premium?† _____ Cash value _____
Amount of loans on policy _____ Face amount _____

*Term, whole life, split dollar, group life, annuity.
†Husband (H), Wife (W), Corporation (C).

SUMMARY OF VALUES

ASSETS

	AMOUNTS*	
	HUSBAND	WIFE
Cash	$ _____	_____
Notes receivable	_____	_____
Bonds	_____	_____
Real estate	_____	_____
Corporate business interests	_____	_____
Stocks	_____	_____
Partnership interests	_____	_____
Sole proprietorship business interests	_____	_____
Farm and ranch interests	_____	_____
Oil and gas interests	_____	_____
Anticipated inheritance, gift, or judgment	_____	_____
Retirement plans	_____	_____
Personal effects and other assets	_____	_____
Life insurance face amounts	_____	_____
Total assets	$ _____	_____

LIABILITIES

	AMOUNTS*	
	HUSBAND	WIFE
Loans payable	$ _____	_____
Accounts payable	_____	_____
Real estate mortgages payable	_____	_____
Contingent liabilities	_____	_____
Loans against life insurance	_____	_____
Unpaid taxes	_____	_____
Other obligations	_____	_____
_____	_____	_____
_____	_____	_____
Total liabilities	$ _____	_____
Net Estate	$ _____	_____

*Joint Tenancy (JT), Tenancy in Common (TC), and Community Property (CP) values should be entered half in husband's column, half in wife's column.

Appendix B

Federal Estate and Gift Tax Tables

The Federal Estate and Gift Tax Rates

Column A	Column B	Column C	Column D
Taxable amount over	Taxable amount not over	Tax on amount in column A	Rate of tax on excess over amount in column A
			(Percent)
0	$10,000	0	18
$10,000	20,000	$1,800	20
20,000	40,000	3,800	22
40,000	60,000	8,200	24
60,000	80,000	13,000	26
80,000	100,000	18,200	28
100,000	150,000	23,800	30
150,000	250,000	38,800	32
250,000	500,000	70,800	34
500,000	750,000	155,800	37
750,000	1,000,000	248,300	39
1,000,000	1,250,000	345,800	41
1,250,000	1,500,000	448,300	43
1,500,000	2,000,000	555,800	45
2,000,000	2,500,000	780,800	49
2,500,000	3,000,000	1,025,800	53
3,000,000	————————	1,290,800	55

There is a 5% surcharge for estates between $10,000,000 and $17,184,000.

In the case of estates of decedents dying during:	The applicable exclusion amount is:	The unified credit is:
1998	$625,000	$202,050
1999	650,000	211,300
2000 and 2001	675,000	220,550
2002 and 2003	700,000	229,800
2004	850,000	287,300
2005	950,000	326,300
2006 or thereafter	1,000,000	345,800

The federal estate tax on various estates during and after the phase-in of the applicable exclusion amount.

Estate tax if death occurs in

Taxable estate	1998	1999	2000-2001	2002-2003	2004	2005	2006
$ 625,000							
650,000	$ 9,250						
675,000	18,500	$ 9,250					
700,000	27,750	18,500	$ 9,250				
850,000	85,250	76,000	66,750	$ 57,500			
950,000	124,250	115,000	105,750	96,500	$ 39,000		
1,000,000	143,750	134,500	125,250	116,000	58,500	$ 19,500	
1,500,000	353,750	344,500	335,250	326,000	268,500	229,500	$210,000
2,000,000	578,750	569,500	560,250	551,000	493,500	454,500	435,000
2,500,000	823,750	814,500	805,250	796,000	738,500	699,500	680,000
3,000,000	1,088,750	1,079,500	1,070,250	1,061,000	1,003,500	964,500	945,000

Appendix C

Spouses Have Rights Too

Throughout the United States, the law has evolved to protect the interests of a surviving husband or wife. Depending upon the state involved, these spousal rights are called a right to elect against the will, a dissent from the will, or by other terms. Their purpose remains the same, regardless of terminology. As a matter of public policy and based on an historical context, society has decided that it serves the public good to prevent husbands and wives from completely disinheriting their spouses.

This appendix includes a brief explanation of the terms used in state laws and a state-by-state synopsis of spousal rights and obligations on death. Remember that state legislatures meet at least every other year; therefore, it is imperative that you contact your estate planning professional to ascertain the current law in your state.

Terminology

The concept that husbands and wives should receive at least a minimum amount of their spouses' property on death is based on English common law. The English common law is the body of principles and customs that was developed in England and was brought to this country at the time of its settlement.

Historically, the first terms used to describe spousal rights were *dower* and *curtesy*. Dower is the wife's right to participate in the husband's estate; curtesy is the entitlement of the husband to share in his wife's estate. Usually these represented limited rights, most commonly life estates. To have a life estate in property means that you are entitled to all income from that property for your life.

A life estate cannot be transferred by will. After the death of the surviving spouse, the property usually reverts, or goes back, to the descendants of the deceased person (decedent). Frequently life estates are expressed in terms of a fraction of the estate; for example, a wife could receive a life estate in one-half of her husband's property. If personal property is involved, it might be placed in a trust by law with income going to the surviving spouse. When real estate is involved, a deed for the life of the survivor is usually prepared.

In the past there was frequently a distinction made between the rights of the husband and the rights of the wife. These differences were based on the way society viewed the roles of men and women at that time. For the most part, those distinctions have been removed, but some states still retain vestiges of this type of sex discrimination.

As the law changed, more and more states decided that the dower and curtesy rights were either outdated or insufficient to protect the interests of the surviving spouse. The right of spouses to elect against the will or to dissent from the will of their spouses was then created by state legislatures. In some states these new laws did not replace dower and curtesy, but merely supplemented them.

To elect against or dissent from the will (synonymous terms) means that the surviving spouse chooses to take what the law provides in lieu of what the deceased spouse's will provides. It is not possible to take under the will and also dissent from it; you cannot have both.

The amount that a spouse receives through a will election varies depending upon the state involved. There are two terms with which you should become familiar. The first term, *augmented estate*, is used in the states that have adopted the Uniform Probate Code (UPC). The augmented estate generally includes all property in which the deceased spouse retained any ownership as well as certain types of gifts. In UPC states, the electing spouse receives a fraction of the augmented estate, usually one-half or one-third.

Another term that is used when the surviving spouse elects against the will is the *intestate share*. This term is derived from the word *intestacy*, which means to die without a will. If intestacy occurs, the law provides the specific share of the estate that the wife or husband receives. This varies depending upon the number of children involved and a host of other factors. In some states, if a spouse dissents against the will, it is as if the decedent left no will. The dissenting spouse receives an intestate share of the estate as prescribed by state law.

Other states use neither the augmented estate nor the intestate share. They may rely solely upon forms of dower or curtesy, or they provide what essentially are the same rights by their law.

If a spouse elects against the will, the election is against probate assets. A probate asset is property the passage of which must be proved in court. In fact, the word *probate* has its roots in the Latin term for proof or truth. Whether the election will reach nonprobate assets is frequently an open question. Examples of nonprobate assets are life insurance policies, pension plans, funded living trusts, and jointly held property.

One type of living trust is a revocable living trust. The person who creates a revocable living trust (the settlor or maker) can cancel, alter, or revoke its terms. The trust is called "living" because it exists while the settlor is alive and is funded with assets, directly or indirectly. This is in contrast to a testamentary trust, which does not exist until after death. The latter type is virtually always included in the elective share. Whether a revocable living trust is included in the elective share or not depends upon the state involved. In almost all UPC states, this type of trust is part of the elective share because the maker retains the right to revoke it as well as other powers.

In addition to the right to take against the will, most states also provide allowances for the surviving spouse. These are generally in addition to the right to elect against the will. The allowances are taken off the top before computing the elective share. In some states the allowances are substantial and they are frequently exempt from other claims against the estate.

The homestead allowance or exemption is based on a legislative desire to preserve the family home. In many states, homestead allowances are inadequate and have been outpaced by inflation. For example, a state might permit $10,000 for a homestead exemption. If creditors demand it, there could be a forced sale of the family home; the first $10,000 would go to the spouse and/or children of the decedent. The balance of the proceeds would be subject to the claims of creditors.

The surviving spouse may be entitled to an allowance intended to support the spouse as well as surviving minor children during the administration of the estate. These allowances are usually restricted to one year but can be extended by court order. The amount and frequency of payment differs from state to state. Sometimes the allowance is intended solely for the spouse. Occasionally, it is a lump-sum payment. This allowance is called a maintenance, family, or support allowance.

Many states provide an exempt personal property allowance that can cover everything from sentimental objects and the decedent's clothing to household furniture and even the family car. This allowance is a fixed amount and it is usually in the $3,000 to $5,000 range.

It is not necessary to elect against the will in order to be entitled to allowances; they are in addition to either the elective share or the share under the will. Proper procedure must be followed to file claims for allowances.

In most states it is required that the decedent be domiciled in the state in order for the allowance provisions to apply. Domicile is a legal term having a different meaning than residence, but one that does not lend itself to a particular definition. If there are any doubts, always consult an attorney to verify the question of domicile.

Frequently, a person will have already made a will prior to marriage. If there is no provision in the will for a spouse, the spouse may receive a share of the estate anyway. This is known as the omitted spouse provision; however, in almost all states, if the person making the will specifically states that the omission is intentional, this law will not apply.

The rules in community property states are different. Most property owned by spouses in a community property state is marital property; however, community property spouses may have separate property. This is usually property that was acquired before the marriage. If a community property spouse attempts to dispose of more than his or her community property interest, the other spouse can usually elect against the will.

In reading the material in this appendix, you will frequently note that the word *descendant* is used. Generally, a descendant is a child, grandchild, or greatgrandchild of the decedent. People in previous generations are referred to as ancestors. People in subsequent generations are referred to as descendants.

Locate your state in this appendix to determine what your spousal rights and obligations are. Remember, however, to always seek the advice of a knowledgeable professional before utilizing any of these concepts in your estate plan.

State Synopses

Alabama. In the state of Alabama, a surviving spouse has a right to the *lesser* of (1) all of the estate of the deceased spouse, reduced by the value of the surviving spouse's separate property, or (2) one-third of the estate of the deceased spouse. The surviving spouse's separate property includes all lifetime transfers from the deceased spouse to the surviving spouse, as well as property the surviving spouse may have received from other sources.

The surviving spouse and minor children whom the deceased spouse was obligated to support or children who were in fact being supported by the deceased spouse are entitled to a reasonable allowance in money from the estate during the period of administration. This allowance applies whether or not the spouse has elected against the estate.

The surviving spouse has a homestead allowance of $6,000, a personal property allowance of $3,000, and rights to miscellaneous other personal property. A spouse may waive the right to the elective share, the homestead allowance, and the family allowance before or after marriage. The surviving spouse may also retain possession of the dwelling house, under what is known as the widow's quarantine, where the surviving spouse lived with decedent before his or her death. The decedent's estate must pay any rent due.

Alaska. The Alaskan augmented estate statute provides for the surviving spouse, husband or wife, to take one-third of the augmented estate. This is all that he or she receives regardless of whether there are children. The remaining two-thirds is divided among the children or, if none, among other family members as provided by law. The Alaskan code generally incorporates the UPC definition of augmented estate, so this would seem to include trust property as well as property owned outright. This is true because the

UPC refers to all assets that are transferred gratuitously, and in which the transferring spouse retained an interest, as part of the augmented estate. There are no sex distinctions in Alaska's election provisions.

There are also various types of family allowances in Alaska. A homestead allowance of $27,000 is available to protect the family home. A personal property allowance is available of up to $10,000. Finally, a family allowance, defined as a reasonable sum for the family, not to exceed $15,000, is available for a period of up to one year. The probate court can, in its discretion, modify the family allowance.

In May 1998, Alaska became the first state to authorize opt-in community property. Under the Alaska Community Property Act, residents of Alaska and other states can establish an Alaska Community Property Trust and selectively choose which assets they would like to convert to community property.

Arizona. Arizona is a community property state. In a community property state, one-half of the property acquired during marriage belongs to the surviving spouse.

Arizona has general allowance provisions. The homestead allowance is $18,000. A personal property allowance of $7,000 is intended to protect such items as furniture. A standard family allowance of up to $12,000 lump sum or $1,000 per month permits a reasonable amount for care of the family for up to one year. There is no distinction between the sexes under Arizona law as concerns these rights. As in most community property states, the right of the decedent to dispose of his or her property is limited to one-half.

Arkansas. The laws of Arkansas that protect the surviving spouse are generally based on dower rights. By amendment in 1981, sex distinction was removed as concerns the election.

The dower right (which would apply to the husband as well) consists of a one-third life estate in the part of the land the deceased spouse owned and one-third full ownership in the personal property. Again, terminology that includes property owned "for his use" would seem to include living trust property. One-third of the personal property is also given to the surviving spouse if a child or children survive.

If there are no surviving children, the surviving spouse can receive up to one-half of the real and personal property as against the other heirs, but only one-third as against creditors.

A somewhat unique provision in Arkansas is that the surviving spouse also receives one-third of any mineral rights.

The homestead provision in Arkansas extends up to $5,000 and can be taken from the sale of a qualifying home. Check with your professional advisers for details.

Another allowance provides that in addition to homestead and dower rights, the surviving spouse is entitled to $2,000 against other distributees (that is, people who would take under the will) and $1,000 against creditors. There is a living allowance not to exceed $500 per month, usually limited in time to a period set by the court.

One final nuance under Arkansas law is that in order to elect against the will, that is, to receive dower, the surviving spouse must have been married to the decedent for more than one year.

California. California is a community property state. In a community property state, one-half of the property acquired during the marriage belongs to the surviving spouse.

Upon the death of a married person domiciled in California, one-half of the property, under the community property system, automatically belongs to the surviving spouse. The other half is subject to the will of the decedent; if he or she leaves no will, the surviving spouse will receive the property subject to the general intestacy provisions.

It is important to know that California uses the concept of quasi-community property as well. Quasi-community property is property that was acquired elsewhere while the person was not domiciled in California but that would have been considered community property if the person had been domiciled in California at the time of acquisition. The effect this has on the estate can be complicated; therefore, it should be investigated early.

California has a homestead provision that apparently has no dollar limitation. It offers protection for the family home. There is also a standard family allowance intended to provide reasonable support for up to one year.

Colorado. Colorado is a UPC state. Either the husband or the wife can elect against the will; the election includes trust property. The share received is one-half of the augmented estate, which is the net estate with certain prescribed additions. This is the share regardless of whether there are children. A supplementary elective share of up to $50,000 may also apply.

There is a $30,000 homestead exemption. The decedent's homestead exemption inures to the surviving spouse or the children if they held the house as joint tenants of the decedent. The exempt property allowance is $15,000 to cover personal property. There is also a reasonable family allowance, which is limited to one year but can be for longer if the court deems it necessary. Under Colorado law, these allowances are in addition to the elective share.

Connecticut. Under Connecticut law, the surviving spouse is entitled to the use for his or her life of one-third of the value of all property, whether it be real or personal, owned by the decedent. It is important to know that the statute refers to property owned legally or equitably and thus appears to include living trust assets. The share is the same whether or not there are children.

A support allowance is provided for the surviving spouse or the family as deemed necessary by the court. The amount is intended to cover living expenses during administration.

Delaware. Under Delaware law, the surviving spouse can receive one-third of the elective estate less the amount of certain transfers of property that are made to the surviving spouse by the deceased spouse by virtue of his or her death (including beneficial interests in a trust created during the decedent's lifetime). Elective estate means the adjusted gross estate as that term is used on the federal estate tax return, after subtracting all transfers that are included on that tax return and that were made with the consent of the surviving spouse. The elective estate in Delaware is highly technical; consult your estate planning professional for the details. The share is the same whether or not there are children.

Also under Delaware law, the surviving spouse is given an allowance of $2,000; this is a one-time fixed amount given to the spouse. The allowance has priority over other debts.

District of Columbia. A family allowance is provided of up to $10,000; the amounts and times of distribution are decided by the court.

The surviving spouse, husband or wife, has a right to elect to take the intestate share against the will. The intestate share is one-third if there are children or descendants. If there are no children, but the deceased had parents, brothers, sisters, nieces, or nephews, the spouse receives one-half of the estate. The spouse could receive all of the estate if there are no descendants, parents, brothers, sisters, nieces, or nephews. He or she may take dower rights in the real estate of the decedent, if desired, in lieu of the intestate provisions affecting real estate. This means that the surviving spouse, if taking dower rights, receives one-half of the personal property outright and a dower interest in the real estate.

Florida. The surviving spouse in the state of Florida may elect against the will and receive 30 percent of the fair market value of the assets in the estate. This does not include real estate located outside the state of Florida. This share is the same whether or not there are children.

The homestead provision in Florida consists of a life estate if survived by a surviving spouse and children and the homestead was not held as tenants by the entirety, which is a special type of legal title to real estate that exists only between husbands and wives. A surviving spouse is entitled to household items up to a value of $10,000, personal effects up to $1,000, as well as all automobiles in the decedent's name and regularly used by the decedent or the decedent's immediate family. Finally, there is a standard family allowance that appears to have a ceiling of $6,000. That amount is for living expenses during administration.

Georgia. Until January 1, 1998, Georgia was the only state that did not have any provision for an election against the will. As of January 1, 1998, the court can make separate awards to the surviving spouse and minor children. If there are no separate awards, the surviving spouse is given the equivalent of a life estate with power to include corpus for support, with the remainder going to the children. The surviving spouse takes equally with the children, except that the surviving spouse's share shall not be less than one-third of the estate. There are also provisions to give up to one year's support for living expenses to the surviving spouse and minor children, for which a minimum figure of $1,600 is set.

Dower rights were repealed in Georgia as of 1969.

Hawaii. Under Hawaiian law, the surviving spouse, husband or wife, receives one-half of the net estate if he or she elects against the will. Net estate means the estate to be disposed of under the decedent's will and therefore appears not to include living trust property. The surviving spouse takes the entire estate if there are no surviving children or parents of the deceased.

A homestead allowance provides up to $5,000 for the protection of the family home, and an exempt property allowance provides $5,000 for personal property items. A family allowance is provided for support of the surviving spouse and any children whom the deceased was obligated to, and in fact did, support.

Idaho. Idaho is a community property state. In a community property state, one-half of the property acquired during the marriage belongs to the surviving spouse; however, if a transfer is made of quasi-community property without adequate consideration, it can be included under the augmented estate provisions of the Idaho law. It should not be assumed that quasi-community property means the same in each community property state, as there are variations. Always consult an attorney before making a decision in this regard. If the election is made, it covers one-half of the property that was transferred and in which the decedent has retained certain types of interests. The share is the same whether or not there are children.

The homestead provision varies: It is $50,000 if set aside during life, or $4,000 if only a spouse survives, or $10,000 if a spouse survives and there are children living with the surviving spouse. The spouse's elective share is taken subject to the homestead exemption. A family allowance provides for living expenses of the family for up to one year. There is also a $3,500 exempt property allowance to cover personal property items and other protected assets.

There appears to be no sex distinction in Idaho concerning the election. The issue of living trust property does not seem to be addressed.

Illinois. Illinois law provides a spousal support allowance for up to nine months. This amount is not less than $10,000, together with an additional sum of not less than $5,000 for each dependent child. There is also a $15,000 homestead exemption for the surviving spouse and minor children.

The surviving spouse may elect against the will. If he or she does so, one-third of the entire estate is given to the spouse if there are descendants; one-half is given if there are no descendants. Descendants include children and their children.

Under case law, it appears that revocable living trusts do not escape the augmented estate provisions.

Indiana. The election against the will in Indiana applies equally to both men and women. The electing spouse receives one-half of the net personal property and real estate, but if there are children from a prior marriage surviving and the surviving spouse has no children from the second marriage, the following provisions apply: The survivor receives one-third of the net personal property and a one-third interest in the real property for life only.

The statute says that the net estate shall consider only property that would have passed under the laws of descent and distribution, which appears to exclude living trust property.

There is a special personal property allowance of $15,000 under Indiana law. If the value of all the personal property is less than $15,000, the remainder can be taken from the proceeds of any sales of real property.

Iowa. A standard family allowance of up to one year is provided for the living expenses of the family. The amount involved may vary depending on needs.

If the surviving spouse, husband or wife, elects against the will, the following provisions are applicable: If the decedent dies leaving the surviving spouse and only children who are issue of the surviving spouse, the surviving spouse receives all of the legal or equitable estate assets, all personal property held by the deceased as head of the family, and all other personal property of decedent not necessary for payment of debts. If the decedent dies leaving issue not of the surviving spouse, the surviving spouse receives one-half of the legal and equitable assets, all personal property held by the decedent as head of the family, and one-half of decedent's other personal property not necessary for payment of debts, but no less than $50,000. Thus living trust property seems to be included.

Kansas. Kansas has a homestead allowance of up to 160 acres if the property is outside the city limits and 1 acre if it is within city limits. This helps to protect the family home, regardless of value. There is a personal property allowance that varies in amount depending upon circumstances, but that cannot be less than $1,500 nor more than $25,000. Consult your professional planner for the details.

The surviving spouse may elect against the will and receive an intestate share, which will vary depending upon whether there are children. If there are no children, the spouse receives all of the estate; if there are one or more children or their issue, the spouse receives one-half of the estate.

Kentucky. In Kentucky, when a husband or a wife dies intestate (without a will), the surviving spouse has a dower right, which is a one-half interest in all surplus real estate, and a life estate in one-third of any real estate owned by the decedent during marriage, but not at death. The surviving spouse also receives a one-half interest in all surplus personal property. A surviving spouse who elects against a will can take a modified dower share, which is identical to the intestate dower share except that the one-half interest in surplus real estate is reduced to one-third.

There appear to be no sex distinctions under the Kentucky election law. The issue of living trust property is not specifically addressed.

There is a $5,000 homestead exemption in Kentucky. A $7,500 personal property exemption to cover household effects and so on is available when the deceased spouse dies without a will or when the surviving spouse renounces the will. There is also a $1,000 spousal allowance to any surviving spouse (except that it will be treated as a charge against the exempt property).

Louisiana. Louisiana is a community property state. In a community property state, one-half of the property acquired during the marriage belongs to the surviving spouse.

Louisiana's civil code is extremely intricate and quite different from any other state's law. Generally speaking, there is no right to elect against the will.

A $15,000 homestead exemption applies. If the decedent died rich, leaving the surviving spouse in "necessitous circumstances," a marital portion in varying amounts may be available up to $1,000,000. However, check with a local estate planning attorney because there are comprehensive changes to dispositions by will, effective July 1, 1999.

Maine. Under Maine law, the surviving spouse is entitled to one-third of the augmented estate, which is the net estate with certain additions. The share is the same whether or not there are children. Maine uses the UPC language, including gratuitous transfers with retained interests, so it appears to include living trusts. Further, in its official comments to the law, Maine legislation refers to New York law, which does include living trusts but excludes insurance, pension plans, and other assets payable to a designated person.

Maine law includes a homestead provision in the amount of $5,000 to protect the family home; an exempt property allowance in the amount of $3,500 for household furniture and so on; and a family allowance to provide for the reasonable living expenses of the family that is limited in duration to one year.

Maryland. The elective intestate share in Maryland is as follows: The surviving spouse, husband or wife, may receive one-third of the net estate if there was issue from the marriage. If there was no issue, the surviving spouse receives one-half of the net estate.

Net estate is defined to mean property of the decedent exclusive of allowances and claims. It is therefore uncertain whether Maryland would include a revocable inter vivos trust as part of the elective share.

There is also a family allowance in the amount of $5,000 to provide for living expenses plus $2,500 for each unmarried child under the age of 18.

Massachusetts. A homestead allowance of up to $100,000 is provided to protect the family home.

Curtesy, the husband's equivalent of dower, has been abolished in Massachusetts, but dower is expressed in terms applying to both sexes. The dower provisions of Massachusetts law permit the surviving spouse to take one-third of all land owned by the spouse for life. This is referred to as tenancy by dower. However, the following are not subject to dower: (1) wild lands not used with a farm or dwelling; (2) equitable interests; (3) assets held in a revocable inter vivos trust.

Other allowances are: a personal property allowance to cover such items as furniture; the right to live in the house for six months with no rent; and an allowance for necessities, apparently as the court orders.

The elective share in Massachusetts is as follows: If there are issues surviving the decedent, the surviving spouse is entitled to elect one-third of the personal property and one-third of the real estate. If there are no surviving issue but there are kindred, the surviving spouse receives $25,000 plus one-half of the estate. Finally, if there are no issue and no kindred, the surviving spouse receives $25,000 plus one-half of the real estate and personal property absolutely, and not as a life estate.

It should be noted that in the first two categories above, if either amount exceeds $25,000, the surviving spouse receives only a life estate and a share of the excess.

Kindred is generally defined in Massachusetts as those members of the family computed according to the rules of civil law; it apparently includes most close family members. There is no distinction between husband and wife provided under Massachusetts law.

Michigan. The elective share is one-half of the amount that the surviving spouse would have received in an intestate estate, reduced by one-half the value of all property derived from the deceased spouse upon his or her death by any means other than testate or intestate succession. The intestate share for a surviving spouse is normally the entire estate or, if there are parents or there are issue who are also issue of the surviving spouse, the first $60,000 plus one-half of the balance. If one or more of the issue are not the issue of the survivor, the normal share is one-half. Remember that these amounts are halved under an election against the will.

Because Michigan law speaks in terms of an intestate share, the inclusion of living trusts is questionable.

The homestead allowance in Michigan is $10,000. This serves to protect the family home. The personal property allowance is $3,500 for assets such as furniture. Finally, a maintenance allowance is provided that is intended to give a reasonable amount of support to the family for living expenses for up to one year.

As an alternative to the elective share, a widow is entitled to power of a life estate in one-third of the property acquired during the marriage that is part of estate.

Minnesota. Minnesota has adopted the Uniform Probate Code, with several modifications. The surviving spouse has the right to a percentage of the augmented estate, graduated depending on the length of marriage, subject to a minimum supplemental amount of $50,000 regardless of percentage. Trusts and wills are treated equally, by statute.

The following allowances are available to the spouse: a $10,000 furniture and household goods allowance; personal property; one automobile; and a family allowance for a period varying from twelve to eighteen months, or longer, at the court's discretion, of not more than $1,500 per month. The surviving spouse is entitled to a life estate in the homestead if the decedent has issue, or the entire homestead if the decedent has no issue. The homestead and allowances are separate from the elective share.

Mississippi. In Mississippi the elective share is the intestate share, not to exceed one-half of the estate. It can be less than one-half if there are children of the decedent. Because the statute speaks in terms of an intestate share, one might conclude that living trust property is not included, but there is no definitive answer to this question.

There is also a separate estate provision in Mississippi law. If the spouse has a separate estate equal to the elective share, he or she will receive nothing. If there is a difference, the elective share will be made up accordingly.

The homestead provision in Mississippi is $75,000; this is intended to protect the family home, up to 160 acres. The spouse is allowed personal property of the deceased spouse up to $10,000.

There is also a support provision for the surviving spouse of one year; it gives him or her a living allowance for reasonable needs.

Missouri. The surviving spouse in Missouri is entitled to elect against the will and receive the following assets: One-half of the estate goes to him or her if there are no lineal descendants; one-third of the estate goes to the surviving spouse if there are lineal descendants. In determining the surviving spouse's share, all property is considered, even if it is not subject to probate. This includes trust property, proceeds of life insurance policies, and other nonprobate assets.

The homestead allowance is $7,500, but is offset against the elective share of the surviving spouse. There is an exempt personal property allowance and a reasonable family allowance for one year, as determined by the court. The personal property allowance includes one car, without regard to value.

Montana. Montana is a UPC state, and therefore it would appear that the elective share includes living trust property. The elective share consists of a percentage of the augmented estate, graduated depending on the length of the marriage, subject to a minimum supplemental amount of $50,000 regardless of percentage. Trusts and wills are treated equally, by statute.

The homestead allowance is $20,000 to protect the family home; the exempt property allowance is $10,000 for personal property; and a family allowance is also provided. The family allowance is for reasonable living expenses for one year. The homestead and other allowances are separate from the elective share in Montana.

Nebraska. In Nebraska, the elective share is one-third of the augmented estate. Again, the augmented estate is defined as including those assets subject to the codes, which probably includes living trust assets. The share is the same whether or not there are children.

The homestead provision in Nebraska is $7,500; the exempt personal property allowance is $5,000; and a family allowance is also provided for under law. That allowance gives a reasonable amount to the family for living expenses.

The general comments to the Nebraska law imply that the views of New York and Pennsylvania law toward will substitutes (that is, that they should be included in the augmented estates) are viewed favorably under the Nebraska law.

Nevada. Nevada is a community property state. In a community property state, one-half of the property acquired during the marriage belongs to the surviving spouse.

Nevada has no elective share provision. There is a homestead allowance of $125,000 to protect the family home, plus a certain amount of personal property reserved to the surviving spouse. A family allowance is provided at the discretion of the court.

New Hampshire. The elective share for the surviving husband or wife in New Hampshire varies widely, depending upon the other survivors. It ranges from one-third of the estate to a one-half interest. If there are children, the surviving spouse receives one-third. There is no mention of living trust assets as includable or excludable from the elective share; however, case law indicates that transfers to a living trust will defeat the statutory rights of a surviving spouse unless it can be shown that the transfers were made for that purpose.

There is a reasonable allowance provision for present support that the court may, in its discretion, count as part of the elective share. This contrasts with most other states' handling of the support allowance.

The surviving spouse is entitled to a homestead of a life estate until remarriage. However, the surviving spouse must waive the homestead exemption when electing against the will.

New Jersey. Under New Jersey law, the surviving spouse has a right of election to take one-third of the augmented estate, which is patterned after the Uniform Probate Code's definition of augmented estate. There is a right to up to $5,000 worth of the decedent's personal property by the surviving spouse, provided the decedent's will does not state otherwise. No other allowances are available, except the right to the decedent's wearing apparel and $5,000 worth of personal property.

New Mexico. New Mexico is a community property state. In a community property state, one-half of the property acquired during the marriage belongs to the surviving spouse.

New Mexico has no elective share at the present time. There is a $30,000 homestead exemption and a family allowance of $5,000 to provide for living expenses. A personal property allowance of $15,000 is also available.

New York. Under New York law, the surviving spouse has an elective share provision as follows: He or she may receive one-third of the net estate if issue survive; one-half of the net estate is the provision if there are no issue.

New York has specifically addressed the issue of the living trust as it relates to the election against the will. Treatment of the matter is divided depending upon when the will was executed. If the will was signed after August 31, 1930 (the beginning of the elective share period), but before September 1, 1966, the statute does not apparently reach living trust assets. The law was amended for wills executed after August 31, 1966 to include living trust assets. The same fractions are involved, that is, one-third or one-half of the net estate, regardless of the date of the will. If the decedent died after August 31, 1992, the surviving spouse may elect for the greater of $50,000 or one-third of the decedent's net estate, taking into consideration amounts passing absolutely by will or trust.

The surviving spouse has the right to certain items of personal and household property of the deceased spouse, limited by various dollar amounts, and may remain in the family home rent-free for forty days.

North Carolina. In North Carolina, a surviving spouse has the right to dissent against an estate when the surviving spouse has received less than one-half of the value of all property passing on the death of the deceased spouse. The statute concerning surviving spouses sets out a complete definition of property passing at death.

Upon making a dissent, the surviving spouse has the right to receive up to a maximum of one-half of the deceased spouse's estate, depending on the number of children of the marriage and other factors. The amount received by the surviving spouse is the same as the surviving spouse would have received had the deceased spouse died intestate.

The homestead in North Carolina is exempt from debts of the homesteader during widowhood of the surviving spouse. The surviving spouse can get an allowance of up to $10,000 for support for a period of one year after the death of the deceased spouse and $2,000 per child up to age 18, or age 22 if a full-time student. If the decedent's estate is greater than $10,000, the surviving spouse may receive up to one-half of the annual net income of the decedent for the three years preceding death.

North Dakota. In this state, the surviving spouse, husband or wife, may receive one-third of the augmented estate. Notes accompanying the North Dakota statute indicate that at least Totten trust funds are included. These are bank accounts that are set up in the name of one individual in trust for another. Whether North Dakota would include regular living trusts is uncertain, although the law notes with approval the New York law on trusts. The share is the same whether or not there are children.

There is a homestead allowance of $80,000 in North Dakota to the surviving spouse for life estate or until remarriage. There is also a family allowance of a reasonable amount for up to one year to provide for the family's living expenses. The exempt property allowance is $5,000 for personal property.

Ohio. In Ohio the surviving spouse can elect to receive the amount of $60,000 plus a share of the balance of the estate, depending upon the number of children or descendants who survive the decedent. The spouse receives one-half of the net estate unless there are two or more descendants surviving, in which case the spouse receives one-third. The $60,000 is reduced to $20,000 if the surviving spouse is not the natural or adoptive parent of the surviving children.

A living trust can probably be used to defeat rights of the surviving spouse in Ohio. State law provides that the surviving spouse has no dower in the corpus of a living trust and cannot reach the living trust as part of the spouse's distributive share or election to take against the will.

The support allowance in Ohio is $25,000 for the living expenses of the family and is deducted before computing the elective share. The surviving spouse may elect to take certain types of personal property not to exceed $2,500, and may remain in the family home rent-free for one year.

Oklahoma. In Oklahoma, a surviving spouse can elect to take an interest in one-half of the property acquired by the joint industry of the husband and wife during marriage, a concept somewhat akin to community property.

The surviving spouse has a life estate in the entire homestead, subject to various conditions. The surviving spouse also has a right to certain personal property. In addition, if the homestead and personal property amounts are not sufficient for the care of the surviving spouse, the court can award a reasonable family allowance for maintenance during estate settlement.

Oregon. The surviving husband or wife may elect against the will and receive one-quarter of the net estate. The share is the same whether or not there are children. The one-quarter elective share is reduced by (1) property given outright by will; (2) the present value of a legal life estate; and (3) the present value of the surviving spouse's right to income or annuity, or the right of withdrawal from any property transferred in trust by will. Thus, it appears that revocable inter vivos trust property is not included.

The allowances for the spouse permit him or her to occupy the dwelling for one year after the death for no rent and to receive reasonable support.

Pennsylvania. The surviving spouse in Pennsylvania may elect against the will and receive one-third of the probate estate.

There is a family exemption of $2,000 in real or personal property; this amount is exempt from creditors' claims. There is no homestead exemption in Pennsylvania.

Rhode Island. The surviving husband or wife may elect a life estate in all real estate instead of receiving property under the will. The share is the same whether or not there are children. When a will fails to indicate an intention that it has made provisions for the surviving spouse in lieu of the statutory life estate in real estate, then the surviving spouse gets the life estate in real estate in addition to the provisions in the will.

There are also family allowances of varying amounts; they cover support for the family and wearing apparel. Also included is a generous provision that permits real estate to go to the spouse as necessary and deemed suitable by the court if there are no issue.

South Carolina. South Carolina has adopted its own version of the Uniform Probate Code. A surviving spouse has the right to one-third of the decedent's estate. This right includes the right to one-third of the assets in a revocable inter vivos trust established by the decedent.

The law allows waiver of the right to elect by either a pre- or postmarital agreement.

There is a homestead exemption of $5,000 and a provision for personal property, both of which can also be waived by agreement of the spouses. There are no provisions for support of the surviving spouse and family pending administration.

South Dakota. South Dakota adopted the UPC for a brief period and then readopted it effective July 1, 1995. As of that date, the surviving spouse may elect one-third of the decedent's augmented estate, and transfers in trust are charged against the surviving spouse's elective share.

The homestead allowance in South Dakota is limited to $30,000 in most cases. There are certain minimal personal property allowances and a family allowance at the court's discretion.

Tennessee. Both dower and curtesy have been abolished in Tennessee.

Personal property allowances and a one-year support allowance for living expenses are provided, and the surviving spouse is entitled to up to $10,000 of the final wages of the decedent, chargeable against the support allowance.

There is also a homestead allowance in Tennessee of up to $5,000 to protect the family home.

The surviving spouse may elect to take a share in lieu of the will, the percentage of which is determined by the length of the marriage. The share is the same whether or not there are children. The position of Tennessee law on living trust property is unclear.

Texas. Texas is a community property state. In a community property state, one-half of the property acquired during the marriage belongs to the surviving spouse.

In Texas, if the deceased spouse attempts to dispose of more than his or her interest in the community property, the surviving spouse may elect his or her interest in the community property. The share is the same whether or not there are children.

A homestead exemption gives the surviving spouse a life estate in the family home, up to one acre in the city and up to 200 acres in rural areas. A personal property allowance covers such things as furniture, clothing, and so on. A cash allowance in lieu of exempt property may be claimed, not to exceed $5,000; and a cash allowance in lieu of homestead may be claimed, not to exceed $15,000. The cash allowance is a one-time allotment. The court may award a family allowance for one year's reasonable maintenance if the surviving spouse and children have insufficient property of their own.

Utah. Utah uses a somewhat complicated mathematical formula for computing the elective share. The husband or wife can take one-third of the augmented estate multiplied by a certain fraction that is determined under that formula. The share is the same whether or not there are children.

The homestead allowance in Utah is $10,000 for the surviving spouse. The law provides a personal property allowance of $5,000 and family allowance of up to one year. The family allowance is limited to $6,000.

The matter of living trust property is not specifically addressed.

Vermont. Under Vermont law, the dissenting husband or wife can elect against the will and receive one-third of the value of all real estate, or one-half if the decedent left only one heir who is also the child of the surviving spouse or was adopted by both. Apparently, both of these provisions are for outright bequests and not life estates.

A personal property allowance and a provision for support during the administration of the estate are provided, including living expenses for the spouse and children. There is also a homestead allowance of $75,000 to protect the family home.

Although Vermont does not specifically address the issue of trust property, the election against the will addresses all real estate and does not seem to distinguish between that which is held in trust and that which is held outright.

Virginia. If a surviving spouse renounces the will of a deceased spouse, the surviving spouse takes one-third of the augmented estate if there are surviving children or their descendants. Otherwise, the surviving spouse takes one-half.

A surviving spouse can elect a one-third dower or curtesy right in real estate instead of renouncing the will.

There is a $10,000 homestead allowance, which reduces any other amounts received by the surviving spouse. In addition, there is a personal property allowance of up to $10,000. A reasonable family allowance can be awarded by the court at its discretion, but is not to exceed the amount of $12,000.

Washington. Washington is a community property state. In a community property state, one-half of the property acquired during the marriage belongs to the surviving spouse.

Washington permits the surviving spouse to elect his or her interest in the community property if the deceased spouse attempts to dispose of it.

There is a homestead allowance of up to $30,000; the allowance helps to protect the family home.

West Virginia. The rights of dower and curtesy have recently been abolished in West Virginia. The surviving spouse may elect a percentage of the augmented estate based upon the length of the marriage. If this amount is less than $25,000, the surviving spouse is entitled to a supplementary elective share of $25,000. The augmented estate consists of the couple's combined assets.

There is a homestead exemption of up to $5,000 and a $1,000 family allowance.

Wisconsin. Wisconsin has adopted the Marital Property Act, which is somewhat similar to the community property concept. A surviving spouse may elect to take a one-half interest in all deferred marital property, including property not subject to probate. Deferred marital property is defined in a relatively complex manner, but generally includes all property acquired during a marriage, excluding individual property. Certain effective dates apply, so consult your adviser for details.

There is a generous personal property allowance that includes clothing, jewelry, an automobile, and certain other property. It will be limited to $3,000 only if claims cannot be paid in full. Property up to an amount of $10,000 can be advanced for support of the family. The court has the discretion to provide allowances for support during administration or for a longer period of time, depending on circumstances. The surviving spouse may also petition the court for a fee or life estate in the family home.

Wyoming. The Wyoming surviving spouse, husband or wife, may elect against the estate and receive from one-fourth to one-half of the estate, depending upon the number of the surviving descendants. If there are no descendants or if the spouse is the parent of the children, the spouse receives one-half of the estate; if there are surviving children or descendants and the surviving spouse is not the parent, the spouse receives one-fourth.

There is a $10,000 homestead allowance to protect the family home and also a maintenance allowance. The maintenance allowance provides for the reasonable living expenses of the family unit.

The issue of living trust property is not specifically addressed in Wyoming.

Puerto Rico. Puerto Rico uses a version of community property. A surviving spouse has a legal share in community property and a life estate in a portion of the remaining estate that varies depending on the number of children.

There is a $1,500 homestead protection for the surviving spouse, children, and other relatives. Certain personal property is exempt, but there are no other exemptions or allowances.

Virgin Islands. Dower and curtesy are abolished. The surviving spouse may elect to take an intestate share, but if the spouse so elects, the share is limited to no more than one-half of the net estate, subject to certain property transferred in trust.

The intestate share of the surviving spouse is one-third if there are issue of the decedent. If there are no issue but there are surviving parents, siblings, nieces, or nephews, the share can be greater than one-half by certain amounts depending on which of these relatives survive. If none of these relatives survive, the surviving spouse receives the entire estate.

There are provisions for homestead and an allowance for family support. There are also exempt property and personal property allowances.

Appendix D

Estate Planning History

Primitive people did not recognize that land could be owned; the land belonged to all people. It was unthinkable that land could be transferred at all, much less on death.

Only personal property was possessed and owned by primitive people, and on death, our early ancestors either destroyed or buried such property with its owner.

When people began to recognize the value in their possessions, they began to become concerned with passing those possessions on death. Perhaps the earliest written evidence of the penchant for passing property on can be found in the hieroglyphics of the early Egyptians. Although our knowledge of these early wills is limited, we do know they passed property to select heirs.

In Babylonia, as a result of the Code of Hammurabi, property, with only a very few exceptions, had to pass to heirs on death. This was true under the laws of Solon in Greece also. Roman law, especially under Caesar Augustus, followed this practice as well. As a matter of fact, it would appear that Augustus was the inventor of the estate tax; he levied a tax of 5 percent on the value of all estates to help support his army.

Emperor Justin of the Byzantine Empire, long recognized as one of the greatest lawmakers of all time, created the Justinian Code. It was this code that prescribed the first formal requirements that attached to wills. The code also allowed a certain form of contract that is remarkably similar to modern-day trusts.

Many of our current will and estate laws can be traced to both Rome and the Justinian Code. Rome extended its rule to most of the known world; its rule included creating a system of law for each territory it conquered, and Great Britain was no exception. Even though the Romans were pushed out of Great Britain by the Anglo-Saxons, much Roman law remained.

Up until the Norman conquest in A.D. 1066, the Anglo-Saxon law allowed people to pass title to most of their property through the use of wills on their deaths. Their laws even provided that in the absence of a will, certain property would pass to heirs. All of this changed, however, after the Norman invasion of England and the advent of feudalism.

The foundation of the English feudal system was that the king owned all the land under his domain. Land was to be disposed of only by the king. Even though the king distributed land among his nobles, he still retained an interest called a military tenure. In fact, the nobles took the property given them by the king subject to their making continuing financial contributions toward the king's war efforts.

The king needed large armies that could only be raised by nobles owning large estates. To prevent the dilution of land into smaller parcels by inheritance, the English law prohibited land from being left by will. Such property passed automatically to the eldest living male heir (primogeniture). Primogeniture allowed wealth to accumulate in a very few hands. It also created a large caste of property-poor nobles and knights.

English feudal wills could, in the main, pass only personal property. There was a constant battle between the church and the king about who had the authority to administer these feudal wills. At first the king took on this task and charged for his services. This charge, or "herriot," covered his expenses of administering the will and created tax revenue for the king's coffers.

When the church began to administer these estates, it also charged a fee. It also inherited substantial property through deathbed persuasion and the bequests that resulted from that persuasion. The king feared the power the church was accumulating by its increased wealth, and the saga of their power struggle began.

Over the years, property vested in fewer and fewer hands because of primogeniture. Events, however, were to change this. Nobles wanted to control the passing of their lands. Primogeniture was too restrictive; it took the fun out of being rich.

Under the English feudal system, two courts and systems of law developed. The first was the system of the common-law courts. Common-law courts applied the king's laws strictly and without compassion. Participants began to appeal to the king for mercy and equitable relief. The second system came into being when the king appointed a chancellor to take charge of his royal courts of mercy or equity. Two court systems were emerging in tandem: common courts of law and royal courts of equity. Often these courts would conflict, but over time their functions became separated. Basically, the common-law courts would say what the law was, and the courts of equity gave relief to litigants under their rules. The law of trusts, as we shall see, grew out of the conflict and confusion between the two systems.

As we mentioned earlier, it was impossible, under feudal law, to dispose of land by will. The common-law courts had jurisdiction in this area.

During this time a new concept was developing that allowed a noble to sell property to a third person (not leave it but sell it while alive). Legal title would be in the name of that third party; however, the property was to be used for the benefit of another person named in the seller's will. This great legal scam to get around primogeniture, with all its restrictions, landed in the lap of the courts of equity. These courts developed a body of law that allowed the transfer of property to one person subject to somebody *else's* use or benefit. This was called beneficial ownership, the beginning of the law of trusts.

Land began to have two title holders: (1) the legal title holder, the person whose name appeared on the deed, and (2) the beneficial title holder, the person for whom the property was held. Can you see the law of trusts emerging?

By the early 1500s, it is estimated that over two-thirds of all land in England was held in the form of a "use" (trust). Uses (trusts) were handy devices. They could *deter* creditors, particularly spouses with claims, and they could also avoid the herriot (transfer fees) of the king.

Now the plot thickens. The king was not happy. Parliament, at the king's bidding, passed the Statute of Uses in 1535. This law attacked and attempted to prohibit these early trust devices. There were too many loopholes in the Statute of Uses, and Parliament acknowledged the public sentiment and passed the Statute of Wills in 1540.

The Statute of Wills, for the first time, allowed a person to pass title to real estate (real property) through a will. By the mid-1660s, all property was allowed to pass by will; and in the latter part of the seventeenth century, the last great statute in this area was passed: the Statute of Frauds.

The Statute of Frauds required that all transfers of land be in writing, signed by the transferor, and witnessed by a plurality of witnesses.

Most of the rules created through this historic process have been adopted in the United States and are referred to as our English common-law heritage. In most states, courts of law and equity have been merged into the courts we have today.

Out of this heritage came the idea and ability for government to tax property at the owner's death. In the late 1700s, England passed the Stamp Act. This Stamp Act required people to write their wills on paper printed by the government. The paper had stamps on it. Different paper and stamps were used depending upon the size of the estate. When the paper was needed because it was will-drafting time, it had to be paid for. When the decedent's estate was administered, the court would check the size of the estate against the stamps on the will paper to make sure that the proper tax was paid. They would also check to see whether any gifts were made in contemplation of death. These gifts were assumed to be death devices and would also be taxed. Thus the first gift tax law came into existence.

The first American attempt at a federal estate tax was the Revolutionary War Tax passed in 1797. The purpose of this tax was to pay the war debt. This was adopted from the English Stamp Act, and the person who inherited the estate paid a stamp duty. This act was repealed in 1802 when the revenue was no longer needed. In 1826, the state of Pennsylvania adopted the first inheritance tax. The inheritance tax was based on the Revolutionary War Tax. Instead of taxing the estate of the decedent, it taxed the recipient of the inheritance. By the late 1800s, nine states had adopted an inheritance tax.

The second federal estate tax was passed in 1862. This also was a stamp tax to raise revenue for the Civil War; this tax was repealed in 1870. In 1898, the Spanish War Tax was enacted, which was a tax on personal property passing by will or otherwise; it was repealed in 1902.

The forerunner of our current federal estate tax was the German War Tax passed in 1916. This tax, like the others, was to raise revenue for the war. This tax, however, did not go away.

The federal estate tax was held constitutional by the Supreme Court of the United States. Article 1, Section 8, Clause 1, of the United States Constitution states as follows:

> The Congress shall have Power To lay and collect Taxes, Duties, Imposts and Excises, to pay Debts and provide for the common Defence and general Welfare of the United States; but all Duties, Imposts and Excises shall be uniform throughout the United States.

In addition, Article 1, Section 9, Clause 4, of the Constitution states as follows: "No capitation, or other direct, Tax shall be laid, unless in Proportion to the Census or Enumeration herein before directed to be taken."

This new federal estate tax was not a direct tax on property. As a matter of fact, the federal estate tax as it was then and is now is merely a tax on the transfers of assets from deceased persons to their heirs. Technically, it is not a tax against property. Thus, unlike the income tax, which had to be added as a constitutional amendment to become legal, the federal estate tax did fit within the strict original confines of the U.S. Constitution.

The gift tax was a natural extension of the federal estate tax. When the federal estate tax began in 1916, it was constantly amended. There was an amendment in 1917, one in 1918, and a major amendment in 1926. In 1926, the gift tax was formally recognized. Prior to 1926, a gift in contemplation of death was not taxed at the same rate as the federal estate tax. It was found that much revenue was being lost because people were making gifts during their lifetimes and these gifts were free from tax. Thus, in 1926, the first gift tax was passed so that there would be a tax on all property that was transferred from the owner to another person without charging a fair market value.

It seems clear to us that most laws historically restricted ownership based on social policy, not revenue policy. In feudal times wealth was held in a few hands for purposes of control and transfer. With the modern concept of centralized government, the "holding together" of estates in the hands of a few was considered antidemocratic and was politically unpopular.

Redistribution of wealth came into vogue for a variety of reasons; it seemed appropriate to have more people own a share of the available wealth.

The United States enacted estate taxes to fund specific military escapades. However, according to President F. Roosevelt, the federal estate tax was based on "the very sound policy of encouraging a wider distribution of wealth," or, in other words, redistribution of wealth. President Roosevelt made this statement at a time most apropos: the introduction of another rise in the estate tax rates in 1935.

President Roosevelt's words have stood for reality for a very long time; but, thanks to ERTA and TRA 1986, the pendulum has swung back in the opposite direction.

Index

About the Authors

Robert A. Esperti and Renno L. Peterson are known internationally for their estate and wealth strategies planning expertise. They live respectively in Jackson Hole, Wyoming, and Sarasota, Florida.

They are the founders of the National Network of Estate Planning Attorneys and the Esperti Peterson Institute of Estate and Wealth Strategies Planning, and are the publishers of CONSPECTUS CURRENT, *The Journal of the Estate and Wealth Strategies Planning Professions.* They are also the senior principals in Esperti Peterson & Cahoone, a National Law Firm and Partnership of Professional Corporations, and Esperti Peterson Consulting, Inc., a wealth strategies design firm specializing in serving the planning needs of the world's affluent families.

Widely known to the general public and planning practitioners in the multidisciplinary professions of law, accounting, and financial and insurance planning, Esperti and Peterson are the world's most prolific and creative estate planning authors. They are the authors of 23 books, including the best-selling *Loving Trust, The Living Trust Revolution: Why America Is Abandoning Wills and Probate, The Living Trust Workbook,* and a number of multivolume professional treatises.

Esperti and Peterson are dedicated to meeting the estate and wealth strategies planning needs of affluent client families, and are widely sought for their practice and lecture skills as they impart the depth of their unique knowledge.